Sociology of Religion for
Generations X and Y

Sociology of Religion for Generations X and Y

Adam Possamai

LONDON   OAKVILLE

Published by Equinox Publishing Ltd.
UK: Unit 6, The Village, 101 Amies St., London SW11 2JW
USA: DBBC, 28 Main Street, Oakville, CT 06779

www.equinoxpub.com

First published 2009

British Library Cataloguing-in-Publication Data

A catalogue record for this book is available from the British Library.

ISBN   978 1 84553 303 8   (hardback)
         978 1 84553 304 5   (paperback)

Library of Congress Cataloging-in-Publication Data

Possamai, Adam.
  Sociology of religion for generations X and Y / Adam Possamai.
    p. cm.
  Includes bibliographical references (p. 206) and index.
  ISBN 978-1-84553-303-8 (hb) — ISBN 978-1-84553-304-5 (pb) 1.
Religion and sociology—Textbooks. I. Title.
  BL60.P59 2009
  306.6—dc22
                        2008024907

Typeset by S.J.I. Service, New Delhi
Printed and bound in Great Britain by Lightning Source UK Ltd, Milton Keynes

Contents

Tables

Figures

Acknowledgements

This book is dedicated to my step children, Natasha and Cameron, who are part of this generation Y. I wrote the book wondering what they would like to read if they were to study sociology when they go to university.

Many thanks go to my wife, Alphia, a Xer who gave me much feedback when thinking and writing this book; and my son and toddler, Addison, a Zer, who got so fascinated with his father writing that he grabbed a few keys with his little fingers and broke my computer keyboard.

My thanks go to my first mentors in the sociology of religion from the Catholic University of Leuven who taught me the francophone aspects of this discipline during my undergraduate years: these are Liliane Voyé, Jean-Pierre Hiernaux and Jean Rémy. During my PhD at La Trobe University in Melbourne, Rowan Ireland and Ken Dempsey opened my eyes to the anglophone sociology of religion. This book hopes to continue their weighty legacy, adapted to the 21st century. I also would like to acknowledge all the students who studied my subject 'Sociology of Religion' and thank them for their involvement over the many years I taught it.

Special thanks go to the School of Social Sciences, the Social Justice Social Change Research Centre and the College of Arts from the University of Western Sydney, which have provided assistance with this project and have made it possible to employ research assistants to help me; these being Brian Salter, Amie Matthews, Joanne Cummings and Deborah Wilmore. Without them, I would have not been able to finish this book within a decent amount of time.

Note

A third of this book is a total rework of some parts of my earlier publications. These include:

Possamai, A. (2000). 'Nature Religions'. In P. Hughes (ed.), *Australia's Religious Communities. A Multimedia Exploration: CD-Rom Standard Edition*. Christian Research Association, Melbourne. [Parts of Chapter 13]

Possamai, A. (2004). 'AASR Presidential Address 2004: Intellectuals of the Other in Religion: Fear and Fascination.' *Australian Religion Studies Review* 17(2): 10–19. [Parts of the conclusion]

Possamai, A. (2005). *Religion and Popular Culture: A Hyper-real Testament*. Bruxelles, Bern, Berlin, Frankfurt am Main, New York, Oxford, Wein: P.I.E.-Peter Lang. [Parts of Chapters 2, 4, 5, 6, 7, and 8]

Possamai, A. (2005). *In Search of New Age Spirituality*. Aldershot: Ashgate. [Parts of Chapters 7, 8, 12 and 13]

Possamai, A. (2007). '"Secularisation" and "Religion" as Zombie Categories?' *The Australian Religion Studies Review* 20(2): 233–42. [Parts of Chapter 1]

Possamai, A. (2007). 'Producing and Consuming New Age Spirituality: The Cultic Milieu and the Network Paradigm'. In D. Kemp and J. Lewis (ed.), *Handbook of New Age*, 151–66. Leiden: E. J Brill. [Parts of Chapter 12]

Possamai, A. and A. Possamai-Inesedy (2007), 'Risk Society, Sustainable Development and Religion'. In Roberto Blancarte Pimentel and Vassilis Saroglou (eds), *Religion, Culture and Sustainable Development in Encyclopedia of Life Support Systems (EOLSS)*. Developed under the Auspices of the UNESCO. Oxford: Eolss Publishers [http://www.eolss.net]. [Parts of Chapter 8]

Possamai, A. (2008). 'Australia "Shy" De-secularisation Process'. In A. Imotoual and B. Spaler (eds), *Religion, Spirituality and Social Science*, 23–35. Oxford: Polity Press. [Parts of Chapter 4]

Possamai, A. (2009, Forthcoming). 'Hyper-Real Religions.Com and the Participatory Culture'. In D. Guttierez (ed.), *Creencias, Religiosidad y Secularizacion en el Mundo Actual*. Mexico: El Colegio Mexiquense. [Parts of Chapter 6]

Possamai, A. and A. Possamai-Inesedy (2009, Forthcoming). 'Scientology Down Under'. In J. Lewis (ed.) *Scientology*. Oxford and New York: Oxford University Press. [Parts of Chapter 1]

I would like to acknowledge the above publishers of these sociological pieces of work for having first presented them in a print format.

Introduction: Xers and Yers as Cohorts of the Post-1970s Generation

Introduction

In an episode of the sitcom *Friends*, Ross is a divorcee who wants to celebrate the Jewish festival of Hanukkah with his son. Ross does not see his child on an everyday basis and would like to share the values that are dear to his heart with him. He does not want to give a rational explanation of the event because he realises that this Jewish holy day competes with Christmas and is far from being as media friendly as the Christian one. He hopes to narrate the story and meaning of Hanukkah by organising something fun and entertaining. Knowing the appeal of popular culture on his generation (X) and his son's (Y), and with the help of his friends, Ross tries to find a disguise similar to Santa Claus to capture his son's attention. Unfortunately, the only costume he manages to find at the last minute is an armadillo; and when his son sees him, he merely wonders about his sanity. However, what makes this episode strong in terms of values is that even his friends who are not Jewish help Ross to celebrate Hanukkah in this way.

This sitcom, has, according to Huntley (2006: 26–27), tapped into the reality of both generations X and Y. Friends, this show tells us, are the family people get to choose; and in a world in which marriages, relationships and jobs can be easily destroyed, friends are the strongest constant in a person's life. In each episode, one has the impression that the six main characters spend more time with each other than with their families and partners. And with generations X and Y in general, religion is not what dominates their lives, but it is occasionally present in one way or another. Ross is never seen practising his faith, but as is common in today's society, he appears to believe without belonging to it. In another episode, two friends are about to marry in a civil ceremony but the person who has been asked to lead the ceremony is delayed. At the last minute they find an orthodox priest to celebrate their wedding. What is of interest is that neither of them shows resistance to having someone from another religion marry them. Thus we are shown that these friends, while not overtly religious, respect other faiths and are even open to them.

Although the episodes described above underline the importance of friend-ship over religion, this book is meant to be a friend for recent generations to understand religion. Whereas many existing books on the sociology of reli-gion are written by Baby Boomers, this one is written by a member of gen-eration X who wants to reach the concerns of both generations X and Y. While outsiders might see these generations as 'apathetic', 'out of control' or 'self-centred', I do not have these views because I write from the inside. Like *Friends*, this book is aimed at tapping into the concerns and needs of post-1970s people who are faced with a changing world and who might be interested in touching or, even better, studying religion in depth like me. This book is designed in such a way that it addresses specific X and Y concerns while giving the knowledge needed to pass a university degree, if needed, and perhaps continue further study in the sociology of religion. It contains the most up-to-date information as well as new ideas that are only slowly emerging in the literature. Before going into what the book is about, I will first explain what I mean by generations X and Y.

Generations X and Y

The term generation X comes from the North American author Douglas Coupland (1992), who refers in his novel *Generation X* to the generation immediately after the Baby Boomers. The 'X' symbolises the namelessness of a generation that was different from Baby Boomers. They are also known as the Baby Busters. Although there is no strong agreement on dates in the literature, for argument sake, Baby Boomers were born between 1946 and 1964 whereas generation Xers were born between 1965 and 1980; followed by the Y generation between 1981 and 2000. Yers are also known as the dot.coms, the millennials, the Net Generation or the Thumb Generation (because of the use of remote controls and mobile phones).

How different are Xers and Yers? Huntley (2006: 5–11) believes there is a sharp break between them. Contrasted to the deep-rooted sceptical outlook developed by Xers during the economic crisis in the 1970s, the Aids epi-demic and threat of global nuclear warfare, Yers think anything and every-thing is possible. Although both generations now live in a world of insecurity, Yers were born into this age of uncertainty and took it for granted whereas Xers had to learn this reality for themselves. While both generations were raised in the heyday of global consumerism, Huntley (2006: 144) sees that in terms of being faithful to a logo in consumer society (that is choosing and having fidelity towards a specific brand as if one could belong to a type of consumer tribe), Xers started in their teen years whereas Yers were already hooked in pre-school. While Xers were brought up on television, Atari video games and the first computers, Yers were born with MTV and played on Nintendo and Gameboys.

The groups are similar in that, except for the conflicts in Iraq (see Chapter 6), neither generation has experienced war. Compared to Baby Boomers who lived through the 'counterculture' revolution of the 1960s, both Xers and Yers are less concerned with rebellion and are closer to their parents (sometimes even referring to them as friends), despite their parents' high rate of divorce. Both are better educated than previous generations and their racial composition is the most heterogeneous since the Middle Ages. Both were born and grew up during globalisation, which has created a feeling of uncertainty through job insecurity caused by the delocalisation of industry from the west to the 'rest'. They do not know if they will live in the same place for the rest of their life and they can never be certain they will last with a partner until their death bed. If there is a constant in the lives of these people it is that they have to live with uncertainty. They are also more likely to be tolerant of religious and belief systems; as many of them embrace the view that there are no absolute rights and wrongs for everybody. They tend to view dogmatic belief systems with suspicion. Contrary to older generations that remain loyal to institutional and doctrinal beliefs (Roof 1999: 52), these generations are more interested in religious experience than theological reasoning. For them, the heart must win over the head. They want to know, but the forms of knowledge they encounter better not be dogmatic, and the more they are presented as a narrative the better. These characteristics are, of course, broad generalisations, but they give us an idea of what is happening to both generations.

Wyn and Woodman (2006) argue that differentiation between Xers and Yers seems to be stronger in the mass media and popular literature than in social reality; thus the two groups should be referred to as birth cohorts rather than generations. They suggest that generations should be located within specific economic, social, cultural and political conditions rather than arbitrary sets of birth years. To understand what they mean by a generation, Wyn and Woodman (2006: 496) make reference to the work of the German sociologist, Mannheim:

> 'generation' was a term that should be applied to people who belong to a common period of history, or whose lives are forged through the same conditions. He (Mannheim) argued for the existence of a 'generational consciousness' that emerged for each generation.

They would rather use the term 'post-1970 generation' as a concept that subsumes or includes generations X and Y because this broader group makes a clear break with the social and cultural conditions that made the Baby Boomers. As Wyn and Woodman (2006: 501) state:

> The post-1970 generation is a label for exploring the concept of generational difference. The extent to which young people entering their twenties now (those commonly labelled generation Y) represent another distinct shift in life priorities from earlier members of the 1970s generation [that is the Xers] is yet to be established.

For the purpose of this book I will therefore refer to generations X and Y as two similar cohorts and sub-groups of the post-1970 generation.

What more can be said in a snapshot about the post-1970s generation with regard to religion? One key aspect is that, rather than asking what they must do to be saved, they ask what they must do to be loved (Miller and Miller 2000: 10). Perhaps because Xers and Yers are still young and not too worried about death, their religious concern is more about the here-and-now than the salvation of the soul. This focus on the here-and-now is further detailed by Davie (2000:180) who writes about institutional religions in Europe:

> It is abundantly clear (1) that the younger generations of Europe have effectively lost touch with the institutional churches in terms of anything approaching regular practice and (2) that the forms of religious instruction provided in the educational systems of modern Europe are moving away from a model based on catechesis to modes of teaching that offer information about rather than in religious beliefs. Given this state of affairs, it is hardly surprising that the knowledge base on younger people in terms of Bible stories, awareness of liturgy, and elementary church history is crumbling – there is very little to hold it in place.

Davie (2000: 180) believes it is important to distinguish between religious knowledge and religious sensibility. She postulates that while allegiance to the knowledge provided by religious institutions is in decline, openness towards the spiritual (religious sensibility) is growing (see Chapter 4). As Miller and Miller (2000: 4) explain with regard to Xers (which can easily be adapted to Yers as well), parents of this cohort hesitated to dogmatically impose religion on their kids. These parents wanted their children to choose for themselves, but this meant that they were often not given any religious education to counteract this lack. This lead to many Xers and Yers searching/choosing a religion and/or spirituality by themselves for themselves. As Bader-Saye (2006:16) argues from a Christian point of view, this generation searches for:

> things like a return to mystery (with a renewed interest in spiritual practices and medieval mysticism), a hunger for spirituality (even if overlaid with 'new age' assumptions and do-it-yourself religion), new models of networked communities (via Internet, cell phones and increased mobility), a desire to find

roots in tradition (in contrast to the modern suspicion of tradition), and a yearning to encounter God through image, ritual and sacrament (in contrast to highly word-centred and often iconoclastic modernist forms of Christianity.

Further, the Xers are the first cohort to be fully raised on television, which has become a moral mentor for them. Today, more than ever before, Christians are less influenced by Jesus as a role model and more by television celebrities such as sitcom and movie characters, singers, sports figures and others. Beaudoin (1998) suggests that, as the religious education of generation Xers is fragmented, popular culture is used to fill the gaps. For example, as a member of generation X who has become a reasonably established sociologist of religion, I must admit that I have far more knowledge of popular culture than institutional doctrine. This is something I have managed to hide from my Baby Boomer colleagues at various conferences, but with this book I am 'coming out' of my closet of ignorance, so to speak. Popular culture can help us to understand the basis of complex ideas, but we must also move beyond works of fiction to get to the core of the issues through sociology. Whatever the generation, there are nevertheless canons of knowledge that need to be transmitted through history; as this book does.

Contents

To take the reader on the path to understanding what is happening to religion in the western world from a sociological point of view, many angles must be considered. Each chapter in this book aims to explore a particular angle or viewpoint.

Chapter 1 (*Religious Diversity and the Politics of Definition*) covers the difficulty of finding an all-inclusive definition of religion without using a specific religious viewpoint. Although Chapter 3 gives some 'faulty' sociological definitions from the 19th century, I argue for the impossibility of such a thing and underline that definitions of religion can be politically loaded, as some interest group might try to gain something out of a definition that might include or exclude certain groups. The case of the Church of Scientology illuminates this argument. The chapter then covers the issue of believing exclusively in one's religion when other religions exist and might have something different to say.

Chapter 2 (*Religion and Popular Culture*) explores popular culture as a central aspect of generations X and Y's religious/spiritual works. Although a few Baby Boomers have used popular culture for their religion, some of these younger generations have included popular culture as a main aspect of their religion, and this is a factor that distinguishes these two generations from others. Popular culture can tell us about who we are in our society, and more specifically who we are in terms of religion and spirituality. This will be a key way to start this book through the case study of one of the most recent innovations in religion, that of using global popular culture as a source of religious inspiration.

Chapter 3 (*Religion and Modernity: Marx, Durkheim, and Weber*) is a basic theoretical chapter to lay down the foundation of the sociology of religion from Marx, Durkheim, and Weber. After having described the case study of people who use popular culture for their religion, this chapter takes a few steps back and uses the classics to help readers to lay down some knowledge foundation to make sense of the current religious context in subsequent chapters.

Chapter 4 (*Religion, Spirituality and the Post-Secularisation Approach*) underlines that religion, contrary to what Durkheim, Marx and Weber have said, is still alive and rich, but is now different than when these authors were researching in the 19th and beginning of the 20th centuries. Unfortunately, as this chapter argues, it took a long time for sociologists to lose their fundamentalist approach to these three thinkers and realise the transformations that were happening to religion. One of these important changes is the use of the term spirituality which has become fluid in popular understanding. The discussion in this chapter has the secularisation debate as a backdrop, which uses Eisenstadt's theory of multiple modernities.

Chapter 5 (*Religion and Postmodernity (Part A): Consumer Religions*) explains our move from modernity to postmodernity and more specifically to the rise of consumerism and individualism. This illustrates the contemporary position of religion which generations X and Y are the most familiar with. Critiques have often been leveled at these two generations for being too consumerist, but the reality is that they are part of the sign of the times which religion follows as well. Instead of raising any value judgment on these changes as has been done by those outside of these generations, this chapter objectively explores how consumerism affects religion.

Chapter 6 (*Religion and Postmodernity (Part B): Hyper-Reality and the Internet*) follows on from the previous chapter on postmodernity and uses the work of Baudrillard (as a substitute for the theories of Durkheim, Marx and Weber) to develop the points elaborated in the previous chapter. It basically focuses on the new phenomenon of hyper-real religion (e.g. Star Wars, Matrixism), which is touched on in Chapter 2. This chapter also investigates the importance of the Internet on our current postmodern society and on religion by arguing that the virtual world is giving opportunities to new forms of religions to exist which could have never emerged in the past.

Chapter 7 (*Esotericism, Its McDonaldisation, and Its Re-enchantment Process*) brings the classical analysis of Weber on re-enchantment to contemporary analyses. This chapter explains the new phenomenon of the McDonaldisation of society, which paradoxically re-enchants our world through consumer society. This chapter is special in the sense that it brings many of the discussions from the previous chapters together into one by showing some of the arguments in a new light. As a case study for this chapter I discuss esotericism, or the cult of mystery in religion. I argue that with the advent of postmodernity, it has lost its fundamental aspect; that of secrecy.

Chapter 8 (*Monotheistic Fundamentalism(s) as an Outcome of Consumer Culture*) then moves the book towards a new direction. If previous chapters have been dabbling with innovative forms of religion, the following four will deal with more traditional aspects of religion that are faced with current socio-cultural changes. For example, as an outcome of consumer culture, certain groups within monotheistic religions are reacting to this aspect of life within the western world and to the way this lifestyle is becoming hegemonic in the world. One of these reactions is fundamentalism. By focusing on fundamentalism within Christianity, Islam and Judaism, this chapter addresses the difficulties of pinpointing this phenomenon exactly because of its many shades of grey.

Chapter 9 (*Buddhism, Its Westernisation and the Easternisation of the West*) is a case study of the changes that can happen to a long established religion when it becomes part of the global phenomenon. A few of these outcomes are the development of some transnational characteristics and more importantly its westernisation. As postmodernity reflects a society full of paradoxes, this chapter argues that while the migration of Buddhism has been westernised, this religion has also been a carrier for the easternisation of the west.

Chapter 10 (*Christianity: Churches and Sects in a Post-Christian World*) argues that Christianity is faced with new issues that it needs to address in this post-Christian world (i.e. a western world no longer fully dominated by Christian values). After explaining the difference between a church and a sect, this chapter addresses the various movements within the Christian world that act and react to our consuming world and the push for churches to get out of their institutional walls and become more part of 21st-century everyday life. This chapter focuses on Vatican II, mega-churches and the emerging church phenomenon.

Chapter 11 (*The Multiple Modernities of Islam*) explores how Islam is trying to re-Islamise societies previously governed by a secularist and 'corrupted' government. The cases of Turkey, Iran, Palestine and Algeria are quickly covered. This chapter also addresses the ways that moderate Islam in the postmodern world is trying to adapt and dissociate itself from fundamentalism(s). This chapter argues that this moderate re-Islamisation is a new form of modernity that fits with Eisenstadt's vision of multiple modernities.

Chapter 12 (*New Religious Movements and the Death of the New Age*) argues that New Religious Movements and the New Age are phenomena that were strong from the 1960s to the end of last century, and were key players in getting spirituality outside mainstream religions. However, because of the authority structure of some of these New Religious Movements and the commercialisation of many of its small loose groups, these are now supplanted with the broader movement towards 'spirituality', which is detailed in Chapter 4. Although these groups still exist, they are poorly growing and not filling the void created by people who have left traditional religions. However, those who are involved in these alternative spiritualities network in what is called the cultic milieu.

Chapter 13 (*Witchcraft, the Internet and Consumerism*) explores the birth of witchcraft, its success and more importantly the tension between 'traditionalists' and 'consumers' of this religion. The case study of teenage witches is presented. This chapter also highlights how the use of the Internet can impact on the structure and practices of this religion.

The Conclusion (*What Do Sociologists of Religion in Academia Do Apart from Teaching and Marking? Their Work as Intellectuals*) analyses the role of intellectuals in social life, which has already been widely studied and theorised. However, there have been few studies of the involvement of the intellectual in the study of religions. This chapter analyses the different types of intellectuals, e.g. Bauman's legislators and interpreters, and the role they take in researching and/or speaking for and/or against the other in religion. It demonstrates that sociologists do more than just teach because they are as involved in the production and reproduction of everyday life as any other social actor.

These chapters cover the most important aspects of what the sociology of religion is today, and what it does, in a language that is relevant to generations X and Y. This book unfortunately does not cover all aspects, as chapters on New Ethnic and Migrant Religious Movements, Hinduism and Judaism would have been important inclusions. It was, however, beyond the scope of this edition. If there is the chance to work on a second edition, some or all of these proposed chapters will of course then take their place.

1 Religious Diversity and the Politics of Definition

Introduction

For any social scientists researching religion, the Internet has become a considerable source of knowledge. Blogs, among other things, are a valuable source of information when it comes to trying to understand the sign of the times. In these Blogs, people write freely about their opinion and can offer a window for looking at what people think. One such blog is 'TheoFantastique', which is 'devoted to the enjoyment and exploration of the imagination and creativity as expressed through Science Fiction, Fantasy, and Horror'.[1] Its webmaster, John Morehead, is interested in intercultural studies, new religious movements, theology and popular culture. As part of his blogs, he interviews people who can comment on his interest. For example, on the 12th October, 2007, he posted his conversation with Dr James McGrath from Butler University who made an interesting comment about *Star Trek*. This will be the thread of this chapter:

> **TheoFantastique:** With the cultural changes in the West in the shift to late modernity or postmodernity [see Chapter 5] do you think there has been an increase in religious or spiritual topics discussed or incorporated within science fiction?
>
> **James McGrath:** Absolutely. The best example (to preempt your next question) is to trace the *Star Trek* series in its various incarnations. The original series took a wholly modern outlook. There was no one with any publicly-visible religious beliefs on the Enterprise. They may have had them, but this was a secular enterprise, if you'll allow the pun. On their journeys they encountered two kinds of civilizations: ones that were enlightened and secular like themselves, and ones that were primitive and in which religion was mere superstition that was used to manipulate people and/or keep them from progressing. If we fast forward to *Deep Space Nine*, we find that postmodernism has radically altered the outlook of the show. On this space station, everyone (except for most of the humans, interestingly enough) has a religious tradition, and everyone participates in each other's traditions and rituals, with plenty of room for putting together one's own eclectic smorgasbord of beliefs. Sci-fi certainly speculates about the future, but it also reflects the present, and because it is the future as seen from the present, it provides plenty of opportunities to reflect on our present values and our aims.[2]

We will come back to the place of the internet in relation to religions in Chapter 6 and the key notions of modernity and postmodernity will be addressed in Chapters 3, 4 and 5. What I would like to focus on for this chapter is the paradigm shift from the Star Trek series and on the fact that works of popular culture reflect changes within our society. There appears to be a change from a secularist outlook (see Chapter 4) of our world, as indicated in the first series, to a view in the most recent one that celebrates religious diversity (see forthcoming sections). As *Deep Space Nine* reflects current cultural shifts in our society, this book also indicates change and does not escape imposition from reality. No matter how hard a researcher works, how much he or she collects, analyses, and writes about data, he or she carries with him or her a specific frame of mind. No matter how well trained a social scientist is, he or she cannot fully blank his or her life story, cultural and social influences, education, movies and books read while conducting research. His or her life story has been greatly inspired by his or her parents, but also by his or her skin and gender, by how people have perceived him or her throughout his or her life, and by how he or she has reacted to this perception.

If we come back to the illustration on *Star Trek*, it becomes easy to find how sociocultural conditions affect what is thought of, written and directed on screen. Writers, like social scientists, are productions of their time and very rarely are the ones who change the times. The ways religion is viewed and practiced, as I argue in this chapter, are also a product of a time. Whatever the message from the gods and/or prophets, whatever the quality of its veracity, the message is always translated in a specific socio-cultural context. And the sociology of religion is no exception as social scientists who analyse the religious message in its practices also follow the sign of the times.

For example, the research I have conducted in the sociology of religion for close to 15 years appears to be a reflection of some facets of my life. I was raised as a Catholic in Belgium by an Italian Catholic father and an English Anglican mother. This country at that time, not taking into account atheism, was deeply mono-religiously Catholic. Because of my father's work, I travelled on many occasions in North Africa and especially Libya (before and during the international embargo) and Algeria (at the beginning of the civil war in the 90s). These trips exposed me greatly to a part of the Muslim world. I then migrated to Australia and discovered a land with a vastly diverse religious landscape which opened my eyes to issues of management of religious diversity and made me an ardent believer in religious toleration and pluralism.

I just went through this very little biographical sketch to let my readers know about my background, and to make them aware of my perspective in my work in the sociology of religion. As a sociologist following a Weberian approach (see Chapter 3), I research the social meaning that movements and individuals give to their action, and the effect of these meanings and actions on the socio-cultural structure of western societies. As a researcher, I work as a translator (See Conclusion) of these social actors' multiple ways of being and thinking by exposing them to the broader community through my publications and involvement with the media. By making these findings available, I wish to contribute to the study and promotion of religious diversity; this book being such an outlet.

This book is designed for both religious and non-religious people. Some religious people might wonder if a sociological book can destroy one's religious belief. Sociology does not make people atheist; it is simply a discipline that analyses religion in society and does not discuss the validity of the religious message. Saying that a religion is not a religion because it does not believe in a Christian God is not a sociological argument. Saying that some religions are in conflict with other religions and that it impacts on the sociopolitical level of a geographical region is worth having a sociological eye on. Like culture, sociologists analyse religion and the various ways it impacts on different levels of our societies. This is why this book will be of interest to religious and non-religious people. It deals with the sociocultural consequences of believing rather than the theological study of the act of believing itself. As one of the many consequences of globalisation, religions and spiritualities coexist in ways not known in the past. But how can we all exist without destructive conflicts between religious groups and between religious and non-religious groups? As Habermas (2006: 4) recently underlined, the challenge is to draw the 'delimitations between a positive liberty to practice a religion of one's own and the negative liberty to remain spared from the religious practice of the others'. In other words, how do we work religious toleration in a way that celebrates religious diversity but does not prevent the freedom for people to be atheist as well?

Religious Toleration? The Case Study of the Church of Scientology

Before starting this section, I will first present a case study which aims to set the underpinning of this book: whatever the religious belief, it should be able to be practised openly as a religion, as long as it does not go against the laws of a country. This case study is of a controversial nature, but is a case in point, as it helps us to understand that at the basis of religious toleration is the issue of how to define/label what religion is.

The Church of Scientology

This church is well known in the media for being the religion of stars like Tom Cruise and John Travolta. It was formed by Ron Hubbard who believed that the human mind could be greatly improved to give people greater mental agility. Hubbard, who was at the time of the genesis of the church a pulp fiction writer, first described his views on the optimisation of the brain in the May 1950 issue of *Astounding Science Fiction*. He then developed his ideas of a new psychotherapy in books, and in 1953, created his church.

The ideal mental state for scientologists to reach is that of being 'Clear'. This is a state in which we are free from all the pains we have experienced in this life and in all the previous ones. All the painful experiences of current and previous lives are said to be stored in our subconscious and are called 'engrams'. These would prevent us from functioning at our full potential in daily life.

Hubbard developed a technique called 'dianetics' to discover the origins of the engrams and clear them away from a person. Part of these exercises include following the indications of some type of religious manual from the church and the reading of an e-meter; a machine inspired by the lie detector. After various exercises, the scientologist is argued to be able to read his or her emotions on this e-meter and detect the unconscious pains accumulated from his or her past lives.

The courses offered are various and can be costly. As people move from one course to another one, they move a level closer to the 'Clear' state. As a typical initiatory religion, members have to move from one level at a time. The Church of Scientology does not offer a religion in which people can come on a Sunday morning and make a small donation. It is rather a religion which charges a specific amount of money for all the various levels required by their course.

The Church of Scientology in Australian Courts

In 1963 following complaints from health professionals, government health authorities and from the public, Scientology became the subject of an inquiry by Kevin Anderson QC. In 1965 a Board of Inquiry from the State of Victoria reported in the first paragraph of its prefatory note that 'Scientology is evil; its techniques evil; its practices a serious threat to the community, medically, morally and socially; and its adherents sadly deluded and often mentally ill' and that Scientology is not a religion. The Board of this inquiry sat to receive evidence and to hear submissions and addresses on 160 days. It listened to oral evidence on oath from 151 witnesses covering 8,920 pages of transcript.

Reading through this report, one can easily discover that the board viewed the church as a pseudo-science affecting the mental health of its members.

In chapter 27 of the document entitled, *Scientology and Religion*, the board said that the church claimed to be a religion to improve their defence tactics by pretending to be persecuted because of their religious beliefs. Further, as stated in chapter 7 of its report, the board could not grasp the religious teaching of the group from a non-Christian perspective.

> Scientology is opposed to religion as such, irrespective of kind of denomination. The essence of Hubbard's axioms of scientology is that the universe was created not by God, but by a conglomeration of thetans who postulated the universe. Sometimes God is referred to as the Big Thetan. Many of the theories he propounds are almost the negation of Christian thought and morality.

It is clear from this statement (and a few others in the same chapter) that the legal system of that time did not reflect the type of autonomous judiciary system (in this case, independent from a Christian perspective) required to ensure religious freedom for minority groups as described by Richardson (2007). This lack of independence from external systems, be it religious or secularist, is demonstrated quite strongly in the conclusions of the report when describing Scientologists accounts: 'These ardent devotees, though quite rational and intelligent on other subjects, are possessed of an invincible impediment to reason where Scientology is concerned'. A further conclusion is also worth quoting:

> Though the practice of scientology has many undesirable features, such is the novelty of many of its activities that it is difficult to classify them precisely as being in breach of existing laws. That scientology practices and activities are improper and are harmful and prejudicial to mental health is evident.

In its recommendations, the board admits that invoking the criminal law in respect to past conduct of the group will be of little significance, 'like prosecuting a bank robber for driving his get-away car against the traffic lights'.

The board then decided that 'in order to control Scientology, it is necessary to strike at the heart of the problem':

> Hubbard claims that scientology is a form of psychology and the evidence shows it to be psychology practises in a perverted and dangerous way by persons who are not only lacking in any qualifications which would fit them to practise psychology but who have been indoctrinated and trained in beliefs and practices which equip them to do more than apply dangerous techniques harmfully and indiscriminately.

The Board envisaged a system of registration for psychologists which would prohibit the advertising and practice of psychology for fee or reward unless registered. It was of the Board's opinion that Scientology's qualifications should not entitle a person to register as a psychologist. It admitted that limiting the practice of Scientology would involve the surveillance of practices and conduct by persons other than Scientologists. This report led to the Psychological Practices Act 1965 (Vict.) which made the teaching of Scientology an offence. However, this Act did not apply to 'anything done by any person who is a priest or minister of a recognised religion in accordance with the usual practice of that religion'. These provisions were repealed in 1982 (Psychological Practices (Scientology) Act 1982 (Vict.).

Later, the Church became recognised as a religious denomination under s.26 of the Marriage Act 1961 in 1973, and was then exempted as a religious institution from pay-roll tax in South Australia, Western Australia, New South Wales and the Australian Capital Territory.

However, in Victoria in 1983, the Church faced a legal battle on the issue of being defined as a religion for tax purposes in the Church of the New Faith v Commissioner for Payroll Tax (Vic.). The court was asked to decide if the Church was a religious institution for the purpose of tax exemption. The Church was first listed as a foreign company as the Church of the New Faith Incorporated in 1969 in Victoria. When the Church of the New Faith was asked to pay taxes from 1975 to 1977, it objected on the basis that it was a religion, and thus its wages were not liable to pay-roll tax. After many rejections to this objection, the 'corporation'/church applied for an appeal at the High Court of Australia. The court investigated whether this 'corporation' was, during the relevant period, a religious institution. Instead of focusing on the writing of Hubbard as was previously done (see above), the court focused instead on whether 'the beliefs, practices and observances which were established by the affidavits and oral evidence as the set of beliefs, practices and observances accepted by Scientologists are properly to be described as a religion'. Taking into account that religion had received little judicial exegesis in Australia since 1943 (Company of Jehovah's Witnesses Inc. v. The Commonwealth), that religions in Australia were no longer exclusively Christian and theistic since it has recognised itself as a multicultural country since the early 1970s, and that protection is required for the adherents of religions rather than for the religions themselves, the court held that the beliefs, practices and observances of this church did constitute a religion in the state of Victoria. Through this case, the legal definition of religion in Australia was redefined by Acting Chief Justice Mason and Justice Brennan to include as its two elements:

- belief in a supernatural Being, Thing or Principle
- the acceptance of canons of conduct to give effect to that belief (though canons of conduct which offend against the ordinary laws are outside the area of any immunity, privilege or right conferred on the ground of religion).

Justices Wilson and Deane, instead of a single definition of religion, referred to some guiding principles. These are:

- a particular collection of ideas and/or practices involving belief in the supernatural
- ideas that relate to the nature and place of humanity in the universe and the relation of humanity to things supernatural
- ideas accepted by adherents requiring or encouraging the observation of particular standards or codes of conduct or participation in specific practices having supernatural significance
- adherents constituting an identifiable group or identifiable groups, regardless of how loosely knit and varying in beliefs and practices these adherents may be
- adherents themselves seeing the collection of ideas and/or practices as constituting a religion.

By applying a definition of religion that is more inclusive of non-Christian faiths, the Church of Scientology was able to be recognised as a religion and at the end won the case. However, it does not mean that once a group has successfully been labelled a religion that it is at peace with the rest of a society. Indeed in the same year as the Church won the case, Gaze and Jones (1990: 222 and 282–84) reported that the High Court offered little help when Scientologists complained about the Australian Security Intelligence Organisation (ASIO) (Church of Scientology v. Woodward (1983) 154 C.L.R. 25 (High Ct)). The Australian Intelligence services were said to have kept them under surveillance and were reporting members' church affiliation to Commonwealth agencies when applying for a job. The matter was heard and ASIO's activities were regarded as not being subject to judicial review. Using this case as an example of ASIO's lack of accountability in the light of the new anti-terror laws, Head (2004) underlines how the agency was shielded from legal scrutiny.

In New South Wales, the New South Wales Anti-Discrimination Board (1984) published an extensive report on discrimination and religious conviction in New South Wales and Australia. It reported in an unprejudicial way, among many other things, that the Church of Scientology was a case study of Australian intolerance and prejudice towards minority religions. According to the Board, the reason for this attitude would be because the public is inadequately informed about religion in general, and minority groups in particular (section 5.5). It underlines that pressure on Federal and NSW Governments to make extensive inquiries into the 'cults' (see Chapter 12) in general has been resisted by both Federal and the State Attorneys-General. Such inquiries, the Board argues, would infringe religious freedom and that specific breaches of the law can be dealt with adequately under existing legislation. It follows the view that 'controversial activities of unpopular minority religious groups belong rather in the province of public discussion than in that of governmental regulation by legislation or other action' (section 5.183). It recommends (section 5.241) educating people working in governmental agencies (e.g. police, local governments, health and education) on issues of religious prejudice.

In 1998, the Australian Human Rights and Equal Opportunity Commission (1998) investigated freedom of religion and belief in Australia and discovered for example that some Scientologists would not disclose their affiliation when applying for accommodation fearing that this would affect their chances (77). This report uses the case of the Church as part of its sub-section 5.2 on experiences of vilification and incitement to hatred for non-mainstream religions and other beliefs (90–93). This sub-section explores the large group of submissions received from members of the Church who complained of vilification and harassment on the basis of their membership. For example, a member made reference to the Church being publicly vilified in a State Parliament by derogatory claims about the Church targeting the recruitment of children through its schools in Australia (e.g. the Athena school). The report also quotes a former member of the Church who surveyed 60 Scientologists and who claimed that despite the gradual recognition and tolerance of the group in Australia over the last 30 years, many still experience intolerance and discrimination.

More recently in 2002, a case[3] in the Australian Capital Territory involved the government's attempt to define Scientology's 'Purification Rundown' as a 'health practice' and thus subject to regulation. The Supreme Court of the Australian Capital Territory ruled that the 'Purification Rundown' is a religious practice because it is 'essentially provided for religious purposes and not for the benefit of the health of participants' (28) and thus public officials are not allowed 'to intrude into areas which predominantly concern matters of religious belief and practice' (24).

Although this last case illustrates that there is still tension between the authorities and the Church of Scientology, especially on how to define religion and religious rituals, we are nevertheless a long way from the 1965 Anderson report.

This explanation has underlined the politics behind the definition of what a religion is in a specific case. The next section gives a broader look at this issue.

Protection and Definition of Religion?

Since the end of the Second World War, the right of all human beings to freely believe in their religion has been supported by many international bodies such as the United Nations and the Council of Europe. Governments are recommended to condemn religious persecution and to protect religious liberties, as long as a religious practice does not contravene criminal law or go against the rights of other citizens. This leads to treating all religions at the same level of tolerance. As Davie (2000:14) mentions about the European case and new religious movements (see Chapter 12) which include the Church of Scientology:

> After all, tolerance of religious difference in contemporary Europe must mean tolerance of all religious differences, not just the ones we happen to approve of. If a country fails in its tolerance of new religious movements, it is unlikely, or at least very much less likely, to succeed with respect to other religious minorities.

It is one thing to say that people should have the freedom to express their religion, it is another to debate what a religion is. With the case study above, the Australian government in the 1960s saw the Church of Scientology as a business rather than a religion. It was not perceived as a religion because it does not have a Christian God and because it reinforces a consumer commitment. However, the Church of Scientology whether we like it or not, is a religion.[4]

This leads us to examine what a religion is. I will first explore this from a Christian point of view and will then fail to achieve a multi-cultural point of view to underline the reality that generalisations about religions are not easy, if not impossible.

Debray (2005) demonstrates how the word 'religion', as we know it in the English language, emerged in Latin with the birth of Christianity. Indeed, the word as we understand it now is not found in Sanskrit, Hebrew, Greek and Arabic. In these languages, Debray explores non-western words such as *dharma* in Sanskrit ['that which carries the universe'], *dat* in Hebrew ['judgement'], *thrèskeia* in Greek ['following of cultural prescriptions'] and *dîn* in Arabic ['debt, obligation to follow God'], that we translate as religion; but these translations are only approximations and do not adequately reflect the meaning of these words in their original context. The author points out how the word 'religion' has become a universal entity emerging from a locality that is the Roman Christian one. Christianism was not born a religion (the notion was unthinkable in the Jewish culture), and did not grow into one during the first two centuries of the Christian era because Christian theologians had their thoughts formulated within the Greek language which ignored this Latin category. It only became a religion – in the sense of the word as we know it – in the 3rd century AD. This was simply a political move for Christians to view themselves as a religion so their faith would become a valid belief system in the Roman world. Before Constantine, the first Roman emperor who converted from paganism to Christianity, Christianity was seen as *superstitio* (pejorative term) and thus perceived negatively by the Roman pagans as, if I may be allowed this divergence, 'cults' are in current western societies. Christianity had to become a *religio* (laudatory term) to be accepted by the mainstream and to be able to develop in the Roman world. In 341, the appropriation of the Latin word *religio* became so successful that Christianity became *religio* and roman paganism *superstitio*. This reversal of perspective that established Christianity as the official religion clearly demonstrates power issues and labelling politics.

It is for reasons like this that Beckford (2003: 13), following a social constructionist approach, thinks that:

> religion is … a particularly interesting 'site' where boundary disputes are endemic and where well-entrenched interest groups are prepared to defend their definition of religion against opponents. The history of anti-witchcraft movements in many parts of the world, particularly the Inquisition, is powerful evidence of the deadly length to which some interest groups go to enforce their definition of 'true' religion.

Defining religion can thus be seen as a site of power in which groups try to impose their personal view and impose their agenda, such as rejecting 'pagan' practices from medieval Christianity, or authenticating miracles and shrines (see e.g. Voyé 1998).

When Christianity was a *religio* in the Middle Ages, it was an exclusivist religion (that is, it forbade its members to worship other gods and religions) and universalistic (that is, it proclaimed itself as the only true religion for all humankind). During that time period and geographical location, religion was bounded to Christianity and had to have an allusion to a supreme being and to the notion of sin. However, in Theravada Buddhism (see Chapter 9) there is no reference to a supreme being or to the notion of sin. In Buddhism, there are acts leading towards and away from the chain of reincarnation (that is the chain of rebirth and suffering) but there is no offence against a god as such which could lead a person to damnation. If in Catholicism there are saints who can intercede in the believers' favor, this is not the case in Theravada Buddhism.

Max Weber, whom we will explore in Chapter 3, is one of the founding fathers of the sociology of religion. He started his leading book on religion by stating:

> To define 'religion', to say what it is, is not possible at the start of a presentation such as this. Definition can be attempted, if at all, only at the conclusion of the study. The essence of religion is not even our concern, as we make it our task to study the conditions and effects of a particular type of social behaviour (Weber 1995: 1).

He started his research with this quote and was not able to define religion at the end of his work. No one definition of religion that takes into account

all belief systems (see the discussion about a substantive versus functional definition of religion in Chapter 3) has been accepted by all sociologists of religion. However, a set of broad and abstract elements are often used to understand what religion is. Bryan Wilson (1995) claims that religion can include some of these items, often leading to various combinations. In his own words, these characteristics are:
- supernatural forces, power(s), beings or goals
- human's ultimate concerns
- sacred objects (things set apart and forbidden) of spiritual devotion
- an agency that controls human destiny
- the ground of being
- a source of transcendent knowledge or wisdom
- the collective character of religious life

The consequences and functions of religion are indicated as:
- conferring group and/or individual identity
- establishing a framework of orientation
- facilitating the creation of a humanly constructed universe of meaning
- providing reassurance and comfort about prospects of help and salvation
- effecting human reconciliation and the maintenance of a moral community

This helps us to understand what a religion is but, like what Justices Mason, Brennan, Wilson and Deane have attempted with regard to the Scientology case in Australia, this is too broad a definition. Unfortunately, even if Newton and Einstein had been sociologists of religion, they would also not have found an appropriate definition which addresses the various creeds in our world. As Beckford (2001: 440) points out, there is no fixed point of view from which both scholars and lawyers can look. In a culturally pluralistic world, religion, like other social phenomena, can take many forms; and to determine what a religion is cannot be drawn from the application of a specific set of concepts coming from one particular religion. To accept what a religion is today means moving beyond old stereotypes like the ones against the Church of Scientology in Australia in the 1960s. It also involves having an open mind on the practices of people who create new religions like Jediism (from the Star Wars series) and Matrixism (from the Matrix trilogy) (see Chapter 2) and by people who re-invent fundamentalist forms of religion (see Chapter 8).

To truly define what religion is, if such a thing is possible, would take an extremely high degree of abstraction that no human being could meet. It would require being able to take into account all religions and express this definition in a language that can truly express this meaning without excluding any others. In this instance, finding the perfect definition of religion is a much harder task than cracking *The Da Vinci Code*.

The Diversity of Revelations: What to Believe?

Since we now live in a globalised world and are exposed to a multitude of religions in city streets, the Internet and in popular culture, it can be hard to argue that the revelations of all religions are equal when there appears to be contradiction between them. If religions were not making truth claims, this would not be a problem; but they do. How to solve this conundrum? How to live with seemingly contradictory religions in our current global sociocultural environment? The Australian philosopher, Max Charlesworth (1997) wrote a great essay on the diversity of revelations which tries to answer this question: 'What to believe in when there are conflicts and contradictions between religions?'

Charlesworth first mentions a continuum in which we have at both extremes a side that is absolutist and exclusive and the other, relative and syncretic. On the absolutists and exclusivist side we have people who believe that their religious system is absolutely and exclusively true and is the only true religion. This implies that all other religious systems are false. It is within this perspective that we find some extremist fundamentalist religions (see Chapter 8) that only see their religion as the right one and view other religions as incorrect (to say the least).

On the relativist and syncretic side, religious people believe that all religions are a particular and partial expression of the universal truth and that they are different paths to the same destination. Within this perspective, there is a belief that at the core of all religious systems, it is basically the same thing. From a theological point of view, this can cause problems when dealing with a belief system. For example, is Jesus the son of God or a prophet? If Christianity and Islam are equal, which version to follow? If going to heaven and reincarnation are the same, what happens in the afterlife? At the grassroots level, this does not cause much problem for people as we will see with New Age groups in Chapter 5 and 12, who pick and choose what feels right to them from various religions and philosophies rather than search for what is true from a theological point of view. They are eclectic in their approach (e.g. mixing tarot cards and Catholicism, Buddhism and astrology) and sometimes believe in conflicting religious matters (e.g. belief in both resurrection and reincarnation).

These are two extremes on a continuum, and there are other positions within it. For example, Charlesworth (1997) points out this paradox: 'I am a

Christian or a Hindu or a Muslim and I believe that the teachings of my religion are true, but at the same time I recognise and accept the fact that there are other religious systems and that other people believe that the teachings of their religion are true.'

From a Christian point of view, he attempts to address this paradox, and believes in two outcomes: Jesus being *totus Dei* (i.e. totally expressive of God) and Jesus not being *totus Dei* (i.e. he is not the exhaustive expression or revelation of God) as illustrated in Figure 1.

If Jesus is *totus Dei*, Christianity is regarded as the religion *par excellence*. The value of other religions can only be seen in comparison to Christianity. For Christians, other religions can have a revelation but not as complete as Christianity. Christianity, from within its perspective, has a privileged position by claiming that God has revealed himself (or herself) most fully (but not exhaustively) to Christians.

If Jesus is not *totus Dei*, we have two sub-types: the theophanies (that is the manifestation of a deity to a man or a woman) are either fragmented or different. If they are fragmented, the religious person believes that other religious systems have received a valid and autonomous revelation of God (or another entity), and that God's revelation will only be known in its fullness when all the revelations from various religions are brought together and the puzzle is completed. However, within this perspective, people do not work on an eclectic amalgam of religious beliefs as in the relativist and syncretic type, but on a kind of puzzle in which the pieces must perfectly fit together before being joined. For example, René Guénon (1886–1951) believed in a great primordial tradition that was once revealed at the beginning of humanity and was transmitted through diverse traditions. For Guénon the only salvation was to find the 'great' knowledge that was once given to humankind. He believed that this knowledge could be discovered through a

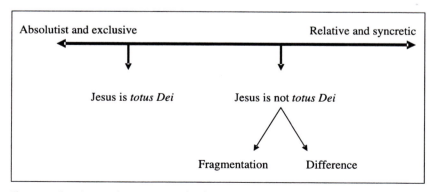

Figure 1 Continuum between an absolutist and a relativistic approach to religion.

type of archaeology of religious knowledge in the great religions which changed the original message after receiving it. In other words, religion as we know it is a layered palimpsest. What he searched for was the original text, the basis of all the palimpsests. He was going beyond his own tradition, not to relativise his faith, but to find the 'real' religion among religions, to find the supreme book among the books of various religious traditions, e.g. what Muslims call 'the mother of the book' (*umm alkitáb*) or the *mutus liber*, the mute book of reality.

If the theophanies are different, we are no longer on various religious paths of the same mountain to salvation like in more relativistic positions (see Figure 2), but we are simply on different paths on different mountains (see Figure 3). This means that one revelation is the source of a set of

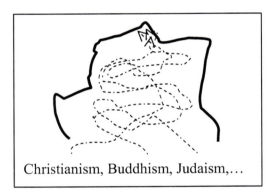

Christianism, Buddhism, Judaism,...

Figure 2 Relativistic approaches to religion (one mountain).

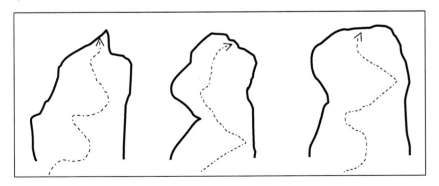

Figure 3 Theophanies are different (many mountains).

religious beliefs, but there are revelations which are more appropriate to specific type of groups and/or people according to their time and specific sociocultural context. With this case, one religious person will see other people from other religions as being in their own faith which does not impact on other people's belief systems.

We live in a multi-creed world in which religions change, react, migrate and create. We are no longer exposed to only one religion but to a variety of them; one simply needs to walk down the streets of a cosmopolitan city or surf religious web pages. Faced with this religious diversity, we are left unsure of what a religion is anymore (Does it need a God? Will a saviour come for us? Am I able to become a god myself? Can the Internet be used as a Church?) and what to believe in if one wants to believe. As discussed above, people can retract into their faith and believe that other faiths are not real whereas others will have the view that all religions are part of the same truth. There are also many zones of grey between these opposite sides as explained above and illustrated in Figure 1.

Conclusion

This book is an attempt to give a sociological explanation of what is happening in the field of religion in today's world but not determine what religion is 'really'. My work follows Beckford's (2001; 2003) social constructionist approach, which is interested in historical and cultural changes that make believers and non-believers change their understanding of what religion and spirituality are rather than an ontological understanding religion.

This book is also a celebration of religious diversity, which must include all religions, even the most unconventional ones that give meaning to its believers as long as they do not contravene criminal law or goes against the rights of others. For example, because of the spread of global and commodified popular culture, some religions use and/or react to this culture. When religious groups use commodified popular culture for their spiritual works, they may make many social commentators raise their eyebrows, or even make them laugh. However, as the next chapter explores, this is nevertheless happening and is in need of being understood as it complexifies conservative understanding of what a religion is.

Notes

1. Internet Site, http://theofantastique.blogspot.com (5/11/07)
2. Internet Site, http://theofantastique.blogspot.com/2007/10/james-mcgrath-on-religion-in-science.html (5/11/07)
3. Vicki Marie Hanna and Church of Scientology Inc v The Commissioner Community and Health Services Complaints Australian Capital Territory [2002] ACTS 111 (6 November 2002).
4. The last chapter of this book will quickly explore the tension between sociologists of religion who support new religious movements as a religion and anti-cultists who claim that the Church is simply hiding behind being a religion to make profit. To see a rather negative account of the Church and of sociologists of religion sharing the ideas developed in this book, see for example, Beit-Hallahmi (2003).

2 Religion and Popular Culture

Introduction

The novels and movies of *Harry Potter* have been so successful that they do not need any introduction in this book. However, what is of interest for this chapter is the graphic novel called *Hairy Polarity and the Sinister Sorcery Satire* published by *The Truth for Youth*[1] which is a Christian evangelical group against pornography, homosexuality, sexual promiscuity, secular rock music, drugs, drunkenness, sorcery and witchcraft. The second page of this book, available on the Internet, is quite telling. A young boy is having an argument with his parents at his home. The boy is aggressive and angry whereas his parents are calm and quote the Bible:

> Young Boy: WHAT!?! You're forbidding me from going out today with Minnie? She's my best friend!! All we do together is read Hairy Polarity books! You ought to be glad I'm finally reading something!!!
>
> Mother: Ari, you've been turning God out of your life lately (Corinthians 11:3)… you don't see your Christian friends anymore…
>
> Father: These books … And Minnie … seem to be a big part of the problem!
>
> Mother: Look, Ari, we've discussed this endlessly! Hairy Polarity is evil! If you can't stop reading those books with Minnie, we don't want you seeing her anymore!
>
> Young Boy: Unbelievable! It's just a fictional story! Nobody actually believes in this stuff… It's just for fun!
>
> Father: Witchcraft isn't fantasy, Ari… It's real. And you don't want to get in-volved in it (Deut. 18:10-11). Like your mom and I were once! A demon was exorcised from us that…
>
> Young boy: "…was bog and blackish. Green and scaly, had a skull-like face, large teeth and things like antlers coming out of his head". YOU'VE TOLD ME THAT STORY LIKE A MILLION TIMES!!!
>
> Mother: Fine. Okay… But the point is… we're trying to protect you, Ari!
>
> Father: Wizards and witches think they're manipulating the world with their magic, but they're being deceived by demonic forces.
>
> Young Boy: I'm just reading a silly book… I'm not a wizard wannabe! And I love Minnie! You're being ridiculous… and cruel!!! I'M OUTTA HERE!!![2]

We have here a conservative religious group that believes popular culture can lead readers and viewers astray. It has therefore created its own work of popular culture to bring people back on the right track, which in this instance, means away from sorcery, witchcraft and Satanism. If the previous chapter of this book explored the politics associated with the definition of religion, this one explores the politics of allowing the 'right' work of popular culture to be read and viewed by people. Since popular culture has become globalised and commodified in today's world, as this chapter demonstrates, some religious groups have used it for their own spiritual work and others have been fighting against it.

This chapter follows from the last one by pointing out that with the use of popular culture, the religious landscape becomes more diversified and it has become even more complex to define religion when, for example, Science Fiction and Fantasy are included in people's spirituality. This process of mixing globalised and commodified popular culture with religion is a reflection of the spirit of our time as it will be developed in Chapter 6.

Popular Culture and Religion

This book does not view popular culture as a sub-culture for the masses, or a form of evasion which leads to a retreat from socio-political activity, or even a form of control of the masses by various groups in power. Popular culture might be all, or some of these, but it is also a medium for the autodetermination of social actors, and more specific to this book, spiritual self-determination. Even if popular culture is part of global capitalism managed by multinational corporations, and even though it provides a form of escapism from our 'anxious' and/or 'hidden' reality like, for example, window shopping does, it is also a platform for our own biography. We live through and with it. We create our lives and view ourselves through popular culture.

Religion and popular culture co-exist intimately, and cannot be seen simply as having a relationship of cause and effect. At times religion creates and regulates popular culture. Indeed, religious actors who express themselves in popular culture are also engaged in shaping popular culture, and in doing so, making possible some experiences and denying access to others. It can take the form of using the content of popular culture to back up their religion, or it can take the form of censorship towards certain narratives. At other times, popular culture can shape the form and content of religion. Some people appear to practise religion/spirituality by creatively reusing the artefacts of contemporary mass-mediated culture – e.g. images, stories, and songs from television, radio, and zines – rather than following the meaning offered by religious institutions. They might view *Star Wars, Star Trek: the Next Generation* or *Oprah* religiously and share with other people fictional or quasi-fictional scenarios. A plethora of distinct popular faiths appear to exist alongside more mainstream religions. Popular culture can be an inspiration for religion as well as amuse, entertain, instruct, and relax people.

As it will be explored in Chapter 4, the time when we were pure social reflections of our parents is gone. Religion, ethnicity, class, political affiliation, tastes and distastes are no longer so easily transmitted from one generation to another. Even if there are exceptions, the trend of today is to create one's own biography/identity. People in this postmodern age pick and choose what suits them for their identity at a specific time and place. As part of this library of choices, popular culture is on the shelf with class, religion, sexuality, significant others… In this process, popular culture, among many other socio-cultural factors, influences the construction of the self, including that of the religious self.

The trend today in western societies is to move away from traditional institutions, and mainstream churches. This process leads many people to seek a sense of spirituality by themselves; to pick and choose what fits with their belief system. In this new diverse and multicultural era, people draw on a vast range of religious resources through consumerism (see Chapter 5). They will pray, meditate and read tarot cards. Crystals and icons will inspire them. They will visit churches and absorb themselves in nature, but also find meaning through popular culture. In short, they are looking for what works for them. As Hume (2006: 11) states:

> Watching movies and television and reading books may engage the individual passively, but what many people want today is an engagement with fantasy that is active. They want to experience the fantasy for themselves. Symbolic arenas are life-like fictions that can move the actor from the realm of play to a lifestyle that immerses his or her total being.

This process would be on one side of a spectrum. For others, on the other side, this world of choice might seem unbearable. Indeed, consumerism can be celebrated by some and disliked by others. While these less consumerist actors do not find answers in mainstream churches, they seek more 'engaged' forms of religion (e.g. some Pentecostal groups) by looking for a stability of commitment in a community with a stronger sense of authority and a tighter system of beliefs and practices; that is, a more structured world/ spiritual view. The way religious/spiritual actors deal with popular culture depends on what side of this heuristic spectrum they tend to be. On one end, we will see that there is a free-market consumption of popular culture as a source of spiritual/religious inspiration. On the other end, the market still exists but it is more restrictive; not in the quantity, but in the breadth of popular culture content (see below).

In Possamai (2005b), I have called the religions that mix popular culture with their beliefs 'hyper-real religions' (that is a simulacrum of a religion partly created out of popular culture which provides inspiration for believers/ consumers). To find this name, I have used the work of Jean Baudrillard, which we will explore at length in Chapter 6. Suffice to say at this moment that hyper-real religions are an example of the sociocultural conditions of our present times, such as the mixing of religion with consumerism (see Chapter 5), and such as finding religious activities outside of mainstream churches (see Chapter 4).

Popular Culture Used for Religious Creativity: Hyper-consumption

By hyper-consumption, I make reference to an avid and eclectic consumption of commercialised popular culture by religious people and or groups. This consumption is not limited to commodities and can be extended to texts and stories sold in global popular culture. As we will see in Chapter 5 on consumer religion, hyper-consumer religious groups such as New Age consume objects from a wide variety of sources (including popular culture) for their beliefs, often with conflicting content. One major characteristic is that the decider of consumption is the consumer rather than the leader, or text, of a specific religious group.

For the purpose of this chapter, I would like to present now a few case studies of what religious groups can do with popular culture. These case studies are meant to show that religious (re)creation is quite active in today's society. Sociologists need to be open and responsive to this religious imagination which, in this case, involves being inspired by contemporary globalised popular culture. As Flory (2000: 241) explains with regard to a common characteristic of generation X, which could easily be transferred to generation Y and to a minority of Baby Boomers as well:

> authentic religious belief is identitified by experience, narrative, creativity, and example, not by rational argumentation for the truth claims of a particular religious belief system. For Xers, rationalistic apologetics are largely irrelevant to their religious commitments, having been replaced by an experience-based epistemology. Thus, religion is not true because someone can construct some detailed argument for it; rather it is what it does, how it makes one feel, and perhaps the commitments that it requires of its adherents that make it so... Thus we see Goths identifying with Anne Rice's vampire

novels, and the existential dilemmas faced by Lestat and Louis, in the midst of their own spiritual crisis.

The Church of All Worlds

The Church of All Worlds is a neo-pagan group (see Chapter 13) founded by Oberon Zell in Missouri, USA. It moved to Ukiah, California, in 1967. This group bases its teaching in part on Robert Heinlein's science-fiction novel *Stranger in a Strange Land,* which narrates the story of Valentine Michael Smith – a Martian living on earth with god-like powers who taught human-kind how to love. The group is not limited to the reading of this novel and even extends its consumption to the *Star Trek* mythos; as one of their members states:

> This whole period (late 1960s) fell under the shadow of the Damoclean Sword of impending nuclear holocaust, and a dominant Christian culture that fully embraced an apocalyptic mythos. For many of us, a powerful anti-dote to that mythos was found in science fiction, and particularly Gene Roddenberry's *Star Trek*, with its Vulcan IDIC: 'Infinite Diversity in Infinite Combinations'. CAW [Church of All Worlds] and Green Egg avidly embraced this vision of, as Roddenberry said, 'a future everyone will want to be part of'.[3]

Neo-Paganism

More broadly to neo-paganism (see Chapter 13), the literature labelled 'fantasy' and 'Medieval romance' seem to express and explore neo-pagan issues (Harvey 2000; Luhrmann 1994; Rose 2006). J.R.R. Tolkiens's *Lord of the Rings*, Marion Bradley's *The Mist of Avalon*, Brian Bates's *The Way of Wyrd*, Terry Pratchett's *Discworld* corpus, and even Gibson's cyber-punk *Neuromancer* and Wagner's operas, are all parts of a cultural reservoir which contribute to neo-pagan thinking. While there is no 'biblical' text of reference in neo-paganism, the construction of the pagan self entails reading works of fiction. These fantasy books describe a pagan world and consequently contribute to the pagan experience of the reader (Harvey 2000).

In Ellwood (2004), we discover how some people involved in the craft use popular culture as a method of practising magic. The author explains how he uses the character of Buffy the Vampire Slayer as a god-form of protection, equality, and magic. Instead of using magic and incantation in the name of a god as is often practised in religions comprising a large pantheon of gods, certain neo-pagans use icons of popular culture. The purpose be-hind these magical practices/rituals is to focus one's energy on the character-istic of this god/pop icon. For example, as the author (ibid: 187) explains:

> Let me give you a quick example. You may want to go on a diet, but know under ordinary circumstances you'd have trouble keeping to it. You can use

the magick of working with a pop culture entity to help you. Who do you use? Were I to go on a diet I'd use the pop culture entity Jared, who represents the Subway franchise. You'll see him a lot on US television and each time he's showing the benefits of a successful diet. So what you do is create a god-form out of Jared. Observe the commercials, take notes on attributes you'd want your Jared god-form to have and then on the first night of the diet and each night after invoke the Jared god-form to help you keep to the diet. Now on a humorous aside you may find yourself having an inexplicable craving for Subway subs, but so be it. As long as you are dieting and reaching your target weight it doesn't matter. What does matter is that you invest Jared with your belief that he will keep you dieting. Use chants, images, and whatever else as needed.

The need for a pop icon, according to this testimony, should only be for the time that one person needs it. After this, the practitioner should move to another pop icon. The danger if this is not acted upon is that the person might start believing too much in the icon instead of using it for a specific purpose.

The Church of Scientology

Another movement clearly inspired by science fiction, and more specifically by Ron Hubbard's stories, is the Church of Scientology (see Chapter 1), which is sometimes referred to as the 'Science Fiction Religion' (Cohen et al. 1987). During the 1940s, science fiction was beginning to explore themes concerning the powers of the mind, and John W. Cambell encouraged such stories in the leading US magazine *Astounding Science Fiction*. The founder of the Church, Hubbard, who was at that time a science fiction and adventure writer, published the article that formed the basis of his religion in the May 1950 issue of *Astounding Science Fiction*, titled 'Dianetics: The Evolution of Science'. Although this article and a book published at the same time *Dianetics: The Modern Science of Mental Health* caused a sensation, many science fiction fans and writers claimed that the creation of the religion has no connection at all with science fiction (Holdstock 1978).

H.P. Lovecraft and the Church of Satan

Horror stories can also provide a reservoir of cultural content to be consumed. In 1966, in San Francisco, Anton LaVey founded the Church of Satan as a medium for the study of the Black Arts. His assumption of the inherent selfishness and violence of human beings is at the base of its non-Christian teaching. Satan, often misunderstood as the long time opponent of God, according to La Vey, is described as a hidden force in nature that can be tapped into. In *The Satanic Rituals,* which is used by some as a basis for metaphysical growth, LaVey (1972) refers to the metaphysics of H.P. Lovecraft, a writer of weird fiction who wrote most of his tales during the 1920s and 1930s. H.P. Lovecraft developed a pantheon of gods, the Ancient Ones – e.g. Cthulhu, Yog-Sothoth and Nyarlathotep – who are waiting in secrecy before coming back to earth to conquer the human race. In 'The Nameless City' (1921), Lovecraft introduced the 'mad Arab' Abdul Alhazred who penned the ancient tome *The Necronomicon*. This book, claiming to reveal all the secrets of the world, especially those of the Ancient Ones, became a standard prop in all later stories, and many readers believed it actually existed (Lacroix 2007). Lovecraft always claimed that his stories were fictional and that he was a total agnostic. However, LaVey (1972), believing that 'fantasy plays an important part in any religious curriculum', developed some rituals for his Church of Satan based on this fictional mythology. The following is a ceremony extract:

> N'kgnath ki'q Az-Athoth r'jyarh wh'fagh zhasa phr-tga nyena phragn'glu.
> *Translation: Let us do honor to Azathoth, without whose laughter this world should not be.*

The influence of Lovecraft is also found in the more recent phenomenon of Teenage Satanism (Lowney 1995) and felt in other groups such as the Esoteric Order of Dagon and the Order of the Trapezoid[4] from the Temple of Set[5], which is a chivalric order of knighthood.

Star Wars

In the 2001 Australian census, 70,509 people, that is 0.37% of the 2001 Australian population, identified with the Jedi religion from *Star Wars (AAP 2002)*. New Zealand followed the trend and had 53,715 people (that is, 1.5% of its population). In the UK, the 2001 census revealed that 390,000 people declared to be followers of the Jedi 'faith': that is 0.7% of the UK population. John Pullinger, the UK director of reporting and analysis at the Office for National Statistics (ONS), claims that Jedi supporters were mostly in their late teens and 20s (anon. 2003).

Is it a joke or does this reflect a trend that social scientists of religion should seriously take into account? The Australian Star Wars Appreciation Society President estimates that about 5,000 people out of these 70,509 would be true 'hard-core' believers of the Jedi religion – most probably at a metaphorical level. He estimates that 50,000 fans would have put down Jedi religion just for fun, and 15,000 people 'did it just to give the government a bit of curry' (Agence France-Press 2002).[6] In one discussion group, one believer in Jediism claims that 'it is important to remember that there is a difference between "Jedi" on a census form and calling oneself a Jediist'.[7]

Moving towards the Internet medium, we discover that the introduction to the 'Jedi Knight Movement' discussion list states:[8]

The Way of Jedi transcends the science fiction series of *Star Wars*. It encompasses many of the same truths and realizations of the major world religions, including Zen Buddhism, Taoism, Hinduism, Catholicism, and Shinto and is both a healing art and a meditative journey that the aspirant can take to improve every aspect of their life.

A messages from the same 'Jedi Knight Movement' discussion list states about 'Jediknightism':

Life on planet earth has become much more complex – the churches, although meaning well, many times fall short of the mark of addressing the complexities. The political arena many times disappoint us and fall short of inspiring either ourselves or others to action.

We can infer from this statement that people who embrace this religion are critical of mainstream religions and political movements. Without these grand narratives, they are left with another type of narrative:

Storytelling is an age-old tradition that has followed mankind for millennia – and has been used effectively for transferring ideals, from philosophers to prophets. It is an ideal medium to both entertain and enlighten simultaneously, which is why it is so powerful and its effects so profound when used expertly.

This site encourages interested people to develop their spiritual potential outside of mainstream religions and governments in an entertaining fashion. Jediism will be further analysed in Chapter 6.

Matrixism

Another spirituality which has popular culture central to its belief system is Matrixism. This hyper-real religion is based on the motion picture trilogy *The Matrix*. It claims to have a history that goes back nearly 100 years. Through an exchange of e-mails with the acting secretary of the group, I was told that Matrixism started at the end of July 2004, went off-line for most of 2005 due to what I have been told were death threats, and is now back on line at http:/www.geocities.com/matrixism2069. In a recent e-mail to celebrate the 2008 New Year, the acting secretary claimed there were 2,000 members around the world. Surfing their site, one can discover a link to the Multidisciplinary Association for Psychedelic Studies and the influence of Huxley's *Doors of Perception* on Matrixism. There are also parallels with the Baha'i Faith to validate the religious aspect of the trilogy.

Heaven's Gate Group and Star Trek

One should not forget the Heaven's Gate group that committed mass suicide in San Diego in 1997. Its members believed that a UFO was travelling behind the Hale-Bop comet and by leaving their physical bodies behind, they would reach the extraterrestrial realm. They watched the *X-Files* and *Star Trek* almost religiously and took fiction seriously. Indeed, as one member expressed a week before the infamous event:

> We watch a lot of *Star Trek*, a lot of *Star Wars*, it's just, to us, it's just like going on a holodeck. We've been training on a holodeck … [and] now it's time to stop. The game's over. It's time to put into practice what we've learned. We take off the virtual reality helmet… go back out of the holodeck to reality to be with, you know, the other members on the craft in the heavens (quoted by Robinson 1997).

Robinson (1997) comments that these members envisioned death as the ultimate Trekkie trip to the final frontier.

It should be noted that because one group has become infamous for consuming popular culture, the whole phenomenon should not be condemned. That would be like repressing the action of all members of New Religious Movements because a small minority have been involved in destructive cults (see Chapter 12).

Popular Culture Used for Policing: Hypo-consumption

By hypo-consumerism I make reference to a more organised and limited style of religious consumerism that is guided by a religious expert or group rather than the individual making a choice for himself or herself. Everything consumed must re-enforce the religious belief system and cannot be in conflict. The popular culture consumed will be one that fits with the religion and the popular culture in conflict will have to be policed. Fundamentalist/literalist Christian groups (see Chapter 8) are part of this consumerism and have become more than just a marketing niche for global popular culture, e.g. Walt Disney promoting its adaptation of C.S. Lewis's *The Lion, the Witch and the Wardrobe* as a 'Passion of the Christ for kids' in an attempt to secure worldwide Christian support for the film (Hastings and Laurence 2005). They are also a pressure group against certain forms of popular culture (e.g. Imax cinemas refusing to show movies that suggest that Earth's origins do not conform with biblical description such as James Cameron's *Volcanoes of the Deep Sea*) and against the use of non-Christian popular culture for religious practice. For example, the Anglican Church in Sydney screened a trailer in 250 cinemas to tell cinema-goers about their website, which challenges the theories in the *The Da Vinci Code*. Described as 'Harry Potter for adults', this movie was banned in a cinema on the Central Coast of NSW because of the way it depicts the Catholic Church.

Some cases of this policing of popular culture by these groups are now quickly explored.

Star Wars

Many Internet sites promote a Christian exegesis of popular culture. An example is the site of Marcia Montenegro,[9] an ex-astrologer who has a sound knowledge of alternative spiritualities. Some of her attacks are strong, such as those against *Harry Potter* and Marilyn Manson, and others softer, such as those against the *Star Wars* movies. Her critique of the Force is that it is a flow of energy that has as opposites good and evil; and these are 'wrongly' equal. In this fictional worldview, the dynamic of opposing forces holds everything in harmony. Whereas the Force has a dark and light side, the Holy Spirit is for Christian good only, does not need to be balanced, and does not fit with the mythology of the Force. Montenegro sees in *Star Wars* a mythos that needs to be re-evaluated as a good platform for parents to discuss various philosophies with older children. Her comments are not at all derogatory and she views many positive aspects as well. As she suggests to Christian parents:

> The Star Wars movies, if seen by parents as well, can be a good platform for a discussion with older children of these various philosophies as compared to Scripture. The concept of the Force versus the personal nature of God; the dark/light dualism of the Force versus the absolute good and evil declared by God; and the emphasis on feelings in Star Wars versus the Biblical mandate to use our minds and love God with our minds, are all productive areas for discussion, and a good way to teach your child to be discerning. The worldviews presented in Star Wars movies may be somewhat subtle, but such views exist in our culture and need to be understood and responded to.

Pokemon and Digimon

Pokemon was created in Japan and became popular around the world in 1996. Pokemon is short for 'Pocket Monsters' and started as a cartoon involving little monsters that have to be caught. Many of these monsters are seen as 'cute' whereas others represent the forces of evil. The popularity of this story is part of a cultural industry that has merged these cartoons with successful card and video games.

In 2001, Saudi Arabia banned Pokemon and anti-Pokemon campaigns happened in Jordan, Egypt, Oman, Qatar and Dubai. Shaykh Yusuf al-Qaradawi, a widely listened to cleric close to the Fundamentalist Muslim Brotherhood, joined the fight by issuing a fatwa on the 30th December 2003. He argued that Pokemon indirectly supports Darwin's theory of evolution and is thus contrary to the creationist view of the world; that the stories are constructed out of the authors' imagination rather than from the surrounding 'real' nature; that the stories always involved battles in which the stronger survives – another of Darwin's 'dogma'; and that there are signs hidden in the series which are connected to the Zionists and Masons such as the 'Hexa Star'.[10] According to Tugend (2001), some Moslem officials claim that the word 'Pokemon' means 'I am a Jew' in Japanese, believing that this consumerist ploy is part of a Jewish-Zionist conspiracy to turn Arab children away from Islam.

Pokemon is also criticised by some Christian groups. Reading a few sources from the Internet,[11] it becomes obvious that the perception that these creatures are teaching children about evolutionary thought and pagan/occult beliefs is strong. Pokemon is claimed to be the result of mystical/occult influences such as Buddhist Mysticism, Hinduism, meditation rituals, Egyptian Book of the Dead, Book of Tao, the Analects of Confucius, the Bhagavad-gita, the I Ching, and the Tibetan Book of the Dead. As one minister states:

> Recently I observed a group of children who were playing role-playing Pokemon. They were making evil faces and chanting their Pokemon character names over and over! One three year old was chasing another boy almost trance like in expression saying in a deep raspy voice: 'bulbasore attack, bulbasore, bulbasore.' They are meditating and projecting their spirit just like practioners of the occult.

Or from another Christian author: 'Children are being encouraged to tap into supernatural power instead of the power given by God'.

Digimon, short for Digital Monsters, is a serialised cartoon close to the Pokemon 'franchise' in which 'good' Digimons try to keep the world safe from 'evil' Digimons. Although the fight between good and evil might appeal to fundamentalists (see Chapter 8), references in some of the shows that wizards can be one's friend and that demons and devils can be innocent are of concern to religious moral entrepreneurs.[12]

The Lord of the Rings and Harry Potter

It has been noted above that, among other works of fiction, Tolkien's *Lord of the Rings* is being used as a source of inspiration for neo-pagans. However, accounts from some other religious actors are different. On a Christian forum,[13] a fundamentalist writes:

> Though [some] would have us believe that Tolkien's books contain simple allegories of good vs. evil, Tolkien portrays wizards and witches and wizardry as both good and evil. For example, a wizard named Gandalf is portrayed as a good person who convinces Bilbo Baggins in *The Hobbit* to take a journey to recover stolen treasure. The books depict the calling up of the dead to assist the living, which is plainly condemned in the Scriptures. Though not as overtly and sympathetically occultic as the Harry Potter series, Tolkien's fantasies are *unscriptural* and present a very dangerous message.

However, not all accounts from monotheistic believers are negative. According to Kilby (1974), the trilogy has indeed a religious meaning, but more specifically a Christian one. Even if Tolkien, himself a devout Christian, claimed to dislike allegories and to have written the story just to amuse himself, there is nevertheless a strong Christian sub-text. According to Kilby (1974), the whole story, even if not a sermon to be preached but a story to be enjoyed, must be given a strong spiritual reading of biblical inference.

From an Islamic perspective, an article posted on IslamOnline[14] acknowledges the credentials of Tolkien as a Roman Catholic (seen as cousins to Islam) Oxford Professor and warns against taking a 'knee-jerk' reaction to Tolkien on the basis that it might advocate sorcery and magic (*sehr*). Claiming that in the wrong hands, fantasy is capable of spreading *kufr* (that is, a disbelief in Islamic monotheism), he does not recommend outright Tolkien's books and the new movie adaptation to Muslims. In his article, he is much less sympathetic to *Dungeons and Dragons* and *Harry Potter*.

It appears from my research that *Harry Potter* has been more controversial than *Lord of the Rings*. Montenegro (2000) is a writer on the Internet whose account of *Star Wars* we have already discussed, and she now provides a way to understand this issue. She makes a difference between fantasy novels that include magical elements and fantasy stories centred on the occult. Whereas Tolkien's stories are just fantasy, Harry Potter would be a fantasy story using occultism. Harry Potter is argued to make reference to occult history and known practices – e.g. Nicolas Flamel and witch spells – and is not a work of pure imagination like the *Lord of the Rings*. As she states:

> There is a difference between fantasy and the occult. Fantasy [e.g. *Lord of the Rings*] can be used in a way that totally leaves out references to the occult. But this is not what happens in this book [*Harry Potter*]; instead fantasy feeds on the occult and is fuelled by it. Yes, this is just a story, but stories can teach and influence. Stories can present ideas and endorse worldviews. Does this book desensitize children to the occult? What happens when they get older and encounter peers who practice magick, cast spells, and attempt spirit contact? These practices are becoming more popular, and are already widespread among adolescents.

Moving now to *Harry Potter* only, we can appreciate this quote:

> Young readers can relate to Harry: he is the underdog hero who manages to triumph, and like so many children today, he longs for a family who will truly love him… Harry Potter contains powerful and valuable lessons about love, courage and the ultimate victory of good over evil. However, children who read the books will also be confronted with two distinctly non-Christian worldviews: occultism and secularism.[15]

Indeed, Harry Potter, a young English orphan who learns about witchcraft at a secret English school for young wizards, is an extremely popular character, and a likeable one. The plots reinforce the idea that evil is real and must be courageously opposed. It also teaches that human beings have to show courage, loyalty and a willingness to sacrifice oneself for others. Even if some Christian commentators, such as Neal (2001), might take a positive view of myth and fantasy and believe that some stories such as Harry Potter convey analogies to the story of Jesus, for many fundamentalist Christian groups, the *Harry Potter* books are training manuals for the occult and have become the method of introduction of Wicca to the very young.

On a promotional Internet Site for a video against Harry Potter, *Harry Potter: Witchcraft Repackaged. Making Evil Look Innocent,*[16] we are told that sorcery is being introduced in all American public schools disguised as children's fantasy literature. The video/DVD is aimed at explaining to parents how to teach the children that spell-castings are forbidden territory. The site then lists a few accounts from children such as 'I feel like I'm inside Harry's world. If I went to wizard school I'd study everything: spells, counterspells, and defence against the dark arts (Carolyn, age 10)' or 'It would be great to be a wizard because you could control situations and things like teachers (Jeffrey, age 11)'. It then concludes by stating: 'Stop and think: what will these children do when invited to visit an occult website, or even a local coven?' And there are the comics warning against the novels and movies which have been introduced in this chapter.

Conclusion

As seen in the previous chapter, religion is a site of contestation when it comes to its definition. This chapter demonstrated that this site of contestation can be extended to other factors such as to the use of popular culture for religious purpose. With hyper-consumerist religious groups, there is a free market available when selecting the type of popular culture that works for the individual in his or her spiritual activities. With hypo-consumerist religious group, the market needs to be restricted, controlled, and policed so as people do not 'wrongly' construct their own spirituality and go astray.

With the case study of the Church of Scientology in Chapter 1 and the case studies of the use of popular culture for religious purpose in this chapter, I have attempted to demonstrate that religion can be very active outside conventional churches, mosques and synagogues. Religion is not bounded by walls but is lived and expressed by a wide range of diverse people with various spiritual needs and wants. Religion, needless to say, has the inexhaustible capacity to surprise even its most astute observers (Introvigne 2004).

This whole book intends to explore what happens to these diverse people with their variety of beliefs; however, before explaining this at length in Chapter 4, this book first needs to cement the background to future sociological debates. For this, we need to explore what our fathers of sociology wrote on religion and modernity.

Some readers might question the structure of this book and wonder about the place of this chapter on popular culture between a chapter on definition and a chapter on classical theories. This chapter has simply been put in this place to pedagogically draw early on the concern and life experiences of generations X and Y.

Notes

1. Internet Site, http://www.thetruthforyouth.com (5/11/07)
2. Internet Site, http://www.thetruthforyouth.com/special/hpcomic/images/HP-page2.jpg (5/11/07)
3. Internet site, http://www.greenegg.org/issues/123/oberonedit123.html (05/01/00).
4. Internet site, http://www.trapezoid.org/statement.html (18/04/00).
5. Internet site, http://www.xeper.org/pub/tos/noframe.htm (18/04/00).
6. At the time of the writing of this book, I have not come across data from a more academic source.
7. Internet site, http://www.jediism.net/forum/viewtopic.php?t=177 (5/08/04).
8. Internet site, http://groups.yahoo.com/groups/Jedi_Knight_Movement/ (25/10/2002).
9. Internet Site, http://cana.userworld.com/cana_contents.html (03/08/2004).
10. See Internet Site, http://www.cesnur.org/2004/pokemon_01.htm (27/02/2004).
11. Internet Sites, http://sureword.faithweb.com/pokemon.html and http://www.godandscience.org/doctrine/pokemon.html and http://www.crossroad.to/text/responses/answerstopokemon.html (27/02/2004).
12. Internet Site, http://www.breakthroughgaming.com/digi_poke.shtml (25/08/2004).
13. Internet Site, http://forums.christianity.com/html/p681045 (23/08/2004).
14. Internet Site, http://www.islamonline.net/english/ArtCulture/2001/12/article12.shtml (23/08/2004).
15. Quoted from Bob Waliszewski by McManus on the Internet, http://www.marriagesavers.org/Columns/C954.htm (27/02/2004).
16. Internet Site, http://www.chick.com/catalog/videos/0127.asp (04/08/04).

3 Religion and Modernity: Marx, Durkheim and Weber

Introduction

In the graphic novel series of Frank Miller's *Sin City* recently adapted for the big screen, the reader is exposed to a revival of the 1940–50s film noir. In these stories, each character is far from being a boy scout. The only heroes, who are themselves criminals or adventurers of the deviant type, are the ones who have managed to keep a sense of honour. Everyone in this Sin City has been corrupted by greed, yet these anti-heroes, somehow, manage to show goodness.

In the first book of the series, Marvin, a sociopath who is not afraid of killing anyone who gets in his way, wakes up in a sordid hotel room to find his blonde companion dead. Instead of leaving Sin City to escape the police who believe he is guilty of the murder, Marvin decides to find the killer. The more information he finds on his path to the truth, the more he realises the extent to which the city is corrupt; especially at very high levels. After killing a few people, including a cannibal with the face of an angel, Marvin becomes involved with a community of prostitutes as powerful as the mafia, and reaches the end of his journey. He discovers that the person behind the crime of his blonde is the most powerful person in the city: Cardinal Roark, a man as capable of bringing down the mayor or getting a governor elected as he is of saying the Lord's Prayer.

Marvin tracks him down and kills him to avenge the death of his lover. In this world, there is no hope of changing society and bringing justice to light, except by going outside the corrupt judicial system as Marvin did. At the end, this anti-hero is eventually caught, condemned, and sent to the electric chair.

In this very negative view of society and religion, we can find undertones of a Marxist vision. For Marx, humans are essentially good, but are corrupted by living in a capitalist society. Indeed, the society of Marx's time was seen as having been built from the expansion and control of economic power in the hand of a few capitalists. In Miller's story, religion is seen to be working hand in hand with capitalist power to generate and maintain profits, and thus corrupt humankind. Although Miller's story fits with a Marxist vision of society, which this chapter explores, this vision is far from what other social theorists such as Durkheim and Weber understood of religion within modernity. Before touching on their work, this chapter explains first what is meant by modernity.

Modernity

The beginning of modernity coincides with the Industrial (*circa* 1800) and the French revolutions (1789). These revolutions created a new form of society in which the old traditional values such as those from religion could no longer influence people to the same extent. Science and fact opposed speculation, intuition, faith and revelation, which, contrary to past practices, were no longer considered relevant sources of knowledge in the public sphere. One could no longer mention having been contacted by the 'other world', or being inspired by the Bible, when making political decisions in parliament or a business deal. Reason became the common *lingua franca* and was seen as the most powerful tool for avoiding the religious wars that had previously decimated the population of Europe. Differences between Catholicism and Protestantism were no longer so relevant, since the language of reason had put the majority of men and women above these disputes.

When studying modernity as a time period between let say 1798 and the 1960s, one must attempt to enter the same spirit to understand the past. The imaginary of progress was so great that postcards were issued for certain factories that were considered to be the pride of their industrial country. In modernity, faith in progress and in industrial power was so strong that the chimneys of factories were said to have replaced the steeples of cathedrals. The dominant thought of this time period was that with reason, humankind would obtain a rational knowledge which would be objective and universal. This knowledge, once tested and proven correct, would lead to the social betterment of all levels of society; something that religion had been criticised for not being capable of.

Without going into too much into detail, sociology emerged around this time and was trying to understand these social and cultural changes. Before the advent of industrial society, order was believed to be kept in control by God. However, with the birth of the modern individual who could make independent decisions, God was no longer seen to intervene in civil matters. But if it was then the role of the emancipated individual to organise society without God, how was order maintained? And further, since modernity brought the new imaginary of progress, was it true that traditions no longer needed to be reproduced for each generation? It then became more important to move a society further along the path to technological and scientific advancement than to repeat traditions. For the first time in history, a society was not exclusively driven by what it had done in the past but by what it could do in the future.

The fathers of sociology attempted to study the beginning of modernity, and principally how western society gave birth to modernity, how a sense of order was maintained in the world, and how progress affected the newly emancipated men free from religion. Basically, since humankind was without God in the public sphere, questions arose about how we were able to stay and live together. And further since the apocalypse was no longer going to happen, social thinkers were asking what was going to eventuate next?

These fathers of sociology laid down the foundations for sociology so well that it took years for sociologists to revise some of the findings that were originally put forward. Indeed, as the next chapter explains, the writings of Marx, Durkheim and Weber were so strong on the decline of religion in their society that many sociologists did not bother to look at the way religion was changing and adapting itself to modernity.

This chapter is now exploring what the fathers of sociology had to say about the place of religion in modernity. These theorists will be divided into two different ways of looking at religion: the functional (Marx and Durkheim) versus the substantive approach (Weber) to religion.

Functional Understanding of Religion

When following a functional understanding of religion, social theorists analyse religion in terms of what it does for the individual, for the society at large, or for both. The problem in defining what religion does, as detailed below, is that it is likely to include secular ideologies such as nationalism and revolutionary faith which have no reference to supernatural beings.

Marx (1818–83) and Engels (1820–95)

Both Marx and Engels viewed religion in a negative way. In their vision of modernity, which stemmed from their conflict theory, they both saw that the means of production were in the control of the upper classes (aka the bourgeoisie) who kept the profit (also called the surplus value) that should have been redistributed equally among the working class (aka the proletariat). For their work, the exploited working class was not given the same lifestyle as the bourgeoisie even though they deserved it. The solution Marx and Engels provided was to plan a revolution which would change the whole structure of society. This new world structure would create a totally new model for sharing goods which would no longer lead to inequalities and which could only work through the mobilisation of a very large part of the population.

They reasoned that if the working class could realise they were exploited, they could reach a class consciousness and unite against the forces of oppression to overthrow the bourgeoisie. This revelation would lead to a dream society where everyone, whatever their background, would have the same income and be protected within a fairer society that would use reason to govern individuals.

Traditional Marxists argued that, during modernity, religion was basically a tool of oppression and legitimation used by the upper classes to contain the proletariat in a subordinate position and prevent them from reaching the class consciousness needed for Marxist revolution. Marx and Engels used the metaphor of opium to illustrate that religion acts like a drug to dull the pain caused by oppression. In other words, religion is used to make the exploited life of the proletariat more liveable. As the famous quote from Marx goes (cited in Lane (1970: 458): 'Religion acts as an opiate to dull the pain produced by oppression. It does nothing to solve the problem: it is simply a misguided attempt to make life more bearable.'

Because of this, religion is also viewed as having a narcotic impact on revolution because it prevents the working class from realising the strength that they would have if they unite. It was viewed as acting as a mechanism of social control reproducing the existing system of exploitation and maintaining class relationships.

In more specific terms, when Christianity makes a promise of paradise and eternal bliss when one dies, it gives hope to oppressed people who can be looking for a more attractive afterlife than their current life. Religion, and especially Christianity, can also engender a sense of virtue in the follower who suffers. If one takes into account the well known passage from the Bible, 'It is easier for a camel to pass through the eye of a needle, than for a rich man to enter the Kingdom of Heave', one might believe that living in poverty provides rewards in the afterlife. Furthermore, if some religions proclaim that the world is about to end, why would someone start a revolution when they believe that everything is about to be destroyed? And lastly, religion can also justify the position of a person on earth by proclaiming that his or her position in a society has been decided by the will of God. God would have determined who should be a bourgeois or a proletariat and since it is the will of God, nothing could be done about it. All of these factors prevent the working class from desiring to implement change, which concomitantly makes the ideal of a revolution unattractive.

Notwithstanding these issues, Engels (1959: 170) analysed the origins of Christianity and discovered that there were strong similarities between the working-class movement in modernity and the first Christians. Both preached forthcoming salvation from bondage and misery, but while Christianity placed this salvation in a life beyond death in heaven, socialism situated it in this world. However, this early Christianity later became a dogmatically fixed universal religion through the Nicene Council (325 AD), which changed the early positive nature of this religion into one that has been negatively commented upon by the above authors.

In simple terms, Marxists see that religion keeps people in their place and acts as a brake towards the revolution to communism. Religion functions as a social mechanism which justifies the higher position of the dominant class in modernity and that of the underprivileged for their suffering. If the communist revolution succeeds, Marxists see no need for religion as there will be no class division.

The problem with this functional definition of religion is that it can include nationalism, revolutionary faith, or any other dominant ideology, as they can act as ideological tools of social control as well. For example, during the Stalinist period, Russians were dominated and controlled in the name of communist revolution, which made them believe their oppressed lifestyle was for the good of their country. Furthermore, it has been common in some countries for political parties or the military to gain power and maintain it to accumulate wealth while promoting a nationalistic propaganda.

Durkheim (1858–1917)

Durkheim is the founder of the functionalist school of thought. In a nutshell, functionalism sees society as a system divided into a series of parts and sub-parts that fit together. As each organ in a human body has its place and function, each institution (e.g. family, religion, government) and other social groups have a specific function to perform for the benefit of a society as a whole. Durkheim believed that a society is more than the sum of its parts because if all parts of a society perform their function and are well connected to other parts like the organs of our bodies, what comes out is a new whole. Indeed, to reuse the biological metaphor, if one can imagine all the body parts put together inside out and piled together in a box, one will certainly realise that it is the synchronised orchestration of all of these various parts that makes up the body and not the piling of its parts. Further, the element that holds all of these parts and sub-parts together is a type of social glue or social cement which Durkheim equated to social norms and values, and as it will be shown shortly, religion is one of these glues.

Durkheim's key work on religion comes from his book first published in 1912, *The Elementary Forms of the Religious Life* (Durkheim 2001). He started his argument with the premise that all societies divide the world into two distinct categories: that of the 'sacred' and that of the 'profane'. As he (Durkheim 2001: 36–37) stated:

By sacred things one must not understand simply those personal things which are called gods or spirits; a rock, a tree, a spring, a pebble, a piece of wood, a house, in a word anything can be sacred. A rite can have this sacred character as well; in fact, no rite exists that does not have it to some degree. There are words, speeches, and formulas that can be spoken only by consecrated persons; there are gestures and movements that cannot be executed by everyone.

As an illustration of this statement, the historian Mircea Eliade (1959), although not a functionalist, gave an excellent example of a stone that became sacred:

[The stone] becomes sacred – and hence instantly becomes saturated with being – because it constitutes a hierophany [i.e. a manifestation of magical powers], or possesses mana [i.e. a type of force], or again because it commemorates a mythical act, and so on. The object appears as the receptacle of an exterior force that differentiates it from its milieu and gives it meaning and value. This force may reside in the substance of the object or in its form; a rock reveals itself to be sacred because its very existence is a hierophany: incompressible, invulnerable, it is that which man [sic] is not. It resists time; its reality is coupled with perenniality. Take the commonest of stones; it will be raised to the rank of 'precious' that is, impregnated with a magical or religious power by virtue of its symbolic shape or its origin: thunderstone, held to have fallen from the sky; pearl, because it comes from the depth of the sea (Eliade 1959: 4).

From this premise of the world being divided between the 'sacred' and the 'profane', Durkheim (2001: 46) then reached for a definition of religion as 'a unified system of beliefs and practices to sacred things, that is to say, things set apart and forbidden – beliefs and practices which unite into one single moral community called a Church'.

Religion, for Durkheim, was seen to act as a social glue that held everyone within a specific society together around these sacred things. But how did this social glue start? Why did people begin to believe in the first instance? To answer these questions, Durkheim analysed the accounts of anthropologists who studied Aboriginal religion, believing that to study a complex phenomenon such as religion one must begin by analysing its simplest form. Like many thinkers of his time, he viewed Aboriginal religion as the most simple and 'primitive' religion (which has, of course, been later proven otherwise, e.g. Hume 2002). Studying the texts available at this time period, Durkheim realised that each Aboriginal clan followed the rule of exogamy (i.e. members cannot marry within the same clan) and each of them had a totem. This totem was an animal or a plant and represented the sign which an Aboriginal group identified itself with, and against other groups with different totems. The totem was also seen as a sacred symbol.

For Durkheim, the totem was the materialisation of the totemic principle or God, and the whole clan was linked to it. He further wondered that since each clan seemed to be attached to this totem like a social glue, the totem might be more than the symbol of God, but could also be the symbol of this society without its members even realising it. Durkheim then took the next step in arguing that through this totem, God and society were the same and one. In other words, he suggested that by worshipping their God, people were in fact worshiping their own society. Society, for Durkheim, was the real object of religious veneration and not God. But how, in Durkheim's understanding, can humankind come to worship society instead of God without them even realising?

Sacred things, according to him, give a sense of awe, inferiority and dependency to humans; which is how humans are in relation to society as well, as society is considered more important and powerful than the individual. The reason why humans do not worship society instead of a god or other sacred people/thing, is because society is too abstract and complex to be consciously materialised into such a thing as a totem. By having people getting together and worshiping society, religion thus helps to maintain the togetherness of these people like a type of social glue. Religion, in this perspective, helps people to share common values and moral beliefs, which for the French sociologist, form the collective consciousness. Without this collective consciousness, there will be no social order, and thus no society. And through the worship of society/God, the values and moral beliefs of a society are thus strengthened.

As Cosman (2001: xx) summarises:

> Religion, then, is a set of beliefs and practices by which society represents itself to itself. It is the way society experiences itself as itself. Divinity and society are one – or rather, god is a figurative expression of society. If we feel dependent on god, that is but a symbolic representation of our dependency on society; if we tremble at god's justice and punishment, that is our regard for society's laws.

Durkheim believed that with the development of modernity, religion would slowly disappear. However, as religion was such a strong social glue before modernity, an alternative had to come to keep people linked together within a society. This new glue was that of civil religion (as defined by Bellah (1967) who was inspired by Durkheim's work to coin this concept). This civil religion is basically a form of religion derived from the nation-state such as nationalism which has no connections to the supernatural world. As part of this civil religion, the state uses rituals, symbols and language to promote a homogeneous national identity. This religion includes, for example, the strong symbolism of the Statue of Liberty and Big Ben which are 'sacred' to their nation in a similar way as the cross is for Christians. Another symbol of civil religion is the tomb of the unknown warrior in Britain and in France, and as Davie (2000: 162) observes,

> In France, this symbol of national pride is located on secular soil; the tomb is placed beneath the Arc de Triomphe in the heart of the capital city and reflects the laïcité[1] of public life (unusually – in European terms – there is no religious inscription on this tomb). In Britain, on the other hand, the same symbol lies just inside the main door of Westminster Abbey, where institutional Christianity (embodied in Anglican form) meets the secular world or indeed the world of popular belief.

With the constant withdrawal of religion from everyday concerns, Durkheim saw in nationalism the new social glue that would hold everyone within a society together. In this case, it becomes clear that Durkheim's functional definition of religion includes belief systems such as nationalism that have nothing to do with supernatural beings. Indeed, as Durkheim (2001: 322) concluded towards the end of his book:

> What essential difference is there between an assembly of Christians commemorating the principal moments in the life of Christ, or Jews celebrating either the exodus from Egypt or the giving of the Ten Commandments, and a meeting of citizens commemorating the institution of a new moral charter or some great event in national life?

Functionalism and Marxism thus share a functionalist perspective on religion which is viewed in terms of what it does for an individual or a society. However, by focusing on the function of religion, which is negative for Marx and positive for Durkheim, religion can be so easily replaced by ideologies such as nationalism and revolutionary faiths which have nothing in common with God and/or other supernatural beings.

Substantive Understanding of Religion

As seen in Chapter 1, trying to find a definition of religion from what social actors have to say is an impossible task. However, this is what a substantive approach to religion does: it attempts to understand what religion means for its believers rather than find out what it does for a society or an individual. Whereas a functional definition of religion is limited because it can include other belief systems which have nothing to do with supernatural entities, a substantive approach to religion, on the other hand, is impossible to complete from a universalistic point of view, as no definition of religion can include all global religious actors' meanings without excluding some.

Weber (1864–1920)

Weber's approach to the study of society is a *verstehen* one; that is an approach that focuses on analysing the meaning that social actors give to their action. Not forgetting that there is a structure imposed from above on these social actors, Weber gave more importance to what actors do of their own will and their social action than Marx and Durkheim did. It is for this reason, as already explained in Chapter 1, that Weber set the task of understanding what religion meant from the point of view of all religious actors, and quickly realised the impossibility of such a project. A universal approach to a substantive understanding of religion was thus impossible.

Weber is also known for another piece of work in which he gave more credit than previous social theorists to the place of religion as a crucial factor within the coming of modernity. In his famous, *The Protestant Ethic and the Spirit of Capitalism* (1904–1905), Weber aimed to demonstrate that it was not the accumulation of profit and the exploitation of the working class that was at the core of the development of modernity (i.e. a materialist view like Marxism) but it was instead due to the development of a new belief system (i.e. an idealist view; meaning that belief systems are more important than economic factors); that of Calvinism.

Weber argued that there had always been in the world's history people who desired to accumulate wealth. Previously, people used profit to make a more comfortable life for themselves or donated it to various religious organisations in the hope of securing a place in heaven. What strongly characterised modernity for Weber was the fact that people started to make money for the sake of making money rather than for spending and enjoying it.

Weber explained his theory through the development of two belief systems that developed hand in hand during the 16th and 17th centuries. These sets of beliefs did not have any relation of cause and effect towards each other; they were simply two belief systems that developed together, and strengthened each other's development, in, what Weber called, an elective affinity.

The first set of values was that of the spirit of capitalism. This spirit was held by the first capitalist merchants and industrialists who had a strong drive to accumulate personal wealth. They developed new rational methods to make work more calculative and efficient such as the use of clocks. The second set of values was Puritanism, and more specifically Calvinism. For Weber, these Calvinistic doctrines had a strong affinity with the spirit of capitalism which created a new drive in capitalism as never before seen; instead of dissipating their wealth, Calvinist capitalists wanted to reinvest it for the sake of reinvestment.

Early Calvinists believed that they were God's instrument on earth and that God had chosen an occupation for them to perform in his glory (i.e. a vocation). For example, some people would have been put on earth to be an artist and paint for the glory of God.

Further, these Calvinists believed in predestination: that is that only certain individuals already chosen by God would be able to enter heaven in the afterlife. If a person truly believes that the most important thing in life is the afterlife in heaven, even more important than life itself, this person will certainly do everything that is right to reach that goal. Their life will be thus be organised towards that ultimate goal; that is their teleology. However, with the notion of predestination, there is nothing that one person can do in their lifetime to influence their teleology as God has already decided before someone is born if this person will go to heaven or not. Among these early Calvinists, this caused some anxiety as they were not able to work on their path to the afterlife or discover if they had been predestined to go to heaven or not. Nevertheless, early Calvinists managed to find a way out of this conundrum, and this, paradoxically, led to the growth and dominance of the spirit of capitalism in modernity as it will be shown below. The reasoning goes as such: if God puts a person on earth for a specific vocation, and if that person is predestined to go to heaven, this person must be excellent at that vocation.

One indicator of whether someone will go to heaven or not is through observation. If an observed person is excellent at what he or she does, there is a strong chance that God has decided that this person will go to heaven. This led the early Calvinists who were involved in business to try to excel in their vocation. They were working hard on being good at what they were doing to find signs of their predestination. If they were involved in business, they were keen to be successful at accumulating wealth. However, since Calvinist theology identified to its believer that they had to live a sober and frugal life, they did not enjoy the benefit of this wealth and had to reinvest the profit they made for the sake of making profit, rather than using it for the sake of living a more comfortable life. This ascetic approach to accumulating wealth was, according to Weber, the basis for the development of the spirit of capitalism and thus modernity.

This protestant theology developed during the 16th and 17th centuries and was in strong affinity with the spirit of capitalism. However, by the 18th century, the type of capitalism that led to the accumulation of wealth for accumulation sake became independent from this religious ethic, and developed in the world without the need for the presence of this protestant ethic. As Weber explained, the spirit of capitalism was routinised, and no longer became exclusively part of the lives of Calvinists, but part of everyone's everyday life.

After this analysis, Weber wondered why only Europe had these conditions in the 16th and 17th centuries, and why did modernity did not start earlier or somewhere else in the world?

Before going further into that question, I first need to take another road in Weber's analysis. For Weber, the only type of people who could be the carriers of the spirit of capitalism were, what he called, inner-worldly ascetics. An ascetic person is someone who follows a religion dogmatically. He or she will execute the will of God as it is portrayed to him or her and he or she will understand the world in a rational way, whereas a mystic, contrary to an ascetic, is a person who seeks to break with the established order. It is a very individual form of religious actor who leads a life of contemplation rather than a life of action.

Other-worldly mystics are people living in great tension with the world. They try to avoid any concerns that deal with everyday life and want to dissociate themselves from the world. The Buddhist monk, withdrawing from everyday life to lead a life of contemplation, is a case in point.

Other-worldly ascetics work on controlling worldly motivations in the interest of 'devotional' goals rather than worldly ones. An example of this would be Christian hermits.

As other-worldly mystics and ascetics are withdrawn from everyday life, no social change can emerge from them. Indeed, if everyone was a mystic or a hermit meditating or praying, there would not be a society, let alone the seeds for the beginning of modernity, as there would not be communication between people.

For inner-worldly mystics, there are no attempts to withdraw from everyday life as is the case for other-worldly mystics and ascetics. Although they live a life of contemplation, they are still active in day-to-day routine such as having a job and being a member of a family.

Inner-worldly ascetics do not seek a union with God through contemplation like mystics, they seek mastery of themselves according to their theology and pursue what they believe is God's will. They see themselves as God's instrument, and this is the type of religious actor that Weber believes changed the world into a capitalist one.

The early Calvinists, for Weber, were inner-worldly ascetics who became the carriers of the spirit of capitalism while following regimentally their theology and acting closely to the will of God. According to Weber, neither of the two forms of mysticism nor other-worldly asceticism was able to carry changes. It was only the inner-ascetics who were devoted enough to apply themselves in their everyday life with a specific ideology who were able to create the type of social change leading to modernity.

For Weber, there were other inner-worldly ascetics in world history, and he was wondering why they were not successful in carrying the spirit of capitalism like the Calvinists. It has to be pointed out that the exploration that we are now taking on other types of social actors is about the possibility of the spirit of capitalism having developed somewhere else. The point is about exploring the possibilities for capitalism to have begun in China, India and Islam before the 18th century. However, it has to be noted that since capitalism has become routinised in the west in the 18th century, it has later expanded in these countries as well without the need of any inner-worldly ascetics.

Other pre-18th century inner-worldly ascetics involved in the accumulation of capital were the Chinese Mandarins who were the bearers of the teachings of Confucius. Both Calvinists and Mandarins were self-disciplined and were both working on the accumulation of wealth. However, the Mandarins were more interested in cultivating themselves as 'gentlemen' who were educated, cultured and withheld highly refined sensibilities. They were devoted to furthering their self-cultivation and did not reinvest their profit for profit sake. The Brahmans in Hinduism were also inner-worldly ascetics but because of the caste system in India, Weber thought that Hinduism could not transform social life the way that Calvinism did in the 16th and 17th centuries. The caste system was too strong a structure and so non- conducive to the development of capitalism that it prevented its creation. In Islam, Weber realised that the close link between religion and the state was not conducive to the creation of a capitalist society.

Many critiques of Weber's work have been published over the last century (see Bendle (2005) for a list), however the very last one is an enlightened account. Barbalet (2008) discovers through a careful analysis of Weber's almost unanalysed previous works and other of Weber's contemporary works, that the importance of Weber's book is not so much in its analysis of the development of modernity but more about the concerns of his time regarding the political education of Germany's middle class. This political education had been conservative over too many years and needed a model and/or a call to develop the nation into a strong one. Through his work, Weber hoped to wake up this German middle class and make them stand up for their desire to build a stronger nation. This is why Weber's book is more concerned with the difference between Lutheranism and Calvinism than between Catholicism and Calvinism (as one would expect), as Lutheranism was a conservative religion dominant in Prussia and Calvinism was a progressive one in the successful capitalist Anglo-Saxon countries. Viewing this book as Weber's personal manifesto, Barbalet states in his conclusion:

> [Weber's] work is personal in a more direct and deeper sense insofar as it is a statement of Weber's convictions not only about the recent past of the German politics of his day and especially its nationalist complexion, but also what Weber hopes for its future including his aspirations concerning a

powerful Germany whose influence is not confined to Europe, and, connectedly and paradoxically, his affections for and loyalty to the image of a world-conquering Anglo-American culture founded on economic power and the clarity of vision and single-minded purposefulness of its peoples and especially their leaders.

Conclusion

This chapter has only touched on what Marx, Durkheim and Weber had to say about religion in modernity. There were also other theorists such as Simmel and Freud who made strong contributions but this is beyond the scope of this book. As these three theorists laid down the foundation for the sociology of religion to develop as a sub-discipline, this chapter was necessary to understand what is covered in the next chapter: that sociologists are living on these theorists' legacy. For example, as the next chapter explores, it is because Marx, Dukheim and Weber claimed that religion would ultimately disappear from western society that sociologists hardly bothered to systematically study the changes happening to religion until the 1960s. As I argue next, this almost fundamentalist reading of our 'fathers of sociology' by sociologists prevented the discipline from fully understanding what was changing in religion during and after modernity.

Note

1. A francophone style of secularist. It is a word which has no clear equivalent in the English language and refers to the absence of religion in the public sphere, notably the state and the school system.

4 Religion, Spirituality and the Post-Secularisation Approach

Introduction

The Seventh Seal (1957) by Ingmar Bergman is one of the must-see movies. It is the story of a knight who comes back to Europe after 10 years on the Crusades. After surviving many battles, the ship that brought him back sank and the movie starts by showing him and his companion dead on the beach. The embodiment of death, wearing a long black coat and hood, and with a face so white that one would believe that there is no blood left in his body, comes to take them to his realm.

In a moment of magical realism, the knight speaks from beyond death and manages to bargain some extra life time; the time of a chess game that will last the whole movie. During this game, which they play bit by bit at night, the knight wanders in his homeland that is ravaged by bubonic plague and wonders about life, death, and God. In a very important scene, the knight who has lost faith in God after having fought in his name during the Crusades, enters a church and starts speaking to a person whom he thinks is a priest. The dialogue is here transcribed verbatim:

> Knight: I want to confess as honestly as I can, but my heart is empty. And emptiness is a mirror turned to my own face. I see myself… and am seized by disgust and fear. Through my indifference for people, I've been placed outside of their society. Now I live in a ghost world, enclosed in my dreams and imaginings.

> The person pretending to be a priest: Despite that, you don't want to die.

> – Yes, I want to.

> – What are you waiting for?

> – I want knowledge.

> – You want guarantees.

> – Call it what you like. Is it so terribly inconceivable to comprehend God with one's senses? Why does He hide in a cloud of half-promises and unseen miracles? How can we believe in the faithful when we lack faith? What will happen to us who want to believe, but cannot? What about those who neither want to nor can believe? Why can't I kill God in me? Why does He live on in me in an humiliating way – despite my wanting to

evict Him from my heart? Why is He, despite all, a mocking reality I can't
be rid of? ...

This dialogue perfectly represents the aim of this chapter; to demonstrate
that even if 'you' want to kill God within 'you' (or within a society), He or
She is a 'reality you can't be rid of'. This chapter first details the secularisation
thesis that claimed that God was dead (or was about to die) and then move
to the new thesis that sees God as coming back to our reality: that is, the
post-secularisation thesis. I then argue that the point is not to claim that
religion is disappearing or not, but that it is changing, such a change being
the current growth of the spiritual phenomenon.

The Secularisation Thesis

With the development of urbanism, science and mass education in western
societies since the Industrial and the French revolutions, some social theorists and commentators in the 19th and 20th centuries such as Comte,
Durkheim, Frazer, Freud, Marx, Spencer and Weber expected religion to
disappear from people's lives. There was a strong belief among atheists in
modernity that western societies were on the path to progress, and that after
having moved from a society dominated by magic (sorcerers) in pre-historical
times to one by religion (churches) in historical times, we were then moving
from religion to science on our path to evolution. With education, it was
believed, people would realise that religion was anachronistic because of its
bloody history and its perceived superstitious practices. As a hurdle on the
path to progress, religion would simply vanish in a few generations.

There are many problems with this vision. First, it is not clear cut to dissociate science from religion. For example, Milbank (1995) claims that science
has attempted to put itself beyond religion, but scientific reason has only
traded places with religious faith and has become for some a belief system as
well. 'Scientific social theories are themselves theologies or antitheologies in
disguise', Milbank (1995: 3) argues. Further, scientific reason did not appear
as a mental construction independent of any faiths, but was paradoxically
related to a shift *within* theology and not an emancipation *from* theology'
(1995: 29).

Russell (1935) claims that although there is a tension between science
and religion, many great scientists were believers themselves and some were
even theologians. The Big Bang theory, which demonstrates that the universe is in expansion following the explosion of a primitive atom, is such an
example. This theory which argues that the universe evolved from an initial
explosion could be in opposition to religious discourses, especially the ones

that literally see the world as being created in seven days. However, an even more fascinating fact behind this theory is that it was elaborated by the Belgian Georges Lemaître (1894–1966) who was not only a physicist but also a Catholic priest.

Furthermore, this new theory of the creation of the universe, which has been seen by many atheists as the proof that God did not create the world, is not as opposed to a religious interpretation as Guitton et al. (1991) underline. Even if it can indeed be explained that the existence of our world was the result of the explosion and its expansion in the universe is a secular process, no scientific theory can explain the reason behind this explosion. This still leaves room for faith to explain that behind this explosion might still be God.

Another issue is that no matter how often someone claims that religion will disappear or that religion is irrelevant in contemporary western societies, religion is not evaporating at all. Although this might seem like an evident comment to make today, the problem is that it took decades for sociologists to realise this fact as they were inspired by the classic texts by Marx, Durkheim and Weber and because they were looking at the wrong places. Indeed, by observing in Europe that less and less people were attending church, sociologists assumed that indeed, religion was disappearing.

Although church attendance has been in constant decline in Europe (see Table 1), the case in the US is different (see Table 2). Indeed, in the new continent, Presser and Chaves (2007) discover that although religious attendance has declined between 1950 and 1990, it has nevertheless remained stable since then. They make reference to the period before the 1950s as one of relative long-term stability, followed by a short-term decline until the 1990s, and we would now be in a period of stability. In Europe, the decline is constant; however, there are recent trends that are indicative of a change among the post-1970 generation. Lambert (2004), for example, discovers that although less young people attend churches, those who declare themselves as Christian are more religious in 1999 than in 1990 and 1981, and are more interested in believing in a religion rather than belonging to one. However, even if there is a growth of religious activity under these circumstances, Europe still has lower indicators of religious activity than other parts of the world.

As it will be demonstrated in the remainder of this book, religion is not confined to churches. This is only the institutional dimension of religion, and as pointed out by Ireland (1988), there are others such as the cognitive (religious identification), the normative (religion as providing norms and values) and the experiential (having religious experiences)[1] dimensions.

Some sociologists started to explore these issues and came to the conclusion that sociology was so entrenched in a way of seeing the world without

Table 1 Decline in religious participation in the EU 1970–98.

	Fran.	Belg.	Neth.	Germ.	Italy	Lux.	Den.	Ire	Brit.	N.Ire.	Grc.	Port.	Spa.
1970	23	52	41	29	56								
1971	27	58	49	39	58								
1973	19	38	33	22	48	48	5	91	16				
1975	22	45	44	26	39	44	6	93	8	59			
1976	23	45	45	30	37	40	6	93	17	60			
1977	22	50	48	26	37	42	5	91	17	56			
1978	18	45	45	23	36	39	5	90	10	64			
1980	14	38	31	21	37	41	5	91	9	69			47
1981	13	36	29	20	35	36	7	91	7	59	27		
1985	12	27	24	19	37	32	6	88	8	58	26		
1988	13	31	36	19	42	30	6	85	7	61	24	39	34
1989	14	29	34	18	44	28	4	83	10	60	21	40	31
1990	13	30	36	21	46	32	4	85	13	62	24	42	35
1991	10	24	35	19	46	28	4	82	13	61	24	39	33
1992	9	22	22	17	43	29	3	79	6	54	26	33	27
1993	12	27	33	15	45	27	4	81	7		25	33	33
1994	11	27	28	16	41	22	3	77	12		24	37	36
1998	5	10	14	15	39	17	4	65	4	46	21	30	20
Beta	-.620	-1.290	-.780	-.589	-.188	-1.041	-.099	-.855	-.233	-.371	-.250	-1.095	-1.303
Sig.	.000	.000	.001	.000	..316	.000	.005	.000	.075	.081	.067	.023	.004
Obs.	18	18	18	18	18	16	16	16	16	13	10	8	9

Note: Religious Participation: Q: *"Do you attend religious services several times a week, once a week, a few times during the year, once a year or less, or never?"* The percentage attending religious services "several times a week" or "once a week". Sig = significance; Obs. = number of observations in the series.

Source: Norris and Inglehart (2004: 72) from The Mannheim Eurobarometer Trend File 1970–99

Table 2 Percentage attending religious services in a given week implied by GSS and ANES, 1990–2006.

Year	GSS		ANES	
	Per cent	*N*	*Per cent*	*N*
1990	42	1,333	41	1,963
1991	42	1,492	—	—
1992	—	—	41	2,475
1993	42	1,568	—	—
1994	40	2,941	42	1,769
1996	37	2,823	41	1,703
1998	39	2,788	41	1,271
2000	36	2,737	40	1,789
2002	38	2,743	42	1,498
2004	40	2,801	39	1,204
2006	38	4,491	—	—

Source: Presser and Chaves (2007: 421) from General Social Surveys and American National Election Studies.

religion that it had forgotten to have a closer look at the world they were supposed to study. For example, Jeffrey Hadden (1987) writes that the secularist principle.

> emerged in Europe and America during a period of social upheaval that left intellectuals personally disillusioned with religion [and] one did not even have to study the process of secularization, since the disappearance of religion became sacralised, and firmly entrenched in the minds of contemporary sociologists (Hadden 1987: 589 and 593).

David Martin (1995: 296) considers that the studies of Durkheim and Max Weber on the religious consciousness crisis were so strong 'that few bothered to articulate the theory in terms of concrete historical analyses and careful examination of statistical data. Since secularization was the undisputed paradigm relatively few sociologists took a special interest in religion.'[2]

This led theorists between the 1960s and 1980s to refine their arguments and to posit that even if fewer and fewer people attend church and even if religion no longer holds the political power it once had, religion is nevertheless not disappearing. It has instead become a private activity/belief and no longer has a place in the public sphere. This softer secularisation thesis has no 'faith' in the complete disappearance of religion and implies the privatisation of religion, and the diminution of religious influence on social organisation (Wilson 1985: 16–19). This approach to secularisation has been defined as 'the process whereby religious thinking, practice and institutions lose social significance'. In this sense, religion is confined to the sphere of individual privacy and is 'observed [to be] as unthreatening to the modern social system, in much the same way that entertainment is seen as unthreatening' (Wilson 1985: 20).

On a similar level, Luckmann (1967) discusses 'invisible religion', a form of religiosity that has emerged in a period when the ecclesial religion was decaying, religion thus becoming a 'private affair'. As Beyer (1991: 373) notes, this idea has been put forward by many sociologists since at least the 1960s, a time in which, for José Casanova (1994: 19), sociologists developed more systematic and empirically grounded theories of secularisation and distanced themselves from the past thesis that religion would eventually completely disappear from modern societies.

Before moving on, it might be useful to clarify certain concepts. If secularism is an ideology about the belief that religion will disappear, secularisation is about concrete changes in terms of religion in society that can be observed. A sociologist from a classical Marxist perspective would generally be a secularist, that is he or she would have the belief that religion should disappear from society, if not, become invisible. If a sociologist from this perspective notices that less and less people attend church in Europe (which is the case), this secularist sociologist will see in this data confirmation of the secularist thesis (which is the belief, rather than the fact, that religion is moving away from the central lives of Europeans). Another non-secularist sociologist (but not necessarily religious) who studies secularisation could see this data as indicating something else: even if fewer people go to church, it does not stop them from believing. This data can be seen instead as an indicator of religious change rather than decline, as the forthcoming sections explore.

De-secularisation Thesis

There is little dispute about one of the facts on which secularisation theory relied: that except for the USA (Warner 1993), traditional institutional religion in the western world is in decline in modern society. If traditional religious institutions have, in this perspective, lost their social significance, there are nevertheless still people feeling and confronting a religious experience they cannot always easily express. It appears that people still believe in God – or something or someone else – and feel they are confronting a religious world beyond church walls. One could recall that Troeltsch already claimed in 1895 that religion was alive and abundant precisely because it was a time of ecclesial decline (Volker 1997).

Since the 1980s, and even stronger since 9/11, secularisation theory appears now to be something of a 'sacred canopy' (Richardson 1985) for a majority of research in the social sciences of religion. Secularisation theory, not religion, now seems to be in crisis. Indeed, for Kepel (1994) there has been a reversal of this process around the world. Around this time period, revived religious traditions no longer tried to adapt themselves to secular values but proposed alternative ways of organising society around sacred values. Kepel analysed some of these movements inside Judaism, Christianity and Islam and describes these religions as containing a high proportion of people who have a secular education but who want to submit reason to God's law. Following this line of reasoning, Casanova (1994: 65–66) uses the term 'deprivatization': 'the process whereby religion abandons its assigned place in the private sphere and enters the undifferentiated public sphere of civil society to take part in the ongoing process of contestation, discursive legitimation, and redrawing of the boundaries'.

In many parts of the world religion has re-entered the public sphere to such an extent that it has undermined the 'hard line' secularisation thesis as predicted by the fathers of sociology. Further, as explored in a forthcoming section, spirituality is on the rise. Since this under a 'hard line' view should not be happening, views on secularisation have been revised. Some (e.g. Bruce 2002; 2006; Norris and Inglehart 2004) explain that secularisation is still happening but in a much less extreme process as first foretold, others (e.g. Brown 1992; Hadden 1987; Kepel 1994; Richardson 1985; Warner 1993) propose that there is a reverse process and that secularisation is losing momentum. In accordance with this latter view which supports the de-secularisation thesis, recent theories in the sociology of religion (Casanova 2006; Davie 2006; Martin 2005) have pushed the debate further by applying Eisenstadt's (2000) multiple modernities paradigm.

To illustrate this paradigm, I am using Martin's (2005) recent work which underlines the different dynamics of secularisation, rather than simply assumes a single one as in many previous sociological studies. The fundamental argument of his latest work is that secularisation is not a clear cut process that happens in all western societies homogeneously or that will happen to all developing countries. Indeed, as the author argues in relation to Christianity:

> instead of regarding secularization as a once-for-all unilateral process, one might rather think in terms of successive Christianizations followed or accompanied by recoils [i.e. a type of de-secularisation process]. Each Christianization is a salient of faith driven into the secular from a different angle, each pays a characteristic cost which affects the character of the recoil, and each undergoes a partial collapse (Martin 2005: 3).

Following this multilateral view of the process of secularisation and de-secularisation, the reader is asked to observe that this process is not only different between North America and Europe, but is also distinctive within each region of these cultural areas (e.g. California and New York State, Belgium and Norway). There is not one secular ending to our history but rather various phases of secularisation and sanctification.

Martin's articulation of 'multiple secularisations' aligns itself with the recent concept of 'multiple modernities' (Eisenstadt 2000). For Eisenstadt,

> The idea of multiple modernities presumes that the best way to understand the contemporary world – indeed to explain the history of modernity – is to see it as a story of continual constitution and reconstitution of a multiplicity of cultural programs. These ongoing reconstructions of multiple institutional and ideological patterns are carried forward by specific social actors in close connection with social, political, and intellectual activists, and also by social movements pursuing different programs of modernity, holding very different views of what makes societies modern (2000: 2).

Casanova (2006) and Davie (2006) used this theory to differentiate the European case with that of the US. For many years, sociologists analysed the secularisation process in Europe believing that the rest of the world, when modernised, would follow this trend. The US, where religion is stronger in terms of church attendance and political activism, was seen as the exception to the secularisation rule. Now, with recent data, these authors have come to the conclusion that religion is thriving around the world (including countries that are modernised but not European). This has led them to reverse the perspective and to view Europe as the exception. The contrast between the European and US case can provide an answer to this difference:

> Crucial is the question of why individuals in Europe, once they lose faith in their national churches, do not bother to look for alternative salvation religions. In a certain sense, the answer lies in the fact that Europeans continue to be implicit members of their national churches, even after explicitly abandoning them. The national churches remain there as a public good to which they have rightful access when it comes time to celebrate the transcendent rites of passages, birth, and death. It is this peculiar situation that explains the lack of demand and the absence of a truly competitive religious market in Europe. In contrast, … the United States never had a national church. Eventually, all religions in America, churches as well as sects, irrespective of their origins, doctrinal claims, and ecclesiastical identities, turned into 'denominations', formally equal under the constitution and competing in a relatively free, pluralistic, and voluntaristic religious market. As the organizational form and principle of such a religious system, denominationalism constitutes the great American invention (Casanova 2006: 16).

Needless to say, both Europe and the US have gone through a modernisation process which has affected their de-secularisation process differently. Earlier in her work, Davie (2002) put Europe and the US on the extreme of a continuum. At one point, she equated the European[3] case with that of state or elite control of religion (in which there is a culture of obligation, e.g. going to Church because one has to). In the US, the case is that of religious voluntarism (in which there is a culture of consumption or choice, e.g. I go to Church because I want to as long as it provides what I need during a period of time I want to invest).

In the US, religion is very diverse and Europe is following this trend as well. For example, Lambert (2004) finds out that according to the latest surveys, the church attendance decline is still happening, especially among the young people; however, this is put into question by the development of Christian renewal and the growth of spirituality. As Davie (2000: 187) wonders, 'Will the growing diversity stimulate the market as it appears to have done elsewhere in the world or will this process simply not work in the European case?'. To this question, she gives three possible scenarios. The first one is that religious activity is so low in Europe compared with the rest of the world that even a growth of diversity will not suffice to awaken a religious market. The second one is the reverse of the first one and new religious arrivals and innovations will act as stimulation to religious growth. The third one lays between these two previous extreme case scenarios: growth might happen but because the European case is so typical, this growth will be specific to Europe's social and historical context and the European type of pluralism might be totally different from other parts of the world.

In between the US and Europe, Davie places Australia and Canada as hybrid cases. For example, Australia, as I explored in Possamai (2008a), in its 'white' historical beginning, saw religion being used as a tool of social control to help build a modern secular society. Religion was used by the state to 'civilise' the prisoner in penal colonies, the free settlers and the indigenous inhabitants of the land. Although Australia was also born as a modern secular state, religion was nevertheless used in conjunction with the state for this modernisation process. Overall, the colonisation process of Australia itself might explain its hybridity between the US (started modernisation without any established church) and Europe (had tension with established church during the modernisation process).

Further evidence of this hybridity is found in Bouma (2006) who claims that religion and spiritualities in Australian are 'a shy hope in the heart'. Religions and spiritualities are diversifying and are being revitalised in Australia, but this happens at a 'low-temperature'. It is not happening in a loud and very visible way as in the US but it is happening to a greater extent than in Europe. There are no overt claims from any religious group to take central stage at the political level, but groups and individuals are discreetly active at other levels.

Rational Choice Theory in a Nutshell

To explain this culture of consumption or choice, a theory appeared in the 1980s and has since been dominant in explaining the religious phenomenon in the US. However, it clearly does not work in Europe and cannot be easily adapted to a case like Australia or South Africa. The working assumption behind this theory is that people act out of reflexive self-interest in the field of religion and are seeking 'rewards' (such as good health, status or material enrichment) while avoiding 'costs'. There would be a free market of religious groups available and people would be weighing the costs and rewards of joining a specific group. Believers would thus be individualists led by rational acts having an instrumental approach to the world.

The leading figures of this paradigm are Stark, Bainbridge and Iannaccone (e.g. Stark and Bainbridge 1987), and they claim that because the 'rewards' that people tend to seek are often unattainable, religion is therefore used as a compensator sought in the religious marketplace. Following this paradigm, we can think of a person who is in physical pain and who cannot be helped by medicine. This person might turn to a religion which offers a rationale behind this suffering or might even offer hope if specific rituals are properly followed. Some might feel that he or she does not earn enough money and will seek a prosperity religious group that will make the person believe that by having faith in God and by living the 'right' way, more wealth might eventuate.

Taking into account that religious actors would see the religious field as a market place, people will be encouraged to change their religion as they change the way they seek 'rewards'. They might also seek for a 'better' religion in this market place that would provide them with greater compensation.

Following this view, they also argue that contrary to Europe where ecclesiastical monopolies or state involvement in religious affairs is strong, the US is a more vibrant place for religious activity as pluralism and diversity increase religious vitality. They thus propose that religion will strongly strive in a free religious marketplace rather than in a more controlled one. However, as we have seen above, even if Europe moves to a culture of religious choice, there is no certainty that it will espouse this US model as the European case may be too specific.

This paradigm in the sociology of religion is followed by a relatively small group of American scholars and tends to polarise opinion in the sociology of religion field of study. Needless to say, many critiques have been raised against this paradigm as reviewed by Rose (2003) but this is beyond the topic of this chapter.

Religion and Spirituality

What is meant by being religious today is no longer what it once was. Religion is metamorphosing into new, renewed and different forms at various levels (Lyon 2000); as seen in previous chapters, the case of the Church of Scientology and that of hyper-real religions are cases in point. As a result of the collapse of collective systems of codes of being, and of the rapid changes specific to our current society (see Chapter 5), there is an increase of freedom in which the individual makes his or her own sense of his or her life. More people claim to have no religious affiliations but they are not necessarily atheist; they believe without belonging and might see themselves as more spiritual than religious. In everyday life/language, religion appears to be connected with institutionalised/organised forms whereas spirituality is viewed more as a self-authored search by individuals who are looking inward. It refers 'to an experiential journey of encounter and relationship with otherness, with powers, forces and beings beyond the scope of everyday life' (Bouma 2006: 12) and is growing in western societies. Being spiritual is more of an individual task, although it can be done in small groups.

The cultural presence of traditional religious institutions has diminished, but the search for a more personal connection to a religion, that is, for spirituality, has increased. Because of this increase, one can find another evidence to support the de-secularisation thesis.

Table 3 Being religious and being spiritual by age cohort in the United States, 1991.

	(Percentage in Each Age Cohort)			
	Oldest	*Born 1927–1945*	*Baby Boomers*	*Baby Busters*
Religious and spiritual	66.8	67.1	64.9	54.9
Spiritual only	14.5	16.7	19.8	22.6
Religious only	11.0	8.9	8.0	8.3
Neither	7.7	7.3	7.2	14.2
N	*310*	*496*	*761*	*288*

Source: Marler and Hadaway (2002: 293)

Table 4 Being religious and being spiritual by age group in Australia, 2002.

	(Percentage in Each Age Group)					
	70 plus	60 to 69	50 to 59	40 to 49	30 to 39	18 to 29
'Religious' and 'spiritual'	40.5	50.6	36.2	41.3	34.3	34.0
Spiritual only	2.6	3.8	11.4	9.1	9.1	11.5
Religious only	19.8	11.4	13.4	8.4	8.8	5.3
Neither	37.1	34.2	39.0	41.3	47.9	49.2
N	*116*	*158*	*254*	*383*	*353*	*191*

Source: Black *et al.* (2004)

Sociologists have suggested that 'spirituality' might have replaced 'religion', as the term seems more adequate for the current religious quest in consumer culture (e.g. Black *et al.* 2004; Roof 1999).[4] However, recent research as seen in tables 3 in the US and 4 in Australia indicates that spirituality is not simply replacing religion. Most people see themselves as 'religious' and 'spiritual' at the same time. These researchers have been able to demonstrate that being spiritual does not necessarily mean not being religious. For example, Wuthnow (2001: 307) claims that 'many people who practice spirituality in their own way still go to church or synagogue'. From a Christian perspective, Cunningham and Egan (1996) make reference to spirituality as the lived encounter with Jesus Christ in the Spirit. For them, spirituality cannot be limited to an exclusively individualistic 'care of the soul' and involves being part of the local and worldwide community. Going to 'church' on Sunday allows this connection, and furthermore, by listening to the Word of God, Christians can enter 'into the story that tells [them] about Jesus the Christ in the Spirit [i.e. being spiritual] and to respond to that story both as individuals and as part of the local and worldwide community' (Cunningham and Egan 1996: 33). Indeed, as seen above, the large majority of the people surveyed claim to be religious and spiritual at the same time, whereas those who claim to be spiritual but not religious appear to be only a small contingent of people. These spiritual (only) actors are not churchgoers and are more likely to be agnostics who experiment with alternative spiritualities and/or Eastern practices. Spirituality does not seem to replace religion at all.

From such research, it appears that there are two types of spiritual actors, the one that claims that he or she is still religious – the majority according to the two tables above – and the one that is not religious. To make sense of this, it is worth coming back to the classics to shed light on this contemporary phenomenon. Troeltsch's work on mysticism has some strange resemblances with the contemporary spiritual trend. Indeed, Carrette and King (2005: 42–43) even point out that the notion of spirituality overlapped with that of mysticism until the late 1980s. Since that time, references to mysticism have been progressively changed to that of spirituality.

B. Campbell (1978: 231) quotes Troeltsch's late 19th-century definition of mysticism as:

> the insistence upon a direct inward and present religious experience. (...) An individualised reaction against highly institutionalised religion, it arises when 'the world of ideas' which makes up the religious belief system has 'hardened' into formal worship and doctrine. Under these circumstances, religion becomes for some people 'transformed into a purely personal and inward experience'.

The author gives a summary of the characteristics of Troeltsch's mysticism as 'an emphasis on direct, inner personal experience; loose and provisional forms; voluntary adherence, usually not formal; a spiritual conception of fellowship; inclusiveness in attitude; indifference toward the demands of society' (B. Campbell 1978: 231). Nelson (1987: 56) also adds that mystics, even if they go through a religious individuation process, get together and do not stay alone in their spiritual ivory tower. They form organisations because of their need for the give and take of intimate fellowship with their religious peers.

B. Campbell (1978: 231) and Garret (1975: 215) have found that Troeltsch writes about two ideal types of mysticism; these are mysticism and technical mysticism.

1. Mysticism occurs in established religious traditions but its experience happens outside the regular forms of worship and devotion to these religions. The experience of the mystics, from this ideal type, is the means by which they realise and appropriate the tradition of the religious organisation in which they belong. They do not detract from the existing sociological forms of religion even if mysticism embodies the form of the highest religious individualism (Bastide 1996: 197–206). They even legitimise and support established ecclesiastical structures.

2. Technical mysticism makes a break with traditional religion. Technical mystics contest the religion within which they have been socialised. They understand themselves to be independent from religious principle, independent of every religious institution and reject the religious morality they have received *cum lacte*.[5] Technical mysticism sets up its own theory, which takes the place of doctrine and dogma by undercutting the form and structure of the established religions. It discovers everywhere, 'beneath all the concrete forms of religion, the same religious germ (...)' (Troeltsch 1950: 231).

This technical mysticism in the narrower sense, with its own philosophy of religion, has also appeared in various religious spheres with a remarkable similarity of form: in Indian Brahmanism and its repercussion in Buddhism, in the Sufism of the Parsees and of Persian Muslims, in the Neo-Platonism of the Greeks, in the varied syncretism of late antiquity which is known as Gnosticism (Troeltsch 1950: 736).

As Garret (1975: 215–26) realises, mysticism and technical mysticism are far from being a unitary phenomenon. The sociological consequences springing from these two analytical sub-types press in antithetical directions: the one legitimating ecclesial structures, the other innovating new forms of religions.

Could it be argued that those surveyed by Marler and Hadaway (2002) and Black *et al.* (2004) who claim to be spiritual and religious would be mystical in Troeltsch's understanding, and that those claiming to be spiritual but not religious are technical mystics? There are indeed clear similarities that can help us to understand this phenomenon. It is thus tempting to call those who claim to be spiritual and religious as spiritual, and those who are spiritual only as technical spiritual. I would like to point out that I do not equate being spiritual with being mystic. I am simply arguing that there are strong sociological resemblances between these two ideal types of actors and that Troeltsch's typology could be usefully translated to the current research on spirituality. By ideal type, I make reference to a typification method, which stresses, links and organises the traits that are common to a specific category of phenomena in an ideal category that does not necessarily fully represent reality.

Troeltsch claimed that mysticism and technical mysticism were at the beginning of the 20th century the secret religion of the educated class, and predicted that gradually in the world of 'mass' educated people, this type of religiosity would be predominant. B. Campbell (1978) saw this in the late 1960s and early 70s with the development of new religious movements (see Chapter 12) as prescient. It is even more prescient today, at the beginning of the 21st century, in which spirituality has become so important and so mainstream.

Conclusion

With the development of social sciences in the 19th century, social analysts were so certain that religion would disappear that few properly studied the changes that religion was going through. If fewer people attended churches, if religion was no longer mentioned in parliaments and taken into account for business deals, it did not necessarily mean that religion was disappearing. As the socio-cultural aspects of our western societies are not static, religion has also changed. One of these changes has been explained in terms of the growth of spiritualities, which is one of the many factors that indicate a process towards a de-secularisation society. One major catalyst of these changes is the advent of postmodernity which we are specifically exploring in the next two chapters.

Notes

1. Which has reported an increase over the last few years (Hay 1990).
2. One consequence of this in the field of sociology is that the 1980s have seen a growth of interest in the cultural dimension of social life and in consequence a development of the sociology of culture while at the same time, a reverse process seems to have influenced the sociology of religions (Featherstone 1991: 112).
3. Although there is a culture of obligation in Europe, it does not mean that people are not committed to their church. As Davie (2000: 136) points out, there are roughly speaking 30 percent of Europeans who remain committed to their Church and the same amount have no connection at all with these institutions.
4. It is interesting to note that the word 'spirituality' was first used in the seventeenth century as a pejorative term to refer to elite forms of individual religious practice (Cunningham and Egan 1996: 5).
5. As the Romans used to say: 'with mother's milk'.

5 Religion and Postmodernity (Part A): Consumer Religions

Introduction

The 1999 version of *The Mummy*, with Brendan Fraser and Rachel Weisz, is a repackaged version of old adventure and horror movies for a younger public. In one scene, a secondary character is faced with the mysterious awakening of a man who has been mummified for thousands of years. The Mummy is ready to attack its human prey, and the man, with no way to escape, shows him a Christian cross and speaks English, hoping it will work as a protective spell. As this does not stop the nightmarish creature, the man then proceeds to use talismans from other religions and finally saves himself by using the Star of David and by speaking in Hebrew. The monster recognizes the language of the Jewish 'slaves' of his lifetime, and finding this affinity, he asks him to help him in his quest. This humorous scene demonstrates how this person is ready to move from one religion to another as seemed fit. In this movie, the person changes his religion many times in the hope of surviving. In current times, as this chapter covers, people change their religion to what feels right to them at a certain time in their life as if they were consuming religions rather than simply following the traditions of their parents.

In another movie, *What Dreams May Come*, Robin Williams dies from a road accident and discovers from heaven that his wife committed suicide after his own death. She could no longer find the strength to live following the death of her husband, and that of her children a few years before. As suicide is a sin punished in the afterlife in Christianity, she is then condemned to hell. Wanting to save her soul, the character played by Robin Williams manages to find her in what is portrayed as Dante's vision of hell, a circle where people are punished for having committed suicide. Dante's portrayal of the afterlife has a strong Christian underpinning and has served as a reference work for Christians for many years through the artistic medium of paintings and poetry. However, at the very end of the movie, having saved her from her condemnation, and instead of living for ever after in paradise, they are reincarnated. And typically in a more than happy Hollywood ending, they rediscover themselves as children in their next life as if they were never apart. When I make reference to this movie with my students, the large

majority of them acknowledge having seen it but did not notice this important paradox: that of mixing one of the most Christian visions of the afterlife
(Dante's vision of Hell) with the theory of reincarnation. A Christian theolo-
gian might be horrified by this; however, my students felt comfortable with
these two exclusive versions of the afterlife put together.

These two movie extracts show that in popular culture, characters can
move from one religion to another without any issue as long as it works in
the story, and can even link together what theologians would see as totally
opposite versions. This is a sign of the times that has emerged with the
advent of postmodernity and consumer culture. It has now become normal
to consume various religions at the same time without worrying about whether
from a theological point of view, they would fit together or not. To explain
this, this chapter first outlines the broader picture of what postmodernity is,
and then move to a discussion on consumer culture.

Postmodernity

Chapter 3 detailed what our fathers of the sociology of religion had to say
about religion in modernity. However, we are now in a period which is called
postmodernity (also called late, high, liquid, or second modernity). It is not
the point of this book to detail the subtleties between the different understandings of what these words mean. Suffice is to say that the world has
changed and for the purpose of this book, I am using the term postmodernity
to describe these socio-cultural changes. It must be noted at this stage that in
Chapter 4 I made reference to the multiple modernities thesis that this book
follows, and that using the term postmodernity might be a paradox as its
term 'post' makes reference to a time after modernity as if it would be
detached from it. Postmodernity, as explained by Eisenstadt (2000), the
father of the multiple modernities thesis, paradoxically has to be understood
as a specific type of modernity, that is, an advanced type of capitalist modern
society. He admits that the classical formulation of what modernity is, which
had been world dominant for the last two centuries, is now exhausted (see
below). There are now new social settings and frameworks that allow for the
construction of new autonomous social, political, and cultural spaces, different from the classical time of modernity. Although some academics would
see postmodernity as diametrically opposed to the modern program, for
Eisenstadt this is not the case as postmodern movements have reconstituted
modernity in a new context, and are basically reappropriating and redefining
the discourse of modernity in their own ways (2000: 24). There are now
multiple interpretations of modernity that go beyond the homogenising

aspects of the original version. Following Eisenstadt's work, I am therefore using the term 'postmodernity' to make reference to a period of history from the 1960s onwards that has moved beyond, not the whole project of modernity, but mainly its classical version.

It is largely agreed among social scientists that the initial project of modernity has failed and is perceived as being in a crisis state. It is no longer a vehicle of ultimate meanings: the dream of material progress proposed two centuries ago and increasingly accepted as common sense has lost its plausibility.

Roseneau (1992: 127–33) shows how, in the later twentieth century, critiques of modern reason, often seen as linked under the rubric of postmodernism, have diffused through western society. Included in these critiques is a questioning of universalist thinking concerning what is called 'modernity', with a greater emphasis on feelings, emotions, intuition, creativity, imagination, fantasy, together with a rejection of what was understood as the totalitarian and oppressive tendency of 'Reason'.

With the emergence of 'Reason', human beings were expected to govern themselves in a civilised way. No longer were atrocious religious wars, such as those between Catholics and Protestant in Medieval Europe, supposed to happen. However, the outcome of the development of 'Reason' has not met its promises. We are now confronted with realities that we never would have expected in the time of Voltaire: the two World Wars, the rise of Nazism, the construction of concentration camps, various genocides, worldwide depression, Hiroshima, Vietnam, the killing fields in Cambodia, the wars in the Persian Gulf, a widening gap between rich and poor, and ecological catastrophes. All these atrocities are an outcome of the dream of 'Reason', and this makes any contemporary belief in the ideology of progress questionable.

Bauman (1994) believes that modernity is no longer a force of liberation, but rather a source of oppression and repression. As he quotes Feingold (1983: 399–400) on the use of 'Reason' with the holocaust:

> [Auschwitz] was also a mundane extension of the modern factory system. Rather than producing goods, the raw material was human beings and the end-product was death, so many units per day marked carefully on the manager's production charts. The chimneys, the very symbol of the modern factory system, poured forth acrid smoke produced by burning human flesh. The brilliantly organised railroad grid of modern Europe carried a new kind of raw material to the factories. It did so in the same manner as with other cargo. In the gas chambers the victims inhaled noxious gas generated by prussic acid pellets, which were produced by the advanced chemical industry of Germany. Engineers designed the crematoria; managers designed the system of bureaucracy that worked with a zest and efficiency more backward

nations would envy. Even the overall plan itself was a reflection of the modern scientific spirit gone awry. What we witnessed was nothing less than a massive scheme of social engineering...

Moving away from this destabilising quote, I would like to clarify some concepts at this stage. The term 'postmodernity' refers to a structural and socio-cultural change that has happened in western societies since around the 1960s. It is about a historical trend which is in collusion with other current changes such as post-industrialism, post-fordism, globalisation and mass consumption. Postmodernism, on the other hand, is a way of thinking. The term 'postmodernism' became popular in the 1960s on the island of Manhattan when artists and writers such as Cage, Burroughs, Hassan and Sontag first used it. These creators were rejecting high modernism, which they believed was 'exhausted' because of its institutionalisation in the museum and in the academy. The movement gained wider usage in the 1970s and 1980s, and discussions between this movement and a new philosophy went back and forth between the US and Europe. This lead to postmodernism as a philosophy with key theorists such as Bell, Kristeva, Lyotard, Derrida, Foucault, and Baudrillard.[1]

However, even if modernity's dream has faded, the belief in 'rational mastery' is still alive. 'Rational mastery', for Castoriadis (1992), is understood as the living logic of capitalism. It is 'embodied in quantification and lead[s] to the fetishization of growth' *per se* and its maximisation process treats other values, such as human nature and traditions, instrumentally. An example of this type of reason is found in bureaucratic companies that seek productivity for the sake of productivity. It would be like having universities and hospitals seeking the best productivity possible for the sake of productivity and cost saving, and forget their duties towards teaching, health and research. When large corporations seek profit for the sake of profit instead of using parts of that profit for a value-goal (e.g. ecology, poverty alleviation, education of the underprivileged), we are making reference to this 'rational mastery' working by itself for itself. Another type of rationality is the one that led to the 'autonomy' of modern social actors at the beginning of modernity, and started as the critique of traditional and religious forces that held sway before the Enlightenment. This 'reason' cleared the way for social and individual autonomy, i.e. 'the affirmation of the possibility and the right for individuals and the collectivity to find in themselves (or to produce) the principle ordering their lives' (Castoriadis 1992). This has been reflected in, for example, debates in parliament and business deals without including the word of God or of a holy book.

For Castoriadis, during modernity, these two 'reasons' shared 'the imaginary of Progress' and its technical-materialist utopia, and were in opposition and tension with one another. This conflict was the means of the dynamic development of western society and the expansion of capitalism. In postmodernity, reason for efficiency and profit sake seems to have won over the reason used to promote universal and human values (e.g. equality and freedom). But in as far as this development of capitalism has been decisively conditioned by the simultaneous development of the project of social and individual autonomy, the early dream of modernity *is* finished. Capitalism developing whilst forced to face a continuous struggle against the status quo, on the floor of the factory as well as in the sphere of ideas or of art (such as before the 1960s), and capitalism expanding without any effective internal opposition (such as in this period of time), are two different social-historical animals (Castoriadis 1992: 23).

As an outcome of the development of this 'rational mastery' for profit sake in postmodernity, consumption has growth so strongly that we are now living in a consuming society; a society from which religion cannot escape.

Consumption

Consumption has always been part of our society, but consumption for leisure and lifestyle was restricted to only a few groups within the dominant class until the postmodernisation of our society. Now, since the advent of mass consumption, which is one of the key aspects of postmodernity, all people from all wages who are included in this society take part in it – those who do not take part, the non-consumers, are simply excluded.

For Bauman (1998), a 'normal life' in a consumer society is the life of consumerism which involves making choices among all the displayed opportunities. A 'happy life' is then defined as taking as many opportunities as possible. The poor in the consumer society of western societies is not necessarily the one who does not have a shelter but is the one who has no access to a normal life and to a 'happy' one. To be one of these is then to be a consumer *manqué*. As Bauman (1998: 38) explains:

> In a society of consumers, it is above all the inadequacy of the person as a consumer that leads to social degradation and 'internal exile'. It is this inadequacy, this inability to acquit oneself of the consumer's duties, that turns into bitterness at being left behind, disinherited or degraded, shut off or excluded from the social feast to which others gained entry. Overcoming that consumer inadequacy is likely to be seen as the only remedy – the sole exit from a humiliating plight.

Consumer culture is the outcome of the massive expansion of the production of capitalist commodity through this 'rational mastery' as seen in the previous section. This outburst of the capitalist system has created a vast reservoir of consumer goods and sites for purchase and consumption to be 'enjoyed' by the various classes of our society that are 'in'. This has led to the growing dependence on mass leisure and consumption activities. This is viewed by some as leading to more egalitarianism and individual freedom (e.g. de Certeau 1988) and by others as an increase in the ideological and seductive manipulation of the masses by the dominant class. This manipulation would distract the masses from considering an alternative to our society which could improve our social relations (e.g. the early Baudrillard and the Frankfurt School).

To illustrate the latter, Langer (1996) discovers that birthday parties have become part of this process. Few people in their seventies and eighties would have celebrated their birthday as children. The first generation to recognise this event were the baby boomers. This new way of celebrating someone's birth even paved the way for mass production of cheap toys. However, these birthday parties were organised at home and entertainment often involved cheap games. This changes from the 1980s and 1990s as birthday parties became part of a service industry. As McDonalds, Pizza Hut, Pancake Parlour, and Timezone now offer special 'party packages' with specialists – e.g. party coordinator, caterers and clown – to take care of the event', it becomes hard to refuse one of these parties to a child under peer pressure. This industrialisation of birthday parties even turns children's parties into an opportunity for 'conspicuous consumption', i.e. the competitive display of capacity to spend money on inessentials.

When Baudrillard (1970) was a Marxist, before his move towards postmodernism (see Chapter 6), he viewed pleasure as being constrained and institutionalised. It is no longer a wish or a desire to just have fun; it is almost a citizen's duty to take part actively in consumer culture. The masses are being socialised into a force of consumption and must learn how to live the pleasure offered by this culture. In this perspective, there is an increase from production society to consumer society for the capacity of ideological manipulation by a type of corporate capitalism.

This view is similar to that of the Frankfurt School which understands the proletariat as a socially impotent force that has lost its revolutionary role. Capitalism has managed to create a society of compliant workers and consumers. This school of thought also coined the concept of 'culture industry' to shed more light on this process. The term was introduced by Max Horkheimer and Theodor Adorno who argue that the arts were no longer independent of industry and commerce. In this culture industry, industrial manufacturing, commerce and artistic endeavour have been fused in such a way that there now remains no difference between companies producing hit songs or movies and the industries that manufacture vast amounts of mass-produced foods, clothing and automobiles. Culture is no longer the preserve of the artist; it is now adapted to methods used in industrial manufacturing and in marketing.

Schiller (1996: 114) brings this concept up-to-date and alerts us to how, since the globalisation of communication in the 1960s, we have seen the growth of transnational media-information corporations such as Time Warner, Disney, Reuters, Sony and Murdoch's News Corporation. As he claims:

> a world-class cultural industry corporation such as Time Warner or Disney, or one of Murdoch's enterprises, can combine a rich mix of information, pop-cultural activities, synergistically spinning one product off another, or promoting one item by incorporating it in another format. TV programs and movies are retailed as video cassettes and their sound tracks move out into their own orbits as records and tapes. To top it off, sophisticated management of a conglomerate like Disney, engages as well in retail business, selling its various creations and promotions that originated as film or television, in shops owned or franchised.

A more recent phenomenon of this cultural industry is the close link between Hollywood and the computer game industry. According to Williams (2003), video games grossed more than the cinema in 2002 in the USA. Furthermore, the computer technologies used to create both movies and games are moving closer and closer together. For example, Tobey Maguire and Willem Dafoe, while filming *Spiderman*, were asked to visit the computer game studio to have their faces scanned so the characters in the games would look more realistic. As the producer of the movie, Brian Pass, states: 'I definitely see a time when you are not going to be able to see a difference between what's been rendered out of a games console and what's happening in a film' (Williams 2003).

However, if we come back to a more positive view on consumer culture (e.g. de Certeau 1988), and we move away from thinking of ourselves as part of the 'inactive mass', we can think of consumers as active agents who create their own identity through consumption. In this case, they are creating a bricolage – literally the activity of self-consciously mixing and matching any disparate elements that may be at hand – which can produce new cultural identities by cutting across social divisions. In this perspective, all consumer behaviour becomes almost imbued with a romantic glow of creativity.

In his analysis of capitalism, de Certeau argues that workers are involved in what he calls '*La Perruque*'. In French, it literally means 'The Wig', and in the author's language, it is the worker's own work disguised as work for his employer; that is, a diversionary practice. This practice can simply be an office worker writing a love letter on 'company time', a factory worker borrowing tools and raw material to build something for his home, an IT officer playing a game, a secretary sending personal e-mails, or an academic reading a graphic novel in his office – *mea culpa*. This practice diverts time that is free, creative and not directed towards profit. The same can be applied to consumer culture, in which consumers divert the original intention of the producers and consume for their own pleasure. For example, Fiske (1989) analyses shopping malls and realises that if their architecture and structure are designed in such a way as to convince people to buy without thinking twice, there are, for example, youth groups who appropriate the space from the mall to their advantage. They use this environment for leisure with their friends without having to consume more than necessary. The same goes for people who learn about the good deals offered in the mall and thus take advantage of the system.

Within this perspective on consumer culture, it can be argued that mass society does not necessarily oppress individuals as the Frankfurt School would like us to think, but that it might be liberating people by offering multiple avenues for individual expression through a range of commodities which can be appropriated by the individual and worked into their own specific style.

This section has given a quick background on the theories of consumer culture and moves now to the field of religion.

Religion and Consumption

Ritzer (1999) makes reference to new means of consumption – e.g. malls, superstores, airports, and cruise ships – as 'cathedrals of consumption'. These cathedrals, in order to attract a larger amount of customers, need to offer a magical, fantastic and enchanting shopping environment. For example, shopping malls can be interpreted as places where people practice their 'consumer religions':

> Malls provide the kind of centeredness traditionally provided by religious temples, and they are constructed to have similar balance, symmetry, and order. Their atriums usually offer connection to nature through water and vegetation. People gain a sense of community as well as more specific community services. Play is almost universally part of religious practice, and malls provide a place for people to frolic. Similarly, malls offer a setting in which people can partake in ceremonial meals. Malls clearly qualify for the label of cathedrals of consumption (Ritzer 1999: 9).

Although it can be claimed that the cathedrals of consumption have a quasi-religious character, some religious groups are specifically following and promoting the consumerist aspect of these cathedrals.

For example, Trueheart (1996) writes about the Next Church, also called mega churches, full-service churches, seven-day-a-week churches, pastoral churches, apostolic churches, 'new tribe' churches, new paradigm churches, seeker-sensitive churches, or shopping-mall churches. Although we will come back to this phenomenon in Chapter 10, the Next Church, at least in its American context, transcends denominations and the traditional way of attending a church. It is evangelical and tends to be Christian literalist. Under one roof, these churches offer pop-culture packaging worship styles to boutique ministries. The latest generation has huge auditoriums and balconied atriums, orchestras and bands playing soft rock, some of them with even food courts, fountains, 'plus plenty of parking, clean bathrooms, and the likelihood that you'll find something you want and come back again' (Trueheart 1996: 49).

Growing churches and congregations, like growing businesses, have a reflexive thirst for market share. They tend to equate rising numbers with self-worth and bricks and mortar with godliness. But growth is also an expression of the evangelical mission.

> When I marvelled to Bill Hybels, of Willow Creek, about his church's phenomenal growth and size – more than 15,000 attend a worship service every weekend – he frowned. 'There are two million people within a one-hour drive of this place', he said. 'In business parlance, we've got two percent of market share. We've got a long way to go' (Trueheart 1996: 52).

Ritzer (1999: 6) quotes the analogy of the 'Wal-Mart-ization of American Religions' when making reference to a pastor of a large Baptist church who hoped to turn his services into a 'fun' event by asking his staff to study Disney World. Following the work of Ritzer on his work on the McDonaldisation of society – that is 'the process by which the principles of the fast food restaurant are coming to dominate more and more sectors of American society as well as the world' (Ritzer 2000) – Drane (2000) argues that the church that follows this process offers uninventive pre-packaged worship and theology.

In the recent book by Carrette and King (2005), the coagulation between religion and consumption is seen in a very negative light as exemplified by this quote:

> Today in most British cities you will find old church buildings that have been sold off to become business offices, supermarkets, public houses, nightclubs and private apartments. However, it is not primarily the sale of buildings that we are concerned with here, but rather of the 'cultural capital' of the religious for the purposes of consumption and corporate gain. From the branding of perfumes using ancient Asian concepts and the idea of the spiritual ('Samsara' perfume, 'Zen' deodorant, 'Spiritual' body-spray) to clothe the product in an aura of mystical authenticity, to the promotion of management courses offering 'spiritual techniques' for the enhancement of one's work productivity and

corporate business-efficiency, the sanitised religiosity of 'the spiritual' sells (Carette and King 2005: 16).

In this perspective, 'spirituality is turned into a product or a kind of brand name for the meaning of life' (Carette and King 2005: 53).

Religion in our postmodern times – whether we like or not – is definitely part of consumer culture. All religious groups produce commodities, or put positive values on some commodities that can be bought by the religious consumer. Some groups are more involved than others and can vary from Hare Krishna devotees selling books at a stall at a university campus or selling vegetarian meals in a restaurant, to Christian shops selling books and other artefacts, to the Church of Scientology asking for a fee for each level of spiritual development, or to New Age shops offering anything that can help the spiritual actor on his or her quest. It cannot be claimed that religion has always been protected from consumer culture until now – one can remember Jesus protesting against the merchants in the Temple. However, what is new in western societies is religion's full immersion into it: some groups celebrating it, others resisting certain aspects of it. It becomes almost a truism to state that for a group to spread its beliefs and values, it now has to speak a language that the majority of people can understand: that of consumption. For example, as found in fieldwork I conducted (Possamai 2005a), Robyn and Roger organise 'New Age' festivals in the hope that some ideas will stay in the minds of the people wandering past the displays:

Robyn: The general people who are searching, even though it's not getting them into the depth of it, but it's obvious that they come to this [New Age festival] because they're searching for something within themselves. And even though you present it in a light, fantastic way and fantasy and fun, there is a depth I believe.

Roger: Definite resonance. Going on within the world.

Robyn: Yes, within them. And that's why they come along. And we have good you know happy people.

Roger: Good vibes.

Robyn: Good vibes yeah. And they go away and even if, you say, did you have a good day, 'Oh we had a lovely day thank you'. But they don't understand the depth of the meaning of what's happened to them, there's something stirring within them. [...] The New Age festivals just get them going and it's up to the person.

Roger: It's a catalyst. It brings it all together.

Robyn: Yes. It just made good some spark in them that gets them going.

Roger: Inspiration.

Robyn: Yes. That's what I believe.

Roger: Even if for some people it will remain out of their conscious awareness, they won't quite understand, remain unconscious, and it gives them some inspiration. Some sort of stimulation.

Robyn: Yes. Something gets into their subconscious there.

Roger: That's right.

As Robyn and Roger remind us, there is a production of symbols in 'New Age' festivals that, according to them, stays in the mind of the religious consumer and may affect his or her beliefs – though the extent of this effect remains unknown.

Post-war consumer culture dominates the western lifestyle with its mass produced commodities. This culture, instead of building a sense of belonging for groups – e.g. class, sub-cultures, political parties – appears to create a fragmented society in which religion is only a part. Indeed, in this consuming world, the individual becomes his or her own authority; the postmodern person in the west no longer tolerates being told what to believe and what to do. Consumer choice is not limited to shopping, but is extended to education, health, politics and religion. People are now 'free to choose' and the market culture might be turning us into consumers rather than citizens (Lyon 2000: 12). He or she is faced with a proliferation of 'spiritual/religious/philosophical knowledges', which he or she researches and experiences. However, as Davie (2000: 172) underlines, when it comes to consumption and monastic discipline, for example, people choose what they like from the rigours of the order (e.g. listening to Gregorian chants) but rarely embrace the whole ascetic discipline.

It is worth noting at this stage that by consumption, I make reference to more than the consumption of commodities, be it religious commodities or 'non-religious' commodities for religious purpose. Consumer society is not restricted to 'material' commodities but to culture as well – which is the very element of consumer society itself (Featherstone 1991: 85). Texts are consumed by the reader, construct who the reader is, and (re)define the reader's self in his or her involvement in this culture of desire. If malls are crowded with shoppers who construct their sense of self through buying commodities, religious actors have the choice to consume other religions, philosophies and even popular culture as seen in Chapter 2, to build their own spirituality (like a *menu à la carte* rather than follow a set menu) which would make sense to their personal narrative.

Sometimes, as found in many New Age spiritualities (see Chapter 12), this religious choice is celebrated; sometimes this choice is a burden of responsibility too heavy for a religious consumer. To this burden, fundamentalism (see Chapter 8) seems to offer a solution. Fundamentalism, according to Bauman (1998: 72), is a postmodern phenomenon, supporting the 'rationalising, reforms and technological development of modernity'. They offer full enjoyment of today's development without paying a heavy price: the price of self-sufficiency, self-reliance and a feeling of never being fully satisfied.

> If market-type rationality is subordinated to the promotion of freedom of choice and thrives on the uncertainty of choice-making situations, the fundamentalist rationality puts security and certainty first and condemns everything that undermines that certainty – the vagaries of individual freedom first and foremost (Bauman 1998: 75).

Even by taking into account various forms of fundamentalism (see Chapter 8) which are a response to a choice-overload within consumer societies (Bauman 1998), it can be argued that all religions are part of consumer culture; however, some are more involved than others. In Zaidman (2003), we are given a comparison between traditional and New Age religion with regard to the commercialisation of religious objects. The findings are based on fieldwork in Israel with pilgrims visiting saints' tombs. While both groups are part of consumer culture, a difference is found in the participants' perspectives on 'the commercialisation of religious goods, the role of marketing agents, and the general characteristics of the market' (Zaidman 2003: 357). In traditional religions, the demand for religious objects is focused on their authenticity. New objects will not be bought unless there is proof that they are authentic for a specific religion, and that they contain the power of a specific source. In New Age, the individual is the main source of meaning attribution, and the authority of the object rests in the individual's decision and/or feeling about the worth of its religiousness. In this context, New Age spiritual actors will seek expanding markets and new sources of religious goods.

From this research, it can easily be inferred that religious consumers are active in different religious groups; however, the point here is to distinguish these styles of consumption. The religious belief will canvas the consumer's choice. In some religious forms, the consumer is his or her own authority in deciding what to consume, in others, there is a reliance on a guidance that justifies the religious values of these commodities. It could be argued that in postmodern times, we have two extremes. On the one hand, some New Age spiritualities[2] (see Chapter 12) are perceived as having no boundaries in their consumption, on the other hand, consumers from some religious groups need to be guided by a recognised authority. In between these two extremes of a continuum, we find all other religious groups. There is consumption on both ends, but on one hand, there is a celebration of choice by the individual (what I call in Possamai [2005b] hyper-consumerism as already touched on in Chapter 2), on the other, there is a control of choice by a recognised authority (what I call hypo-consumerism). Hyper-consumerist would be people who embrace the changes brought by postmodernity whereas hypo-consumerist people would resist, or at least attempt to not be swayed by, the forces of mass consumption. However, it is not because someone is a religiously hypo-consumerist that he or she will not be active in consumer culture. Indeed a recent research (Park and Baker 2007) found that biblical literalists, which is a form of fundamentalism as it will be explored in Chapter 8, consume 16.8% more genres of religious goods (i.e. religious fiction, movies, cloth, stickers, cards) than non-literalists, but these goods are specifically marketed to the Christian belief system of these people and are legitimised by an authority.

Cultural Consumption, Lipovetsky, and the Postmodern Individual

For Lipovetsky (1987; 1993) consumption is about the construction of individual identity. The French author gives an analysis of postmodernity, and argues that if roles, norms, and class were at the focus of the older social world, we now live in a social world in which life is organised around the individual as consumer. In this culture, the individual is autonomous, seeks his or her potential, constructs who he or she is, and is part of the great adventure of the self.

Lipovetsky (1993) refers to a second revolution of individualism that occurred in postmodernity[3] which is characterised by narcissism. In this revolution, the knowledge of oneself is central (Lipovetsky 1993: 91). Those caught up in these changes mainly focus their attention on themselves and do not invest in 'macro identities' such as class, gender, ethnicity, and religion as much as in the past. They focus on constructing their own identity, their own personality, and on generating their own 'narcissistic' knowledge. Indeed, in today's times, it is no longer important to be of the same class, religious background and education to that of our parents. If before we inherited our social characteristics from our family and kept them as part of our identity for the rest of our life, today, it can be argued, we make ourselves who we want to be. For example, in the sphere of religion, we can even explore different religions and pick-and-mix various parts electively and make it a personal spirituality. As an illustration, in many western countries, it is now less important to be an Irish Catholic like our parents. We can still remain Catholic, but we can also explore and choose à la carte other religious elements to create a personal identity and spirituality; or move away from Catholicism and still consume à la carte, such as studying astrology, being interested in Tibetan Buddhism, re-reading the Bible and re-watching the Star Wars saga. This activity is more a lifestyle than a way of life.[4] Chaney (1996) describes the sensibilities employed by the social actor in consuming and in articulating these cultural resources as a mode of personal expression. In this sense, we could speak about a postmodern religious lifestyle when dealing with these bricoleurs.

These new forms of sociability enrich the realm of private activity and pleasures, and consist of the ramification of modes of individual consumption; indeed, leisure-time is extended and resources are mainly devoted to private consumption and pastimes, including religion.

It is tempting, indeed, to bring the quest to understand this cultural consumption to a close by concluding that this consumption is essentially and exclusively individualistic: there is nothing shared except the exaltation of individual eclecticism. Lipovetsky (1987) would describe this as a frivolous economy, that is, consumers set their own goals and design their own lives guided only by hedonistic values. These consumers eschew available macro-identities. They are mobile and their tastes fluctuate.

Postmodernity has been defined not only in terms of cultural traits, as described above, but in terms of a broad personality profile. Rosenau (1992: 53–54) describes the postmodern individual – an ideal-type portrait:

> The post-modern individual is relaxed and flexible, oriented toward feelings and emotions, interiorization, and holding a 'be-yourself' attitude. S/he is an active human being constituting his/her own social reality, pursuing a personal quest for meaning but making no truth claims for what results.

We can understand from this description that these spiritual consumers seek their personal quest for meaning by consuming diverse parts of various religions.

She summarises the description of this postmodern individual as:

> S/he looks to fantasy, humour, the culture of desire, and immediate gratification. Preferring the temporary over the permanent, s/he is contented with a 'live and let live' (in the present) attitude. More comfortable with the spontaneous than the planned, the post-modern individual is also fascinated with tradition, the antiquated (the past in general), the exotic, the sacred, the unusual, and the place of the local rather than the general or the universal.

This understanding of this postmodern individual can easily be adapted to characterise generations X and Y as explored in the introduction of this book.

Conclusion

To be religious in postmodernity is different from living in modernity. If the fathers of sociology as seen in Chapter 3 gave a complex and accurate account of what religion was or did in their time, we now live in a different time period which needs new sociological understanding. One of these understandings is to accept that consumerism is now part of time, whether we like it or not. Although religious messages are believed to have been given orally or in a written form from a place beyond time, the way the message is interpreted and acted upon is strongly included in a time period whose culture and social structure will affect what religious actors do and think. This current culture and social structure is strongly marked by consumerism. In this time period, religious actors make choice about what to believe or what not to believe. In the western world, the choice to have ultimate choice can be made by an individual, or the choice to have less choice can be relegated to an authority, be it a person, group of people, or a text.

This chapter has just explored what it means to be a postmodern individual surrounded by a culture of choice; however, to be able to have a wider picture of postmodernity, we need to move to the next chapter and explore what reality (or should I write, the lack of reality) affects religious actors. This (lack of) reality is now strongly inscribed on a new media support never found before, the Internet; and this will strongly affect what it means to be religious in the near future.

Notes

1. In case the reader was wondering, I am a modernist in my way of thinking following more specifically a Weberian approach. However, I study the sociocultural changes brought by postmodernity in our western world.
2. One should not think that all of these spiritual groups fit with that mold. There are sites of resistance to consumerism that can also be found in the 'other' wing of New Age that is not involved in pro-capitalism, is counter-cultural to modernity, and refuses to be involved in capitalist mainstream, as described by Heelas (1993; 1996).
3. For Lipovetsky, the first revolution of individualism happened with modernity, but this individualism was mainly restricted to the economic sphere and to some artistic *avant-garde* movements.
4. A way of life tends to be typically associated with a more-or-less stable community.

6 Religion and Postmodernity (Part B): Hyper-Reality and the Internet

Introduction

In the Redux version of the war movie *Apocalypse Now* by Francis Ford Coppola, 49 minutes have been added. Part of the extra footage is a surrealist scene that is perfectly appropriate to illustrate this chapter. Three Playboy playmates are touring various army camps during the Vietnam War to boost the morale of the US soldiers. They become stranded with their manager in an almost deserted camp in the pouring rain. Their helicopter, which has run out of fuel, cannot take them away from this hellish situation. The anti-heroes of this story, a small group of soldiers going up a Cambodian river on a secret mission, find them and offer their assistance. The soldiers bargain to spend two hours with them in return for a couple of barrels of fuel – two hours beyond having a cup of tea in their company. One of these soldiers is alone with Miss May who shows him what she offered to the camera for the Playboy magazine. He is in awe about having an intimate moment with a woman whom he has been fantasising about for so long. Holding the almost worshipped copy of the magazine, he is more concerned with the pictures that made her famous than the reality of her naked body. He asks her to pose in exactly the same way as she did in the magazine, and to wear the same wig, so that reality can replicate these pictures, rather than the other way around.

This movie moment, depicting a soldier more interested in the representation of a naked woman than the naked woman herself, is a reflection of the times. This is not to say that all Playboy bunnies are doomed for ever to live a normal everyday life. What I am suggesting is that the 'reality' promoted in popular culture through the media and consumer culture might have superseded 'real reality'; thus creating a sense of uncertainty when deciphering the real from the copy.

The previous chapter focused on two aspects of postmodernity which have affected religions: that of consumerism and that of the second revolution of individualism. This chapter addresses another aspect of contemporary society: that of the implosion of reality (called hyper-reality). It seems that for spiritual consumers, the real and the unreal might have imploded, and this may have blurred the distinction between them. The way in which Baudrillard (1988) has theorised this implosion is helpful in understanding this new spiritual phenomenon. This chapter shows how the practice of mixing popular culture with religion is part of the spirit of the times and that further development of this coagulation can be expected with the Internet.

Baudrillard and Hyper-reality

With the proliferation of communications through the mass media, particularly television, and the full emergence of consumer society, Baudrillard moved away from a neo-Marxist perspective to a postmodern one (e.g. Baudrillard 1979; 1983; 1988; 1995).[1] For the French sociologist, the result of this proliferation is that culture is now dominated by simulations – these are objects and discourses that have no firm origin, no referent, no ground or foundation. In consumer culture, signs get their meanings from their relation with each other, rather than by reference to some independent reality or standard. In our society, consumer capitalism appears to govern the circulation of images in a way that has never happened before, and has forced consumption to become compulsory. Indeed, Baudrillard's theory of commodity culture removes any distinction between objects and representation. In their place he pictures a social world constructed out of models or 'simulacra' which have no foundation in any reality except their own. For example, the current theme parks representing Hollywood movies or Mickey Mouse cartoons which are very popular in the western world do not represent any 'reality' other than the world of Hollywood and of Disneyland. In these parks, the signs on offer have no grounding in 'reality' but are rather connected to 'Mickey Mouse' fiction.

In the fantasy computer game *Kingdom Hearts*, the codes of the game have as expected no clear connection with 'reality' as it is constructed in the traditional fantasy genre, but on top of this, the reference to 'reality' is even pushed further with the introduction of commodified 'Disneyesque' worlds. The traditional fantasy style has a specific set of codes and sub-texts and stories which always use classical mythology (e.g. Greek, Roman, Norse, Hindu, Pacific, African, Icelandic, Arabian and British), and/or history (e.g. antiquity and Middle Ages) and/or other established fantasy stories (e.g. *Lord of the Rings*) as referents, but never before Disney movies. Classical genre references are blurred in this computer game, and the connection with 'traditional' fantasy is obscure, but the reference to the commodified Disney characters and worlds is clear.[2] Fantasy has never been 'real', however with the addition of Disney characters and thus another layer of fiction, the 'real' (in this case the 'clear' connection with traditional fantasy plots) seems to be greatly broken down.

Daytime television viewers, according to Baudrillard, tend to speak about soap opera characters rather than 'real' people. Indeed, how many times have people been speaking at dinner table about characters from movies and/or television series, rather than 'real' people? I, for example, have moved towards this trend when I lecture. I tend to speak about movies and their characters when illustrating diverse sociological and philosophical theories rather than 'real' life stories and characters. The introductions to each of the chapter of this book are also a case in point.

Popular news broadcasts are now more about entertainment than providing information about 'real' social issues; this process has even been called 'infotainment'. In the world of news, 'reality' is now adapted for popular consumption. For this reason, Baudrillard sarcastically claims that the Gulf War of the early 1990s never happened because it was visually created for television (e.g. computer simulation, manipulation of images) before any event took place in Iraq. As Cubitt (2001: 124) states 'throughout the war, TV stations around the world carried digital images from cameras not just carried by reporters or military personnel but mounted in pilotless weapons and 'smart' bombs, images that, in their resemblance to console games, earned the conflict the nickname "Nintendo war"'.

As the same author mentions (Cubitt 2001: 128), there is such a strong proximity between war games and war reality that it seems simulation is taking part in today's warfare, and is thus making war hyper-real (see below). The theory is that these days, the 'model' precedes the event and exhausts it totally in advance, which means that behind this virtuality, the 'real' event might be nowhere to be seen. As per the example introduced in the beginning of this chapter, the photograph of the model from the Playboy magazine preceded the meeting with the real woman, and the reality was there to be seen but was secondary to the representation.

In this society of spectacles – that is, a society in which social relationships between people are mediated by images (Debord 1995) – there is no fixed meta-code. Modern society is saturated by images with the media generating a 'non-material', or 'de-materialised' concept of reality. It seems we live in an economy of signs in which signs are exchanged against each other rather than against the real.

If Marx's vision of society was a giant workhouse, Baudrillard's vision is that modern society is now structured by signs and symbols in which it becomes difficult to distinguish the real from the unreal: from this, hyper-reality (that is, a situation in which reality has collapsed) takes over. We can take as examples the Imax theatres which make us feel we experience a certain place without having to travel. We can now visit Mount Everest and feel it through these images without undertaking an ascetic voyage. Further, the images that are created for the viewers become 'reality' rather than what this place is, that is the 'real reality' that is not shown (e.g. long waiting hours, smell of sweat, pollution on the side of the panoramic view) does not become part of our conceptions. It is easy to imagine a kid seeing a place/building on television and later, confronted with the 'real' place, who does not think it is 'real' because it is not like the one on the television. In pornography, the images that are shown create a new kind of reality about sex (Baudrillard 1979). Close-ups of certain positions that we are not able to see while we make love (at least for one who is not a contortionist) create a sense of reality that is more real than reality (that is, hyper-real) just by showing everything.

This vision accurately portrays current western postmodern times in which people seem to seek spectacle more than meaning. Indeed, as explored in Chapter 2, some spiritual consumers are inspired by horror stories (e.g. H.P. Lovecraft), science fiction stories (e.g. *Star Wars*, *Star Trek*), and fantasy stories (e.g. Tolkien and his *Lord of the Rings*) to support their spiritual works, and this chapter is now coming back to the study of religion in the light of Baudrillard's theory.

Through the use of his theory, I have called these religions inspired by popular culture, hyper-real religions (Possamai 2005b). By hyper-real religion I thus refer to a simulacrum of a religion created out of popular culture which provides inspiration for believers/consumers at a metaphorical level. This type of religion is currently embryonic, however we can expect a growth in the near future as religions become more active on the Internet.

Jediism as a Case Study of a Hyper-real Religious Phenomenon

Although the case of Jediism has already been touched on in Chapter 2, in light of all the theories developed in previous chapters, it is worth studying this hyper-real religion in more detail. On 'Jediism: the Jedi Religion',[3] an Internet site dedicated to presenting Jediism as a religion, we can find that the site's specific view of the *Star Wars* mythos does not base its focus on the myth and fiction as written by the movie director George Lucas, but upon the so-called 'real life' examples of Jediism. As explained:

> Jediism is not the same as that which is portrayed within the Star Wars Saga by George Lucas and Lucasfilm LTD. George Lucas' Jedi are fictional characters that exist within a literary and cinematic universe. The Jedi discussed within this website refer to factual people within this world that live or lived their lives

according to Jediism, of which we recognize and work together as a community to both cultivate and celebrate. … The history of the path of Jediism
traverses through which is well over 5,000 years old. It shares many themes
embraced in Hinduism, Confucianism, Buddhism, Gnosticism, Stoicism,
Catholicism, Taoism, Shinto, Modern Mysticism, the Way of the Shaolin Monks,
the Knight's Code of Chivalry and the Samurai warriors. We recognize that
many times the answer to mankind's problems comes from within the puri-
fied hearts of genuine seekers of truth. Theology, philosophy and religious
doctrine can facilitate this process, but we believe that it would be a futile
exercise for any belief system to claim to hold all the answers to all the serious
questions posed to seekers of truth in the 21st century. Jediism may help
facilitate this process, yet we also acknowledge that it is up to the true believer
who applies the universal truths inherent with Jediism to find the answers they
seek.

The site, which reflects the pick-and-choose consumerist attitude explored
in the previous chapter, then lists different resources on meditation for Jediism
such as the Force, the Temple Jedi, and the seven steps guide – which are
seven steps towards effective prayer. Malhotra (2001) in his introductory
book on yogic philosophy draws some close similarities between this mythos
and his philosophy of meditation.

Becoming a Jedi Knight, or working towards such state of being, appears
attractive to anyone who wants to develop his or her spiritual abilities. Since
Jediknightism, or Jediism, is presented as an old religion re-mythologised for
a contemporary public, old techniques for development of the self such as
meditation, prayers, yoga, and shamanism are used to progress towards this
Jedi path. But what is that path?

In Possamai (2000), I discovered three ideal types of works towards spiritually developing oneself: that is, what I call the teleologies of the being (see
Figure 4 in Chapter 12). The first type is illuminational development. This is
a quest for a direct inner personal experience of the divine within, or for
greater individual potential which includes greater insight, body awareness,
and communication with others. It leads to personal growth and development of latent abilities. Spirituality here is an end in itself. The second type is
instrumental development. It refers to some techniques an individual uses to
better himself or herself, and to become more effective and efficient in
worldly pursuits. This teleology leads to wanting to become a more 'powerful' person in everyday life and focus attention, not on an inner experience
specifically, but on concrete effects, e.g. to develop intelligence, charisma,
and to feel better in one's body. Spiritual development, in this sense, is a
means to external ends. The third type of development is entertainment.
Some people will work on their spiritual self to develop their higher self
(illuminational development) or to gain more power (instrumental development), but others will be involved in some practices just for a good time.

Thus, if spiritual consumers believe in developing their inner spiritual abilities in the hope of developing the spiritual self, they will consume in relation to this goal, e.g. use Jediism for meditation. If a person fixes a goal in everyday life to reach a state of well-being or realisation, they will consume differently, e.g. they might use Jediism to diminish stress. Furthermore, a person can be involved in this practice for an entertainment purpose, e.g. use Jediism to socialise and have fun. These three types are of course deeply interrelated and many individuals may easily fit with more than one ideal type.

Coming back to Jediism in general, it is worth mentioning that it is not just a fan community discussing issues from the *Star Wars* movies. It is also a global spiritual movement expressing itself via the Internet.[4] There are references in these chat rooms to a Jedi Temple represented in cyber place where people can learn about this new spirituality. Although it is present in cyberspace, there were records on some old forums (closed in Oct/Nov 2003 due to hosting problems) of an attempt to raise money to establish such a building in the UK and US. Membership is small for a religion, but significant for a chat room – 287 people were registered on the lists on the 18th January 2004. However, not everyone contributed to a 'serious' discussion on Jedi rituals. On the previous discussion boards, a hierarchy of Jedi ranks could be achieved by members by training in various online courses. A member could progress from a trainee (a person simply required to participate in discussions) to a Jedi Knight (a fully fledged member), all the way up to High Councillor, which is a high rank authority recognised by leaders of the Jedi community. This arrangement was not included in new lists as it was believed that such a progression distracted members from their 'inner' development.

Perhaps Jediism will grow into a fully organised religion in the near future but this would be hard to predict. Some quotes from different chat rooms are listed below to inform us about how some of these social actors see the concrete way of becoming a Jedi Knight in their everyday life.

The first quote deals with Jedi Budo: the all inclusive Jedi martial art which brings into existing techniques the power that can be gained from working towards becoming a Jedi Knight.

> Jedi Budo is more than a system of techniques to control the force (ki, chi, qi). It is a mystical journey of Light, a means to integrate body, heart, mind and soul in one focused release in keeping with the Four Quadrants (Physical, Mental, Emotional and Spiritual). ... Although Jedi Budo covers a broad curriculum including some of the best and most effective techniques found within many of the best martial arts – Kenpo, Kung Fu, Ju Jitsu, Judo, Aikido, Karate, Tae Kwon Do, T'ai Chi Ch'uan – it also includes within it the disciplines encompassing mental clarity, emotional solidity, and spiritual awareness.[5]

The following quotes illustrate that becoming a Jedi is not about fighting choreographically with a laser sword but is seen as an ascetic path towards self-development:

> A Jedi strives to excel physically, mentally, emotionally and spiritually, and can put these in motion instantly. (From the Maxims of the Jediism code).[6]

> Meditation is essential on the path of Jediism… Meditation is a key which can open the door to higher perception, unlocking the perfect wisdom on our hearts.[7]

Below, we can find some comments from people who have just joined the list and who are interested in following this path.

I've just signed up and become a jediist follower

> I've just become a jedi a few days ago and have begun my life under the ways of becoming 1 with the force. I understand that this is not a star wars rip-off site and am quite glad. Jediism makes a huge amount of sense and has already begun to make an impact on my life. i no longer seek new partners or self-privileges. I've begun to offer help to those who need it and oppose those who act for themselves at the expense of others. I'm beginning to meditate and act as i am meant to by the will of all life for the benefit of all life (human or otherwise). i am 14, coming on 15, and I'm beginning 2 already understand the purpose of all that is about me. I would like to thank the creators of this site (www.jediism.net) for opening my eyes and showing me lifes purpose.

> If you could take the Samurai, Arthurian knights, even the Babylon 5 Rangers, and meld them into a single 'mystic warrior' order you'd get something resembling what Jedi means to me.

> … being a Jedi is really a work in progress of improvement in your self and your ability and desire to help others and your self to understand what it is they should do based on what they want, and if what they want is something that they should want.

The last quote reflects perfectly well the placement of this spirituality within our consumer society in which people pick and choose their religion/spirituality to create their own bricolage. In it we find a neo-pagan/witch (see Chapter 13) expressing a strong affinity with Jediism:

Wiccan Jedi

> Hi everyone! I recently found out about Jediism, read, and re-read the website and decided that i love Jediism ☺ I am actually Wiccan, but as Jediist's morals are excellent as well, i decided to merge the two belief systems so I'm a kind of Jedi Witch.

This consumerist approach of mixing and matching is a clear example of what Lipovetsky, as seen in the previous chapter, refers in his own negative words to as a frivolous[8] economy: that is, consumers, and in this case, spiritual consumers, set their own goals and design their own lives guided only by hedonistic values. As an example of this fluctuation of taste for Jediists, the release of the movie *Star Wars: Attack of the Clones* appears to have caused some members to exit from Jediism. This film introduces previously unknown concepts in the Star Wars franchise that took some believers by surprise, such as renouncement of social attachment, the maintenance of chastity and a pursuit of a type of neo-Franciscan poverty. These ideas conflict with the lifestyle of most would-be adherents and created a drop out in the participation of Star Wars Internet rituals (Anonymous 2002).

From the exploration of certain Internet sites, it becomes clear that the character of the Jedi Knights (a type of super-humans) builds an imaginary doxa[9] of developing oneself spiritually and physically. When the spiritual actor moves from the realm of the imaginary doxa to 'reality', we see in the case of Jediism that the characters of fiction are adapted to already existing 'real' religions. The label 'Jediism' simply becomes a new etiquette for already existing spiritualities and religions, and in that sense, Jediism, in terms of its content, should not be seen as new (Possamai 2005b).

It seems that for these spiritual consumers, the real and the unreal might have imploded and created an unclear sense of distinction between them. Jean Baudrillard who has theorised this implosion in the previous section has indeed been helpful in understanding this new spiritual phenomenon. One should be aware that Baudrillard worked on his theory of hyper-reality before the booming of the Internet; and as seen with the case of Jediism as a hyper-real phenomenon, the Internet is a strong support, if not necessary, for the spiritual experience of its adepts.

Hyper-real Religions.com and the Participatory Culture

As detailed in Chapter 2, case studies of hyper-real religions are not a specific phenomenon of the 21st century. The earliest cases appeared in western societies in the 1950s and 1960s with the Church of Scientology, the Church of All Worlds, and other neo-pagan groups. These 20th-century hyper-real religions have their spirituality – somewhat – defined independently from popular culture which is used as a source of secondary inspiration. As far as I am aware, there are no Lovecraft or Discworld spiritualities; however, there is now a Star Wars and Matrix spirituality. Indeed, in Jediism and Matrixism, the works of popular culture appear to be used as a first hand source of inspiration.

How do we explain what appears to be a shift from using popular culture as a source of inspiration (that is secondary source of inspiration) to having popular culture appropriated as the spiritual work in itself (that is primary source of inspiration)? Based on my exploration of the case studies in the literature and on the Internet, my assumption is that the catalyst for such a process is the Internet which is a haven for the hyper-real phenomenon. There are certainly other social factors that would have caused this shift but without more research, this chapter will remain silent on them.

As pointed out by existing research on the Internet such as Ross (2005) and Murphy (1996), and more specifically on the Internet and religion (Krüger 2005), there is a clear connection between the use of this medium with hyper-reality. Many issues with the use of religion on the Internet are relevant topics of study, but are beyond the scope of this chapter. Such issues include playing with one's on-line and off-line identities, supposed democracy in chat rooms, and the practice of religion on-line, off-line, or both on-line and off-line. We will, however, come back to these issues in Chapter 12 when dealing with neo-paganism and cyber-covens.

The use of the Internet by religious people and groups can be traced back to the 1980s (Campbell 2005). Since that time, the way religion is discussed and practised on the web has gone through recurrent transformations. Karaflogka (2002) studied the various typologies of religious activities but has seen her conceptualisations changing over time following changes on the web itself. These changes are due to the fact that cyberspace is no longer the preserve of the computer specialist and it now supports an inclusive (at least for those who can access the hardware) social space. She also distinguishes what she calls religion *on* cyberspace and religion *in* cyberspace.

> What I call 'religion *on* cyberspace' is the information uploaded by any religion, church, individual or organisation, which also exists and can be reached in the off-line world. In this sense the Internet is used as a tool. 'Religion *in* cyberspace', which I call cyberreligion, is a religious, spiritual or metaphysical expression which is created and exists exclusively in cyberspace, where it enjoys a considerable degree of 'virtual reality' (Karaflogka 2002: 285).

Employing this distinction, it can be argued that when religions started on the Internet, they tended to be religions *on* cyberspace as they mainly posted information, calendar of events or even sermons. However, with the democratisation of access to the Internet and the use of its full potential, religions *in* cyberspace are emerging and involve the full participation of cybernauts such as actively taking part in chat rooms and/or performing rituals on-line. These cyberreligions, or what Karaflogka terms 'New Cyberreligious Movements', are a recent phenomenon and, even if they mainly exist and function online, they can nevertheless mobilise a large part of the population.

Hyper-real religions that use popular culture as a primary source of reference such as Jediism are case studies of the growth of these New Cyberreligious Movements. There are thus sources in the sociology of religion that explain the presence of these hyper-real religions on the Internet but nothing on the reason why or how popular culture is now being used as a primary source of reference for hyper-real religion on the Internet.

The research literature on media studies might provide an element of explanation. Jenkins (2003) studied the participatory phenomenon of the Star Wars culture, and although he did not address Jediism, strong similarities can be drawn from his research with that on hyper-real religion. Jenkins discovered on the Internet that Star Wars fans emulate/parody some of the Star Wars stories and create their own work (e.g. home made movies, pictures and stories). For example, a database on the Internet for fan film production has close to 300 amateur-produced Star Wars films. These works are no longer photocopied and/or recorded from tape to tape, sent via (snail)mail, and thus only accessible to, for example, a few dozen people; but are put on the Web to be reached by the very broad 'logged-on' world. This allows for alternative media productions to become more visible in mainstream culture, and opens a door to cheap and high distribution of this creativity, which could be regarded as an alternative to dominant media content. These artists/fans create their own stories which do not have to be moulded by the imperative of consumer culture (e.g. editing with a commercialist vision or marketing to a specific public with buying power), which could be interpreted by some as questioning the hegemonic representation of their culture. To reflect this process amplified by the Internet and its online circulation, Jenkins uses the term 'participatory culture':

> Patterns of media consumption have been profoundly altered by a succession of new media technologies which enable average citizens to participate in the archiving, annotation, appropriation, transformation, and recirculation of media content. Participatory culture refers to the new style of consumerism that emerges in this environment.

It can be argued that participatory culture also encompasses hyper-real religionists. They now have the ability to discuss their spiritual works on the Internet and share them with others; something that would have been difficult to accomplish to such an extent with the use of a photocopier. Indeed, the Internet as a vehicle allows people to share their construction of self (e.g. through photographs and biography) with the world. Some of them include their view on spirituality (Smith 1999). This can attract other people towards these idiosyncratic spiritualties in a way that was not possible pre-

Internet times. In the past, in certain socio-cultural contexts, it was more believable for some to claim that he or she received the message from an envoy of God, print pamphlets, and even make video to promote their vision. But someone who claims publicly that he or she is in touch with Yoda becomes ludicrous. However, if people put messages on the Internet simply stating that the Star Wars stories are a source of inspiration not to be taken literally and thus manage to get people chatting on the Net (rather than listening to someone on a soap box), such a religion becomes more acceptable in today's society. Further, since people on the Net do not use their real identity and can create new on-line selves, Jediists do not have to face any harassment or embarrassment off-line. The fact that popular culture can be used as a primary source of inspiration, I believe, could not have happened without the Internet.

It becomes tempting to argue that because this form of cyber-support was not available at the beginning of the second part of the 20th century, popular culture was only used at a secondary level for hyper-real religions. Indeed, as already explained, the Church of All Worlds, the Church of Satan and Neo-Paganism use popular culture as an aid to their religion. Whereas with the hyper-real religions of the 21st century, and as part of the participatory culture, popular culture can become the main hero; that is the religion itself. Jediism and Matrixism have become a spirituality in themselves contrary to the stories of Lovecraft and Robert Heinlein, which have remained a source of inspiration for other spiritualities. Of course, one should not negate the fact that some people might have attempted in the past to use popular culture as a primary source of inspiration; however, I have not found any trace of this in my research. Perhaps participatory culture on the Internet will allow these 'older' hyper-real religions to emerge in the near future.

I would thus like to argue that with the advent of the Internet and the boom of participatory culture, hyper-real religions have allowed popular culture to move from being secondary to one's spiritual work to becoming central. And in this sense, the Internet has allowed these religions to become part of the hyper-reality described by Baudrillard in a stronger fashion.

As Jenkins argues about the Star Wars participatory culture, the Web has allowed a return to a type of folk-understanding of creativity that was present before the industrial revolution. Before this revolution, folktales, legends, myths, and ballads were built up over time as people transformed them to add more meaning to their own concern. But with the industrial revolution, culture became privatised and copyrighted. This, after a time, led to corporations controlling 'their' intellectual property and thus imposing on the general population the need to become consumers only rather than participants in the culture as well. As Jenkins (2002: 309) describes this phenomenon:

The mass production of culture has largely displaced the old folk culture, but we have lost the possibility for cultural myths to accrue new meanings and associations over time, resulting in single authorized versions (or at best, corporately controlled efforts to rewrite and 'update' the myths of our popular heroes). Our emotional and social investments in culture have not shifted, but new structures of ownership diminish our ability to participate in the creation and interpretation of that culture.

As in the case of fan culture, Star Wars fans are now able to participate in the formation of, and discussion about, the Star Wars culture using the Internet in the same way as happened within folk culture before the industrial revolution. Coming back to hyper-real religions, and including for the purpose of this chapter folk theology as part of folk culture, similarities can easily be drawn with folk theology, which is generally characterised by decentralisation, oral liturgies, dynamic and syncretic belief systems, and consensus-based leadership (Houk 1996). More work has been done to compare and contrast folk theology with hyper-real religions (see Possamai 2008b); but suffice it to say that with the advent of the Internet, the folk aspect of hyper-real religions is web based. This has given an opportunity for people to create a religion out of popular culture and, more importantly, to share it on-line with like minded people as 'ownership' of religion and spirituality diminishes. This process, it appears, has allowed hyper-religionists to use popular culture as a primary source of inspiration and to share their spiritual work with the on-line community at large. As part of this process, they express their religion *in* cyberspace and are fully part of these New Cyberreligious Movements.

Conclusion

Chapters 5 and 6 covered various facets of today's condition within what is called postmodernity; and by postmodernity (which could also be called high, late or liquid modernity), I make reference to concrete changes in the socio-cultural aspects of our western society. Religion did not escape these changes and is now a part of consumer culture. Believers are more individualistic than they were in the past and they make choices about what to believe in or not. Very often this choice becomes an eclectic mixture of many spiritualities and religions found in the religious marketplace. Further, some of these religions have so much embraced postmodernity and its hyper-reality that they are mixing popular culture with established religions and philosophies without any concerns about the truth of any message or the origin of the belief system. However, not all religions embrace postmodernity to such an extent. Some, like fundamentalism (see Chapter 8), rejects parts of it, while other more traditional groups like moderate Buddhism (Chapter 9),

Christianity (Chapter 10) and Islam (Chapter 11) are dealing with it without going to such extremes.

The next chapter brings together some of the theories developed until this chapter with the case study of esotericism. By studying what happened to esotericism when it entered modernity and postmodernity, we will be able to cement some of the knowledge previously developed. Further, by bringing Weber's notion of the disenchantment of the world into the current context, a kind of loop will be formed with Weber, as seen in Chapter 3.

Notes

1. Because of this move, and because of some of his bold statements which will soon be explored, Jean Baudrillard's theories could sometimes be seen closer to science fiction than sociology (Rojek and Turner 1993). However, as there are elements of truth in his theories that make sense of contemporary changes in the religious landscape, his work will be used.

2. This, without any doubt, exposes children and young teenagers to the conspicuous consumption – that is, the competitive display of capacity to spend money on inessentials – connected with the Disney world.

3. Internet Site, htpp://www.jediism.bigstep.com/ (7/03/03).

4. However, one might wonder if being involved in Jediism is a move forward from belonging to a Star Wars fan community.

5. Internet Site, http://www.jedibudo.com/about.html (04/02/2004).

6. Internet Site, http://www.jediism.org/generic.html?pid=0 (09/09/2004).

7. Internet Site, http://www.jediism.org/generic.html;$sessionid$IKH0DHIAAA GLXTZENUGUTIWPERWRJPX0?pid=5 (09/09/2004).

8. I would rather use the term 'liquid'.

9. That is a general desire grounded in everyday life fantasies which have been created by works of fictions. We could imagine specific forms of imaginary doxa – that is, as wanting to be beautiful and sexy like certain soap opera characters, or as being as sexually active as certain characters in pornographic movies, or being as skinny as certain models in magazines. This fantasy created by works of fiction – a space where affective relationships and identities can be articulated – makes people dream, and makes them wish for some out-of-wordly outcomes, and might, to a certain extent, influence people's everyday life (see Possamai (2005b)).

7 Esotericism, Its McDonaldisation, and Its Re-enchantment Process

Introduction

The last two chapters have described important changes to our western society that have impacted on religions. This chapter follows on from these findings and uses esotericism, which refers to secret religions and/or religions attempting to discover the secrets of the universe, as a case study to illustrate how changes at a larger scale in society can also impact on the most hidden religious groups. This chapter argues that the impact of modernity and postmodernity has been so great that it has now become hard to claim there is much secrecy left in esotericism. However, one unintended consequences of the growth in transparency of esotericism has also been a re-enchantment of parts of today's world. Indeed, esoteric groups are at the core of the mysterious and the magical and have been the repository of some enchanted parts of our world during the many intrusions of the rationalisation process. Before moving to a discussion of Weber's notion of enchantment and disenchantment, I am first illustrating this term with a recent movie directed by Guillermo del Toro.

The movie, *Pan's Labyrinth* (2006), is based shortly after the Spanish civil war of the 1930s in which the dictator Franco (1892–1975) took power. A little girl is brought to a village which is controlled by the Franquists in order to meet her stepfather who comes from a line of proud military men. In this setting, the little girl, Ofelia, is exposed to the reality of a cold and rational world. Her stepfather is a calculating man who is the epitome of a cruel technocrat. She is also in the middle of a fight between the value of two modern and rational movements (Fascism, as represented by the military, and Communism, as represented by the guerrillas from the Spanish Maquis) which have brought with them a non-magical understanding of the world. However, even if the world is rational, there is a yesteryear labyrinth close to the village of which no one knows the origin. The labyrinth is built in a way that no matter how rational and technocratic the world can be, there is always a place hosting mystery nearby. It has been designed in a way that people would believe that it hides secrets. It also reminds the viewer that no matter how rational or technocratic a world can be, there is always a place hosting a dose of mystery. The little girl is slowly dragged into a world of magic when she is contacted by creatures from the labyrinth. She is told that she may be the princess they have been waiting for but to prove this, she needs to undertake various missions that are found in their magical realm. During the whole movie, the viewer is exposed to this magical world which is seen living side by side with a rational one. It is only at the end (after realising that no one else but her can see this world) that the viewer wonders if she is the only one who can reach it, or if it is the fruit of her imagination. Even if it is the fruit of her imagination, the labyrinth is present in this story to add a touch of mystery to the rational and violent world of the civil war in Spain.

The question in this chapter is not about whether the magical, the mysterious, or the uncanny exists. Sociologists are ill equipped with their social scientific tools to understand this. However, what is of importance is the fact that while modernity was growing and Weber thought that it would completely negate this world of fantasy, some religious groups were embracing a rational view of the world and mixing it with their understanding of the magical. They, as I argue in this chapter, started to re-enchant the world, and even increased this process when they entered postmodernity and its consumer culture.

The Disenchantment of the World

Weber saw the changes that drove western society from a traditional to a modern context as a process in which the timeless magic of the universe might be removed and kept outside of people's everyday life. This, according to Weber, might have reduced human perception and experience of the world to that of a banal parade of predictable actions in a society of arid routines which he called the disenchantment of the world. This process describes the state when

> the natural world becomes increasingly less mysterious and is defined instead – in principle at least – as knowable, predictable and, perhaps most importantly, tameable. In a disenchanted world, Weber argued, 'the ultimate and most sublime values have retreated from public life'; the magical, 'mysterious incalculable forces' give way to 'calculation', 'scientific rationalism and bureaucracy'. It is a world in which the sky is emptied of angels (Wallis 2006: 32).

At the time that Weber was writing, he saw industrialisation as characterised by rationalisation and by the disenchantment (also called the demagification) of the world. For him, mystery and magic no longer permeated his world, and the supernatural was banished.

For Weber, magic has a rational aim which is pursued by irrational means (e.g. such as making a love potion with menstrual blood, which is casting an irrational spell to produce specific and rational outcomes). In this sense, magic uses a spontaneous way of thinking (salvage, magical and mythopeic) which is different from a domesticated one (civilised, rational and logical). Religion, on the other hand, is characterised by an irrational aim (e.g. going to heaven, becoming enlighten) but with rational means of salvation (e.g. do not sin, act in a righteous way).

It is important to note at this stage that a society might be religious but nevertheless disenchanted. Indeed, rationalisation is a process widely used in science, and in religion as well. The disenchantment of the world, for Weber, did not start with modernity, but with Judaism; a religion that emerged amidst pagan religions and which completely broke with magic. Jewish prophets distanced themselves from previous polytheist religious traditions as they became the tools of the one and only God whose decision could not be interfered with. Pagan gods, on the other hand, could help people in their everyday life. In this new worldview, nothing magical was allowed to exist as there was no point in expecting God to help people in their everyday life.

Later, in contrast to Judaism, Catholicism re-enchanted parts of the world with, for example, the introduction of saints who could intercede in people's favour through a prayer or through confession as compensation for the sin that the believer had committed. The worship of saints' relics and some forms of pilgrimage can also be viewed sociologically as magical actions rather than religious.

In the history of Catholicism, Durand (1996) points out a crucial moment in history that could have enchanted the world of Catholics even more. Ca. AD 1300, after the Dark Ages, penetration of Arab texts into the Latin world was very advanced. These works were remnants of Ancient Greece and became the basis of a return to mythopoeic thought in the Renaissance. They were also the basis for new synthetic developments in Christianity. Christian theologians had to decide which works among these numerous translations were suitable for expression and elaborations of their credo. They finally adopted the Latin Averroism, being the thought of the Arab Ibn Rushd Averroës (AD 1126–98), an Arab living in Spain who was the interpreter of Aristotle. This was chosen instead of the influence of the Persian Avicenna (AD 980–1037) who, by a combination of Aristotelianism and neo-Platonist ideas, praised the idea of a *mundus imaginalis* and its consequence, the active imagination/intuition.

Aristotelianism then became hegemonic in the western world. Its adaptation to the Bible story was so complete that to claim that Aristotle's work, as translated by Averroës was wrong was to claim that the Bible was wrong. What the Bible could not explain, only Aristotle could. For example, the Galenic system that was inspired by a blend of Hippocrates' and Aristotle's theories could not be criticised, even if a sick person was dying from a blood-letting, i.e. a Galenic prescription. Proposing a heliocentric view of the universe was not a danger to Catholic exegesis in itself, but was a crime because Aristotle's system was geocentric.

Later, Protestantism moved away from what Weber saw as a magical practice and put in place another disenchantment process which would lead to modernity, as already seen in Chapter 3.[1]

Although there have been many disruptors of the 'enchanted' in the western world as detailed above, modernity, with its rational outlook, was for Weber the strongest catalyst for the disenchantment of the world. However, as will be detailed in the next section, some groups that were involved in magic also went through this rationalisation process brought about by modernity without, paradoxically, losing their 'enchanted' element. These later became carriers, among many other groups, of a re-enchanting process in the western world.

Esotericism

In numerous studies, the concepts of esotericism, occultism and Gnosticism are used in many different ways that prove confusing. Riffard (1990) provides an interesting analysis of the word in its various interpretations by different groups. For example, in Gnosticism esotericism was called gnosis; in Pythagoreanism it was synonymous with philosophy (Riffard 1990: 97), and it was described as magic by the Iranian Mazdeism . In 1883 the word was consecrated for the western public in a book by A.P. Sinnet, *Esoteric Buddhism*, and was then used to express the doctrine of the Theosophical Society (Riffard 1990: 78–79). For Foster Bailey (1974: 10) of the Arcane school, esotericism is the secret knowledge found in the work of the founder of the Theosophical Society (see below), Helena Petrovna Blavatsky. For other esotericists, such as René Guénon, Blavatsky was a charlatan who knew nothing about esotericism. The word thus has a diversity of denotations. It is also often strongly valorised by a variety of esoteric groups who appropriate it to establish their credentials with their peers and their public.

Riffard (1990) argues that the most visible characteristic, the affirmation most often renewed among esotericists, is the cult of the secret. However, Faivre (1994) warns us of the danger of reducing this multi-dimensional term to the secrecy dimension.[2] I will argue later that when esotericism entered modernity, it attempted to reveal all of its secrets and later became part of a religious/magical mass market during postmodernity. However, before reaching that point, I need first to describe this tradition from the Renaissance.

In the Renaissance, the Church finally started to cede sovereignty to the temporal rulers and kept only its spiritual power. The notion of time changed with clocks first used by merchants and astronomers, and works from antiquity were discovered through the Crusades and meeting with the Arabs. In the same period, the Kabala was christened by Pico della Mirandola. Paraclese wrote book after book and was inspired by the doctrine of correspondence. Nostradamus received his visions. John Dee, the astrologer to Queen Elizabeth and the magus who inspired Shakespeare's character Prospero in the Tempest, believed he was in communication with angels through a mirror[3] and was a very pious Catholic. But these people had to be careful. If they were living in a Papist land, they could not deny the teaching of the Fathers of the Church. If they were under the rule of a Prince, they had to be careful that he did not think that they were fighting against his power. If they were recognised as being thaumaturgic, they could go to jail, because people were afraid of them, or because people wanted their supposed power.

This was also the time when people started to see the world without Christendom at the centre and when magical practices were in union with what would later be called science. Astrology was studied and taught hand in hand with astronomy in universities. Isaac Newton studied physics and also practised alchemy. Science was mainly mathematics, physics and cosmology at this time, but was also combined with magic, kabala and alchemy.

> It was this same necessity that obliged knowledge to accept magic and erudition on the same level. To us, it seems that sixteenth-century learning was made up of an unstable mixture of rational knowledge, notions derived from magical practices, and a whole cultural heritage whose power and authority had been vastly increased by the rediscovery of Greek and Roman authors. Perceived thus, the learning of that period appears structurally weak: a common ground where fidelity to the Ancients, a taste for the supernatural, and an already awakened awareness of that sovereign rationality in which we recognize ourselves, confronted one another in equal freedom (Foucault 1970: 32).

According to Faivre (1987: 161), esotericism again became a marginal phenomenon by the end of the seventeenth century. 'The scientific community's break with esotericism is symbolised by the exclusion of astrology in 1666 from the new Academy of Sciences founded in Paris'. Riffard (1990: 743) refers to the 17th century as the era of ruptures between esotericism and culture. If esotericism had a certain freedom of expression (depending on its context) in the Renaissance, science took over this independence and relegated esotericism to the backstage of society. The sleep of reason was now supposed to produce monsters.[4] *Le siècle des lumières* created a new kind of shadow. Transparent algebraic signs replaced symbols and their constructive opacity (Durand 1996: 25), and the mechanical world supplanted the symbolic one.

While the world of science developed reason until reaching a consensus about method, and while Cartesianism introduced in French philosophies the distinction between clear and distinctive perceptions, and obscure or confusing ones to establish the primacy of the latter over the former (Bastide 1996:189).

However, this process did not eradicate esotericism, which adapted itself to the changes of the time. The advent of modernity saw the birth of modern Spiritualism in 1848 when the Fox sisters discovered a way of communicating with the spirit of a dead person through mysterious raps and knocks. They began their careers as spirit mediums through newspaper journalism and toured throughout America. Their popularity created intense interest and controversy and was the starting point of the modern Spiritualist movement.

Contacts with entities from the other world are not new phenomena in the history of esotericism. Shamans experience a trance and speak with 'astral' people; mediums let their body be possessed by a spiritual entity and become transmitters of the supernatural. Before Spiritualism, this was called nekyomancy, necromancy or divination by consultation with the dead. What really makes the difference with the appearance of modern Spiritualism is that suddenly people no longer need psychic power or long training to communicate with the world of the spirit. No longer does an individual need to be a shaman and experience a trance to speak with astral 'people' or be a medium and let their body be possessed by a spiritual entity. Everybody is now considered able to contact the spirit of the dead and there is no longer a need for the presence of an intermediary.

Léon Rivail (1804–69), under the pseudonym of Alain Kardec, tried to unify and codify Spiritualism to make it a religion 'tinted with sentimentalism and rationalism' (Faivre 1992: 86). Having positivist beliefs, without being an orthodox positivist, he employed the scientific method of observation, comparison and evaluation to systemise Spiritualism. He was among the first – if not the first – to reintroduce the theory of reincarnation in the West since its condemnation in AD 533 by the Fathers of the Church. However, he reintroduced it with the law of constant progress, i.e. blended with a significant spiritual borrowing of Darwinism, which is a strong narrative in symbiosis with that of modernity. After Kardec's work, the large family of Spiritualism divided into two main tendencies. One, often referred to as Spiritism, followed his work and led to the formation of groups such as the Brazilian Spiritist Federation created in 1874. The other refused his systemisation and turned to predecessors of the movement, like Swedenborg for example, to rationalise Spiritualism with a Christian faith.

Later, in 1875, the Theosophical Society, a movement diverging from modern Spiritualism, followed the same ethos of offering the secret of the other world(s) without the service of intermediary elites such as Brahmans and the priests of Memphis, Eleusis and Orphism. One of the founders, Helena Petrovna Blavatsky, synthesised a new eschatology which was based on evolutionism and the theory of reincarnation in her *magnum opus, The Secret Doctrine* (1888). Blavatsky did not reject Darwinism but insisted that it had omitted the spiritual side of evolutionism in favour of materialism. Inspired by a Darwinian evolutionist discourse, she adapted and westernised the concept of reincarnation by syncretising it with the concept of spiritual progress. In the east, reincarnation is not only progressive – i.e. allowing the possibility of a better embodiment in the next life – but it can also be regressive. In the west, the cultural transaction between evolutionism and the theory of reincarnation allowed only for progressive reincarnation: that is a type of progress on a symbolic spiritual ladder until the final theomorphic stage. Reincarnation is not, in this sense, a fate from which humans may have to be liberated as it is in the east (see Chapter 9 on Buddhism), but a factor of progress. Thus the theory of progressive reincarnation explains how utopia is attained: one day the whole of humankind will have developed its divine sparks and built a world similar to that of Adam and Eve before their fall. However, this time, according to the early members of the Theosophical Society, is still far away. Serious spiritual progress still needs to be achieved over thousands, maybe millions of years.

The Theosophical Society and Spiritualism were the two movements that not only democratised themselves, but also gave the opportunity for women to experience esoteric culture. Previously esotericists had been mainly male who seldom let women participate in their rituals unless there were needed for a sexual purpose. In modernity, women had the opportunity to express themselves religiously.

If the Theosophical Society was mainly based on westernised eastern philosophies, modern Occultism was strongly influenced by the Kabala. For example, Eliphas Lévi (1810–75) and Papus (1865–1916) did not condemn scientific progress or modernity and even integrated science into their teaching against materialism. They planned to elucidate all the mysteries lying in the esoteric traditions and wanted to unveil all the secrets.

Alphonse-Louis Constant, under the pseudonym of Lévi, created a movement to fight against materialism in France. He was also a romantic, a communist, and a one-time Catholic priest. Gérard Encausse, using the *nom de plume* of Papus, was considered the 'Balzac of Occultism' because he wrote 260 titles. He was a physician and an initiate of numerous occult groups. He believed the body could be cured through treatment of the aura. Patients queued for hours in front of his consulting room and he even received a medal of honour from the *Assistance publique* of France. He was also the spiritual teacher of Nicholas II in St Petersburg. This movement attracted apparently diverse personalities who did not condemn scientific progress or modernity but who integrated science into their teachings against materialism. They planned to elucidate all the mysteries lying in the esoteric traditions and wanted to unveil all the secrets. Many new initiatory orders were created from this movement, e.g. the Golden Dawn by Samuel Mathers.

Occultism kept intact the concept of initiatory groups – contrary to Spiritualism and the Theosophical Society – but published many books in 'clear' or non-cryptic language unveiling all the information that was formerly kept secret. So just as modern science attempted to explain the secrets of the empirical world using a logical method, Occultism attempted, by open scientific inquiry, to unlock the secrets of the non-empirical world.

Wallis (2006) studied Spiritualism during modernity in light of the disenchantment debate, and I would like to expand his conclusion from this specific group to all the groups that we have just explored. These esoteric groups grew out of modernity rather than against it and they represent a fusion of science and religion that 'sought to (re-) enchant sites within modernity that from a Weberian perspective would be seen as carriers of disenchantment, specifically science and technology' (Wallis 2006: 40).

In this period of esotericism, as characterised by the birth of Spiritualism, the Theosophical Society and modern Occultism, it was no longer necessary to find hierophants to learn. This type of spiritual dependency was no longer needed because semi-mass produced books then explained the knowledge. Riffard (1990), however, sees this as a vulgarisation of esotericism.

Through the years, we can posit that this process changed from the idea of sharing the 'secret' doctrine (in modernity) into the ethos of simplifying it (in postmodernity). As an example, I compare the book by the modern Occultist Papus (1994), *The Tarot of the Bohemians*, which, even if it supposedly answers the secret of Tarot Cards, is difficult to understand. In comparison to a kind of do-it-yourself-in-five-minutes-Tarot-cards-reading book or a computer program on the same cards that appeared in New Age shops, I see a profound difference of complexity. The former still involves serious work by the reader and proposes some notion of universal knowledge, and the latter is faster to grasp through focussing on easy and quick information about the cards without entering into any theoretical underpinnings. The tendency in postmodern esotericism was to reveal the secrets and to present purported universal knowledge in what Riffard (1990) calls Esotericism Simplified. This period of esotericism that includes contemporary alternative spiritualities (e.g. New Age in Chapter 12 and Neo-Paganism in Chapter 13) simplifies what was already revealed a century ago and encourages the practitioner to develop the knowledge of himself or herself. In today's world, esoteric knowledge is no longer secret (Schlegel 1995; Trevelyan 1984) and even appears to have become a public commodity (Werbner 1995; York 2001). There is no more need to access 'secret wisdom' in groups because the access for individuals is now facilitated thanks to the structure of consumer culture. Every spiritual technique – e.g. astrology, numerology, and occultist rituals – is now easy to find and to learn and there is no need to belong to any secret group.

On the Internet, Steve Cranmer (1995: 4) warns people wanting to become a member of an occultist group: 'Don't count on having "secrets" revealed to you. Ninety-nine percent of them are already published, in some form, somewhere'. Secrecy, a key element of esotericism, has thus been opened up, and is now on the shelves of New Age bookshops, and even on the Internet. As Zygmunt Bauman (1998) notices, if transcendence was once the privilege of an aristocracy of culture such as mystics, ascetic monks, dervishes or occultist leaders, now this transcendence is within every individual's reach. It is part of consumer culture and is thus commodified. I want to point out here that what I express is a majority tendency. Of course, there are spiritual actors who engage in very profound spiritual research, and/ or are in search of universal principles, but what is emphasised is that the simplification of esotericism has given the opportunity for everyone to have access to this knowledge. This access is now offered in a commercially prepared form that is quicker and easier to obtain. So what does this imply for social actors involved in these spiritualities? What does it mean for a 'secret knowledge' to be commodified?

Seeking 'Secret Knowledge' in Postmodernity

Two short case studies from an earlier fieldwork (Possamai 2005a) can help us to understand what it means to seek 'esoteric knowledge' in postmodernity. Anne was a confirmed atheist until her mother gave her a 'New Age' book written by Ruth Montgomery. This book made sense to her so she began to seek to experience the different aspects of the religious and spiritual field. First, she was introduced to Christianity by a born-again Christian, but decided to leave the group she joined. She continued exploring the religious market and decided to follow different 'New Age' workshops. She tried many different practices, including regression, to discover who she was in her previous life. She said:

I've tried to be regressed. Which didn't work on me. But then they say it can take many sessions before you sort of [experience something], and you need to feel comfortable with the person and whatever, which I never did. And at something like [AU] $120 a session you don't want to go to too many sessions before you know that something's happening.

She also went to a Buddhist monastery and was ready to become a Buddhist monk. She left this place because she perceived that the monks were not completely 'authentic' at times; they were watching the *Star Trek* series on television too often. She admits that she was attracted by the 'glamorous part' of the esoteric/New Age market which offers 'mystical knowledge', and hoped to become enlightened. Although she has never had any mystical experience, she still hopes that one day the 'light' might come to her.

Steve has performed rituals in occultist groups for years. Tensions occurred in those groups and some people wanted to gain more power. Steve felt that politics was taking too much time away from the ritual of magic. He is now involved in a networking form of neo-paganism and calls himself an urban shaman.

He strongly criticises the idea of people obtaining a 'universal knowledge'. He said: 'It's not uncommon for a third degree witch – which is the highest thing in most witchcraft systems – to say that she can solve all your problems because she has access to universal knowledge. Absurdities like this are common.'

He also makes a link between this 'universal knowledge' and the ephemeral nature of certain groups: 'People are in one group and they go to another group, another group, another group. It's very common. And there's lots of groups around too and everyone's claiming hidden knowledge and all this sort of rubbish.'

Unlike Anne, Steve claims to have had many spiritual/mystical experiences such as shamanic trances, astral travelling, etc.

From these two examples, it can be seen that this kind of spiritual actor lives in a world of choice, which is part of the consumer society as seen in Chapter 5. In this world, the individual becomes his or her own authority; the postmodern person in the west no longer tolerates being told what to believe and what to do. He or she is faced with an over-proliferation of 'esoteric knowledge' which he or she researches and experiences. However, in this phase of 'esotericism simplified' as we have seen above, occult knowledge is now easily accessible and not controlled by some 'intellectual of the esoteric'. It could thus be argued that the majority of spiritual actors are now faced with what could be called the McDonaldised[5] Occult Culture, which is an arena of esotericism and occultistism in consumer culture where anything goes. In such a culture, esoteric philosophies, such as Swendenborg, Guénonism, Christian Kabbala, are mixed with conspiracy theories, alien intelligences, and Jedi religion; for example the X-Files with Kabbalah (Winslade 2000). In this arena, half-truths are classed as scholarly work.

The McDonaldisation of Occult Culture is a process defined by Koenig (2001) and its central quality is fragmentation of knowledge. The Internet, which he uses as a case study, appears to be a strong medium for this type of knowledge and could be argued to be an element of Techno-Magick.

> Techno-magick is what articulates the channels of discourse that disseminate occult knowledge. Not only is technology caught up in the trope of magic, it becomes the medium through which this formerly hidden knowledge is now available to any individual with access to the internet (Winslade 2000: 96).

With Techno-magick, 'The knowledge is always fluid, disembodied and haunting, never fully locatable, accessible at many different possible nodes, and available to anyone who wishes to engage in practice of magic' (Winslade 2000: 97).

Because of this fluidity – on the Internet more specifically, but also in everyday life – the gap between high culture and mass culture has never been so narrow (Possamai 2005b). This allows the blending of 'serious/high/philosophical' esoteric knowledge with more popular and commodified versions and a move from restrained magical practices to mass-produced magical commodities.

This reduction of facts to hallucinatory speculations leaves no room for the controlling influence of 'truth', and results in an endlessly fragmented labyrinth of unlimited choices. The McDonaldised arena leaves only an aesthetic way of stimulation and navigation in order to find one's path. In this McDonaldised culture, esoteric knowledge appears to have become hyper-real. It is no longer connected to reality but to a consumer culture which mixes esoteric philosophies with popular culture such as the *X-Files* as we have seen with the case of hyper-real religions in Chapter 2 and 6.

If it can be argued that this over-proliferation and commodification of 'esoteric knowledge' together re-enchant western societies by making magic widely available for sale, it might, paradoxically, have a negative effect on over-consumers of this knowledge: that of leading to a blasé attitude and a feeling of disenchantment. Inspired by Simmel's (1858–1918: 414) work on 'The Metropolis and Mental Life', it could be argued that over-seeking mystical pleasure and 'esoteric knowledge' in this McDonaldised occult culture might make seekers feel *blasé*, because this process 'agitates the nerves to their strongest reactivity for such a long time that they finally cease to react at all. [...] An incapacity thus emerges to react to new sensations with the appropriate energy.'

For example, in Lewis's (2001) survey on Satanism, one of his respondents claims that participants tend to leave the movement after realising that it does not keep up with Hollywood stereotypes. As one respondent claims:

> I feel that some people stumble into Satanism thinking they will be able to do as they wish from powers given to them by the devil (Satan) and when they realize that there is actually thought and intelligence within, they feel bored. Most want to be able to curse and kill or hate for no reason. Those who stay are sound in mind and spirit, and have a very strong will for life, or anything they do in life.

Another example is that of a neo-pagan group from Australia that decided to end its activities on the Internet because of the ways their beliefs have been commercialised. They left only a few web pages to explain this situation.[6]

Although Drane's (2000: 157) comment is focused on Christian spirituality, it encompasses the spirituality under investigation and is telling of this process:

> Though pre-packages consumerist spiritualities (both Christian and others) may appear to work for a time, they will not ultimately quench the spiritual thirst of the human spirit any more than the non-stop consumption of food or household goods can meet the fundamental needs of those who are struggling to make sense of the personal emptiness that can be induced by a commercialized commodity culture. [...] One of the consequences of the McDonaldized culture in which this search is taking place is that, for the most part, people are less likely to be concerned about the discovery of universal spiritual truths than they are about following what can seem to be just the latest spiritual fads.

As in consumer society in general (Edwards 2000: 39-40), and more specifically in this McDonaldised occult culture, the insatiability of limitless consumption of 'esoteric knowledge' might be reached when the freedom of the market becomes the ultimate non-freedom, where nothing is ever enough. Indeed, the case might even have been made that the purest form of religious experience, the essence of religion itself, is also tainted by this process where even having mystical experiences does not seem to exclude consumerist motives. As Daniel, one of my respondents (Possamai 2005a), said:

> At around 20 I started developing an interest in various forms of yoga and I think in a lot of ways you definitely have to say I was a little bit compulsive, obsessive with it. I mean maybe I was too intense about it because I would do [...] for instance, exercises until I would get like a nose bleed sometimes. It was like you know striving almost too hard to achieve some goal, God knows what that was. I think they have a term for it these days: Spiritual Materialism. Every time you have a spiritual experience you get a little mark, you know, or a higher rank. I must admit I was very much like that.

What happens if a consumer of this McDonaldised Occult culture has a *blasé* attitude and becomes disenchanted? I am tempted to argue that we can expect four ideal types of reactions to this culture.

Case 1 – Seekers leave this McDonaldised Occult culture and join a more mainstream group, or religion such a Christianity or Islam. For example, I encountered a case study in my research and read the account of Pastor Meyer[7] who were so dissatisfied with this culture that they moved to the Pentecostal church.

Case 2 – They push their dissatisfaction even further by becoming atheist.

In these two cases, people would be the most disenchanted with this culture.

Case 3 – They can find a New Religious Movement and settle down, e.g. the Theosophical Society, the Anthroposophical Society, Spiritualism, etc. They may still consume spiritualities and not adhere to any article of faith, but there is a sense of following an acceptable authority such as a text of reference or the doctrine of a spiritual leader.

Case 4 – They persevere on this 'McDonaldised' path, but still have faith in one day discovering the truth and understanding the mystery of things by themselves only; this being the case of Anne and Steve (see above).

In these last two cases, and more specifically the last one, people would appear to have a calling. Max Weber (1970), in his essay on 'Science as a Vocation', concludes that the quest for a scientific knowledge, in a society which undermines research and its workers, is a 'Vocation'. He says, in other words, that people wanting to do an undervalued and undermined job must have a calling. It could also be said that the search by *blasé* actors for 'secret knowledge' in consumer culture, comprising all the problems and constraints as underlined by Anne and Steve, can also be viewed as a vocation.

We have just touched on the implication of having a culture that has been secret for centuries revealed progressively when entering modernity and being then simplified and McDonaldised when being immersed in the consumer culture of postmodernity. This move to consumer culture has had the effect of bringing popular culture to an almost equal footing with more traditional esoteric knowledge. We have seen that these religions became part of a rationalisation process (i.e. the McDonaldisation of society) and can bring to people a feeling of disenchantment.[8] However, paradoxically, I will now argue that this process had an unintended consequence; that of re-enchanting the world… for some.

A Re-enchantment from Below?

Many researchers have commented on the fact that there is a collective move away from the over-rationalisation of everyday life to re-enchanted forms of public and personal spaces. Westerners are facing the return of spiritual/magical thinking in their everyday life which produces a sense of the mysterious, the weird and the uncanny. It brings back imagination and the possibility of magic in westerners' everyday life (Hume and McPhillips 2006). For Tacey (2000) it is a reconnection with nature – e.g. indigenous landscape – which is at the heart of the re-enchantment process; for Maffesoli (1996) it is the identification with our fellow humans practised in a culture of festivities where people play with their multiple identities. Phillips and Aarons (2007) claim that westerners who engage with Buddhism are expressing their disenchantment with the west. I have claimed that with hyper-real religions, we are seeing a hyper-real re-enchantment that mixes global and commodified popular culture with the magic and the mysterious in everyday life (Possamai 2005b). This chapter has argued that esoteric movements have democratised access to the mystery when entering modernity, thus making this access more popular. And when esotericism entered postmodernity, this same access became even more democratised through its commodification. The move of esotericism in modernity and postmodernity would have re-enchanted parts of the western world. In this sense, re-enchantment represents

> the means by which the hidden or unrecognised powers of human con-
> sciousness are made explicit for the purpose of transcending the limits of the
> secular world… To be re-enchanted means to leave behind the structures
> that bind individuals to the mundane logic of this world and to reclaim the
> powers that invigorate the manifestations of other realities (Lee 2003: 358).

From this interconnection between religion and postmodernity, as already explored in this book, I would suggest we might be seeing a re-enchantment (*Wiederverzauberung*) from below.[9] For Mike Featherstone (1991: 67–68) and Maffesoli (1996), a feature of the times in advanced western societies (or in the global village) is an aestheticisation of everyday life. This is a consequence of the rapid flow of signs and images in contemporary society. Among these signs, which are central to the development of consumer culture, are those of popular culture used by some spiritual actors. For Ritzer (1999), the development of consumer culture itself – with its dizzying proliferation of cathedrals of consumption such as shopping malls, electronic shopping centres, superstores, cruise ships, and casinos – is enchanting our world. These actors, arguably, imbue aestheticised sensibility with a sense of mystery; an invisible power that might be harnessed in consumer and popular culture for the purpose of enchantment. As explored in previous chapters, the move of western societies to postmodernity has affected some religions in that they are part of consumer culture and hyper-reality, and are active on the Internet.

Conclusion

This chapter has recapitulated some of the findings discussed in previous chapters in the light of the case study of esotericism. The move of esoteric groups in modernity has rationalised access to the mysterious and has democratised the use of magic. With the move to postmodernity, this access to the uncanny was simplified and has been commodified. This commodification has been referred to as the McDonaldisation of occult culture and while it can re-enchant parts of the world, it can also, paradoxically, create a feeling of disenchantment for some people who have become blasé with this over-proliferation of magical commodities.

The next chapter moves to the analysis of a contemporary phenomenon known as fundamentalism which is antagonistic to magic. However, as we will see, these groups have something to say about the anxiety brought by consumer culture and do not offer a *blasé* answer.

Notes

1. As an example, see Johnson and Payne 2004 for a detailed and groundbreaking account of the tension between Protestantism and the practice of astrology.
2. This approach has been refined in Possamai (Possamai 2005a).
3. The mirror is nowadays at the British Museum. When I asked a museum guide in 1996 where this mirror was, she answered: 'the magician who was in contact with ETs?' I was quite surprised to discover another level of interpretation.
4. Reference to Goya's etching and aquatint of 1799.
5. Ritzer (2000) claims in his book to have related his analysis of modern society or McDonaldisation to Weber's bureaucratisation in terms of the rationalisation of society. He defines McDonaldisation as 'the process by which the principles of the fast food restaurant are coming to dominate more and more sectors of American society as well as the world'.
6. Internet site, http://www.fortecity.com/victorian/russell/457/clan_raven_moon.html (22/02/2002)
7. Internet Site, http://www.harrypottermagic.org/big_deal_hp_2.htm (19/03/04).
8. This paradox of the re-enchantment process is not a new phenomenon as Wallis (2006: 40) has discovered.
9. What Maffesoli (1996: 66) calls a postmodern re-enchantment.

8 Monotheistic Fundamentalism(s) as an Outcome of Consumer Culture

Introduction

The recent movie *American Dreamz* is a satire of American society and the Bush administration, but its sub-text strongly reenforces hegemonic ideas. A Muslim fundamentalist is sent from his training camp to Southern California. He stays with his uncle and auntie while waiting for further orders from his terrorist cell. Although this character lost his mother in an American attack in the Middle East, he has nevertheless always loved American popular culture, and especially Hollywood musicals. He hides this from his Muslim 'brothers', and is secretly happy to move to the 'Mecca' of movies. Initially he is critical of consumer culture and wonders why his cousins need to go to the mall more than once a week, but he gradually embraces the American way of life. Through sheer luck, he is selected to take part in a talent quest similar to American Idol, which the President of the United States is expected to attend in its last episode. The terrorist is ordered to take this as an opportunity to blow himself up and kill the President, but at the end, he decides otherwise because he has become fully entrenched in his new western life.

One interpretation of this movie is that however critical a non-American Muslim fundamentalist might be towards the American way of life, he can become moderate if he leads a life bombarded with popular and consumer culture. This view, however, opposes the many studies on religious fundamentalism that have found this phenomenon to be a reaction to the excesses of western consumer society. The previous three chapters in this book have focused on new religious phenomena that have embraced their immersion in postmodernity. They have adapted to it, and to some extent are even carriers of, these changes in western societies. This chapter deals with religious fundamentalist groups which are partly reactive to these changes. These groups are far from being pre-modern in their nature as they are specific reactions to some of today's social and cultural changes.

Focusing now on Christianity in our western world it needs to be remembered that what it means to be religious today is no longer what it once was. Religion is metamorphosing into new, renewed and different forms at various levels. As already analysed, there is an increase of freedom in which the individual makes his or her own sense of his or her life and of the rapid changes specific to our current society. More people claim to have no religious affiliation but they are not necessarily atheists; they believe without belonging and might see themselves as more spiritual than religious. One of the many reasons for this gain in freedom of faith is the development of consumer culture which affects, whether we like it or not, religion as well. To have a normal life in this consumer society means to make choices among all of the displayed opportunities. Post-war consumer culture, instead of building a sense of belonging for groups – e.g. class, sub-cultures, and political parties – appears to create a fragmented society in which religion is only a part. In this consuming world, the individual becomes his or her own authority. People are now 'free' to choose and the market culture might be turning us into consumers rather than citizens. Consumer choice, it must be said, is not limited to shopping, but is extended to education, health, politics and religion. Our identity as a worker, a family member, a partner, a follower of a party, a believer of one religion, is in constant flux. The religious person is now faced with a proliferation of spiritual/religious/philosophical knowledges in our pluralist western societies. Sometimes, as found in many New Age spiritualities, this religious choice is celebrated; sometimes it is a burden that creates a sense of insecurity and anxiety. What to choose? What to be? Fundamentalism seems to offer a solution to this burden by providing hope and confidence in an anxious world by re-packaging pre-modern modes of conduct and beliefs in a format conducive to contemporary inspirations. Fundamentalism is a phenomenon of today supporting the rationalising, reforms and technological development of postmodernity, while at the same time providing an island of security in this choice-overloaded consumer society.

Monotheistic Fundamentalism(s)

The term 'fundamentalism' is as imprecise as a ruler without measurements. It refers to religious groups that claim their religious system is the truest – if not absolutely and exclusively true – and that no other religious system can compete with its sole true way of life.[1] It is a term that includes an array of religious groups. It is also a negative label applied by some religious groups to point out groups more conservative than them. It also can be used to silence and marginalise some religious groups by labelling them as anti-intellectual, bigoted and intolerant. As terms evolve in the use and misuse of language and appellation, a new appellation has even come out to distance ultra-conservative groups even further from lesser ones; 'fundagelism'. This term comes from a Christian context and is a compound of 'fundamentalist evangelism'. It embraces people who believe in the future as foretold by the book of Revelation; i.e. the destruction of Babylon (Iraq) and the immanent mass conversion of Jews.

Fundamentalist groups might accept the scientific and technological components of postmodernity yet simultaneously reject its cultural components such as secularism, pluralism, relativism, permissive morality and liberal individualism. Since traditions are always socially constructed and contested, these groups are therefore not traditional in the sociological sense, but are committed to the restoration of what the group regards as 'tradition'. Because they have emerged successfully and grown at a fast pace since the 1970s, they could be considered more as a response to postmodernity and its consumer culture than the continuation of a long line of traditions.

Tamney (2002) equates fundamentalism to traditionalist religions. These are groups that are trying to regenerate religious tradition and make it socially significant which is quite different from traditional religions. He discovered that what these groups try to preserve above all is the group above the individual. Collectivity is valued above individual life and viewed as superior to all other institutions in society. As seen in Chapter 4, the modernisation process has created a structural and cultural differentiation between institutions in western societies. Religion is no longer the overarching institution but one among many others. Fundamentalist groups are resisting this process and want to come back to the way traditional religions (i.e. religions like Catholicism and Anglicanism) were before the advent of modernity. As Tamney (2002: 13) states:

> Unlike premodernists, then, traditionalists feel alienated from a hostile world. In traditional society, there is one important group whose religion is an undifferentiated part of its culture. In modern society, traditionalists fight against a dominant group that defines the traditionalists as inferior. The latter either tries to separate from this hostile environment or seeks to gain control of it. The goal is to approximate the premodern situation. Individuals are to identify with their religious group; this group is to control the state, and through it all other institutions; the group's values and beliefs are to infuse and dominate all of culture. If successful, traditionalists would create a society unified by their religious culture and organization, and in which each individual's identity would be unified by religious values and rules. Traditionalists would create Christian societies, Muslim societies, and so on.

They might reject some postmodern values, but also accommodate others. As discussed in Chapter 10 on Christianity, and in Chapter 5 regarding mega-churches, they try to make their liturgy more popular by, for example, using popular music to make rituals more enjoyable. They often embrace facets of postmodern cultures and new technological discoveries such as the Internet. Although they hope to revive some premodern values, they are not seeking to live in the world as it was before the advent of the industrial revolution.

Fighting Psychological Pressure in Postmodern Culture

Melucci (1996) writes about our contemporary time as being multiple and discontinuous, for it entails the never-ending wandering from one set of experiences to another, from one network to another and from the knowledge and habits of one social sphere to those of another, which is semantically and affectively very different. Due to this, the uncertainty that generations X and Y have become accustomed to might have paradoxically become the only stable component of our new behaviour since we cannot move from one context to another while drawing on what we have already acquired elsewhere. While everything seems to be in a permanent state of flux, uncertainty does not change.

> Change [...] is a goal we find desirable and towards which our search for the new and the different is directed. But at the same time, change poses a threat to our security and to our established and habitual rules. [...] Consequently, the paradox of choice creates a new kind of psychological pressure, confronting us with new problems (Melucci 1996: 45).

What is this new type of psychological pressure? If we work on a crude continuum which can illustrate the reaction of social actors to our contemporary social malaise, we find at one extreme a person who faces constant existential anxiety in their everyday life. This person would be an ontologically insecure individual and would be characterised by an obsessive exaggeration of risks to personal existence, extreme introspection and moral vacuity. On the other end of the spectrum we might find a person who experiences ontological security; that is, a sense of reliability towards persons and things, aided and abetted by the predictability of the apparently minor routines of day-to-day life. He or she is not troubled by, or may even be oblivious to, existential questions. Faced with a predictable routine, they are unable to cope effectively with risk situations, personal tensions and anxiety. This state incorporates trust in the reliability of persons and things. Trust, therefore, may be regarded as a means of dealing psychologically with risks that would otherwise paralyse action or lead to feelings of engulfment, dread and anxiety. Only a small part of the western population is close to these ideal type extremes. The large part of the population is moving back and forth between the two extremes depending on the life they are experiencing at a specific moment.

Not surprisingly, of the people who experience existential anxiety, many wish to reaffirm their threatened self-identity. Any collective identity that can offer a way out of this anxiety has the potential to attract these individuals. According to Kinnvall (2004: 742), nationalism and religion are two 'identity-signifiers' that strongly provide this source of security because they 'convey a picture of security, stability, and simple answers'. If the levels of ontological insecurity increase, it is likely that the search for securitised subjectivity will also rise (Kinnvall 2004: 757).

> Institutionalized religion often concurs with the nation as being territorially defined, as it refers to bounded entities such as churches, organizations, or political parties. In this form, religion, like nationalism, supplies existential answers to individual's quests for security by essentializing the product and providing a picture of totality, unity and wholeness. The fact that God has set the rules and made them difficult to contest relieves the individual psychologically from the responsibility of having to choose (Kinnvall 2004, 759).

Religion is no longer part of the public sphere the way it used to be in yesteryears, and it no longer provides a close-knitted system of beliefs united with, for example, a nation. Religion is now part of consumer culture. In this consumer culture, more and more people make a decision about what belief system to follow, be it religious or not. While mainstream religions and some New Religious Movements (Dawson 2006; Possamai-Inesedy 2002) might offer parts of an island of security in the adversity of ontological insecurity, fundamentalism appears to be better equipped to offer a whole island of security. In this sense, there is a type of religious market available in which fundamentalism is situated. And it is the argument of this chapter that in choosing a religion in terms of what it can offer to alleviate the ontological insecurity for those who join, fundamentalism appears to be the 'best product' on the market. Paradoxically, it could thus be argued that some people make a choice to have less choice.

According to Bauman (1998), fundamentalist religions offer a stronger sense of ontological security to their members than hyper-consumer religions (e.g. New Age and Hyper-real religions). This does not mean that being involved in alternative spiritualities does not provide a sense of ontological security. The argument at hand is that these spiritualities, being hyper-consumerist, do not provide a clear threat in their belief system. Fundamentalist groups, on the other hand, even if they are also consumerist, are focused on a clearer and a more established message, e.g. as found in the Bible or the Koran. For fundamentalists, religious consumerism can still be of high intensity, but it does not happen outside of their religious group.

This form of consumption is simply due to the belief system of the group. New Age, for example, is a relativist and syncretic spirituality/religion in which the believer would claim that all religions are different and yet equal paths. On the other hand, fundamentalism(s) are absolutist and exclusivist religions in which believers claim that their religious system is absolutely and exclusively true and no other religious system can compete with it. They will only consume religious objects and texts within their own group; and will not shop around like New Agers. There are, of course, many shades of grey between these two extremes, as already explored in Chapter 1.

Fundamentalism can be found in all religions and has different characteristics according to the faith where it is situated. In Protestantism, for example, fundamentalism can be equated to Christian literalists who believe that the Bible contains the actual words of God and directly applies entirely to contemporary life. People who join these fundamentalist groups tend not to find answers in mainstream churches. They seek more 'engaged' forms of religion (e.g. certain forms of Pentecostalism) by looking for a stability of commitment in a community that gives a stronger sense of authority and a tighter system of beliefs and practices: that is, a more structured world/spiritual view. As Bauman (1998: 74) states:

> In a world in which all ways of life are allowed, yet none is safe, they muster enough courage to tell those who are eager to listen what to decide so that the decision can remain safe and stand up in all courts that matter. In this respect, religious fundamentalism belongs to a wider family of totalitarian or proto-totalitarian solutions offered to all those who find the burden of individual freedom excessive and unbearable.

Religious fundamentalism would be the type of religion that provides the biggest island of security for people looking to have less anxiety through religion. As fundamentalism is a growing phenomenon in both the south and north of the world, one could thus expect it to rise even stronger as collective anxiety grows (Possamai and Possamai-Inesedy 2007b). There is a multitude of fundamentalisms around the globe, however it can be argued that these are three large types. According to Lawrence (1998), these are Christian, Muslim and Jewish fundamentalisms.

Christian Fundamentalism

The first main type of religious fundamentalism is Christian Literalism, which is a subspecies of the Evangelical movement. Evangelicalism (i.e. the practice of spreading the Christian Gospel) is a large protestant group that emphasises the Bible as authoritative and reliable: salvation is only possible through being born again and thus having a personal trust in Christ. Evangelicals are asked to follow a life of moral conduct, personal devotion (such as Bible reading and prayer), and a zeal for spreading the Gospel. Christian fundamentalism, as a sub-species of evangelicalism, started in the USA in the 1920s and emerged as a reaction against theologians who wanted to modernise their religion and adapt their faith to the changes brought by secularism.

Kaplan (1992: 4) argues that fundamentalist groups did not have much impact on American life between the 1920s and 1980s. During that time, these groups were mainly contained in a few US rural localities and had a very limited influence on the nation.[2] However, they started to be strongly represented in US political life when the Moral Majority was formed in 1979. This group was led by Jerry Falwell, who was one of first to start a television ministry. This political coalition of fundamentalists and other conservatives have had access to large television ministries since that time.

These contemporary Christian fundamentalist groups are combating 'modernist' theology and secularist cultural trends. They aim at counteracting the decline of family values, morality, God's law and the truth of the Bible. They have also successfully revived the anti-evolution crusade (the argument that the earth is no more than 10,000 years old) and supported anti-abortion movements. After 9/11, the aforementioned Christian fundamentalist leader, Jerry Falwell, publicly stated that America got what it deserved because it has allowed gays and lesbians to gain more rights, and woman to have more choice when it comes to abortion (Schick *et al.* 2004). More recently in the USA, the Bush administration, which had some contacts – to say the least – with some of these fundamentalist groups, funded sexual health projects that teach children erroneously that HIV can be contracted through sweat and tears, and touching genitals can result in pregnancy.[3]

In the Christian world, even if fundamentalism is perceived as a conservative evangelical Protestant phenomenon, we should not forget that this happens within Catholicism as well. However, as Coleman (1992) comments, this phenomenon should be called Catholic integralism rather than Catholic fundamentalism. Whereas with fundamentalist Protestant groups, the Scripture is the infallible authority, for Catholic integralists, the infallible authority is the Pope. Examples of these integralist groups are Opus Dei (see Chapter 10), Archbishop Marcel Lefebvre's Fraternity of St. Pius X who believes there has not been a legitimate Pope since Pius XII, and Italian groups such as Communion and Liberation. Further, one should not ignore the fact that the yearly number of Catholics who convert to evangelical fundamentalism is sizeable, and that some Catholics view themselves as 'born again' Bible Christians.

In the USA specifically, the line between evangelical and fundamentalist has become difficult to discern. Although the categories are quite different, there is nevertheless some overlap. Groups within these two categories do not speak with one voice and embrace different views with regard to social life and issues. This is reflected in surveys that indicate the difficulty of labelling people from various religious groups as fundamentalist as the last section of this chapter will address. Not only is there diversity between being evangelical and fundamentalist groups, but also within sub-groups of fundamentalism. Not all groups are ready to push their beliefs to extremes and act on them. Groups that do act in such a way include Operation Rescue and the Lambs of God, which engage in terrorist tactics to intimidate women and physicians who are pro-choice, and the Coalition on Revival which advocates the execution of adulterers and homosexuals (Schick *et al.* 2004: 5). The tension between believing in extreme ideas and acting on them will be explored in the following sections.

In western societies, fundamentalism is a sign of the times. It is one of the many answers to the anxiety and sense of insecurity created in part by the advent of consumerism – at least for Christian fundamentalists – and there is no indication that this trend will slow down in the near future.

Muslim Fundamentalism

The second type, according to Lawrence (1998), is Muslim Terrorism [sic] which encompasses a diversity of groups that view the west as an enemy and tend to be active in terrorist acts. Such groups attempt to re-Islamise the society they see as 'corrupted' by the globalising effects emerging from the western world. They also attempt to purify Islam by targeting Sufism and various popular forms of the Muslim religions (see Bendle 2003).

I would argue that it is erroneous of Lawrence to call this branch of Muslim fundamentalism 'Muslim terrorism', as terrorism is an extreme case of fundamentalism in all religions and not all forms of Islamic fundamentalisms are so extreme. Some less extreme forms aim to make their society more Islamic by focusing on non-violent means such as education, preaching, and publication. There are, of course, many other Islamic movements that attempt to re-Islamise their society, but are not necessarily fundamentalists, as explored in Chapter 11. These moderate groups tend to look at the past as a philosophical model and not as an everyday life way of living. They are not necessarily anti-western, but are mainly interested in contesting negative aspects of their own political system, such as nepotism, corruption, and poverty, often wanting to mix Islam, modernity and democracy.

Applying the term 'fundamentalism', which originated from a Christian context, can be problematic when applying it to the Muslim religion. As Greifenhagen (2004: 64) points out, a literalist reading of the Bible is seen as an indicator of fundamentalism in a Christian context, whereas 'Muslims traditionally regard their scripture, the Koran, as inerrant and read it literally as God's word'. What would make Muslims fundamentalists, for Greifenhagen, is not their literal reading of the Koran, but more their political activism towards the establishment of an Islamic state. However, this distinction is not sufficient, and I am now turning to another author who studies this difference more carefully.

Douglas Pratt (2007) describes 20 interrelated factors that separate what he sees as a quirky, atavist, benignly eccentric type of fundamentalist group from one that is critical, aggressive, and engaged in terrorist activities. There is no doubt that religious terrorism derives substantially, if not solely, from an ideology of religious fundamentalism. However, many different factors affect the move of a fundamentalist mindset from the quirky to the critical, from atavism to aggression, and from benign eccentricity to outright terrorism. It is beyond the scope of this book to cover each of these factors, however, the three phases that encapsulate them will be touched upon. Needless to say, these phases and characteristics could be applied to other fundamentalist religious groups and are not limited to Islam.

Phase 1: Passive Fundamentalism is basically connected to a mindset that identifies a religious text and/or authority as only one true and authentic narrative that accounts for all ways of being. In this instance, the Koran would provide immediate truth or value without error or ambiguity. Fundamentalist people in this phase do not engage in political activities and are far from being motivated by terrorist activities; they simply hold sympathetic views with fundamentalism.

In **Phase 2: Hard-Line Fundamentalism**, there is a deepening of fundamentalist ideology and its application. There is evidence from people who would be categorised as being part of this phase of a growing condemnatory stance taken in respect to any opposition or competition. One would expect a Muslim fundamentalist of this type to think that not just all Muslims should live according to Islamic Law, but that all members of the society in question, irrespective of religion, should live according to it as well. This phase of fundamentalism excludes religious liberalism. There is also a strong deprecating attitude towards others, such as Jews or gays, and a weak social intercourse with people who are not part of their hard-line views.

People involved in **Phase 3: Impositional Fundamentalism**, can commit extreme actions such as violent behaviours. Acts of terrorism may be contemplated, advocated and engaged. It is a phase in which we find a form of enacted extremism. Assertions of self-superiority over all opponents and extreme violence are legitimated. They publicly advocate their views and policies within their society.

Not all fundamentalist groups necessarily become impositional, and the more impositional the group (e.g. extreme and militant Islamic fundamentalism) is, the more on the fringe of the whole Muslim phenomenon it is. As Pratt (2007: 212) insists: 'Not all fundamentalists are terrorists. Yet, given a progressive ideological development, it is arguably the case that religious fundamentalism may – as indeed we know that it does – produce a terrorist'. For him, there are three cumulative phases for someone to move from being a passive fundamentalist to an impositional one. Within each of these phases, there are also various levels that this book has not addressed; for example, an impositional fundamentalist is not always an extremist and it is only at the last of Pratt's twentieth characteristic that he or she becomes one.

The beginning of this chapter gave some sociological explanation with regard to the appearance and growth of fundamentalism. However, when it comes to Muslim fundamentalism, another factor is specific to this case. As will be seen in Chapter 11, all Muslim countries in the world went through a secularisation process after WWI – a secularisation that some equated to westernisation. Many Muslim states that emerged from the colonial period became secular. However, the secular approach to governing Muslim countries often did not work due to the presence of a high level of corruption, nepotism and bureaucratic deficiency. The specific catalyst that legitimised this perception of the weakness of secular governments in Muslim countries was the Six Day War in 1967 between Israel and the Arab countries Egypt, Jordan and Syria. The Arab forces suffered humiliation against the army of the new Israel, especially when East Jerusalem was taken. This war became symptomatic of the crisis in modern Muslim societies as Greifenhagen (2004: 67) explains:

> The model of the secular nation state was not working: Muslim societies continued to suffer corruption and misrule despite independence. The reason for this decline, from a religious perspective, was either that Islam had failed Muslims because it is an outmoded religion, or that Muslims had failed Islam, being seduced away from it by the empty promises of modernism. It is the second explanation that was increasingly embraced. The cry was raised that Islam – not nationalism or some other ideology or concept imported from the West – was the solution to the problems of the modern Muslim world.

A sense of betrayal began to be felt among Muslim movements towards the ideals of western societies and the failed adaptation to these ideals to their own secular governments. The solution to this issue became an Islamic renewal; a renewal which has seen a wide variety of types emerges, including moderate and fundamentalist versions.

Jewish Fundamentalism

The third broad type for Lawrence (1998) is Jewish Political Activism. This type aims to use the state to legitimise the use of force. Today, Israeli politics and religion can be so profoundly interconnected that there are some political parties influenced by religious fundamentalist ideas. Some of them tend to work towards an Israel (including the West Bank of the Jordan River and the Gaza strip) for Jews only, and adhere most strictly to the tenets of the religious law – Halakhah.

For example, Pace (2007) studies extreme Jewish messianism and, more specifically, the Habad religious movement within the Hasidic branch of modern Judaism. The group's headquarters is in Crown Heights, New York. During the Six Day War in 1967, spiritual assistants from this group were sent to the front to establish the theological legitimacy of the State of Israel, which had been regarded by many ultra-orthodox Jews abroad as an artificial creation. The Rebbe (i.e. the leader of this group) wanted to convince his followers that for the holy borders of the Promised Land (*Eretz Yisrael*) to be reestablished, this war had to be won. This group claims that when these borders are fully redefined, the Jewish Messiah will arrive. After the Yom Kippur War in 1973, the group stated that Israel had the divine right to annex the occupied territories.[4]

It should be noted that this type of Jewish fundamentalism is a more recent one. Since the 1930s another type of Jewish fundamentalism, the Neturei Karta ('Guardian of the City') group, has been against the creation of the State of Israel. Its members view the exilic past in Eastern Europe nostalgically and want to continue to live in that fashion as a minority group in the world. They have no political ambitions within Israel (Friedman 1992).

Although Lawrence (1998) makes reference to that type of religious fundamentalism as mainly politically involved, it has not stopped some of these groups plotting the destruction of the el-Aksa mosque (Islam's third holiest site after those in Mecca and Medina) and the Dome of the Rock (which stands on the place where Mohammad ascended to heaven). In 1995, Yigal Amir, who had some ties to the Gush Emmunim (an expansionist Jewish fundamentalist group), murdered the then Prime Minister of Israel, Yitzchak Rabin. This act was meant to stop the Oslo accords (see Chapter 11) and the withdrawal of Jews from Palestinian cities in the West Bank.

These three types suggested by Lawrence provide us with a typology of global fundamentalism, but one should not forget that there are countless hybrid forms within each of them.

The Difficulty in Identifying Forms of Fundamentalism (a Bit of Forensic Theology)

Tamney (2002: 18) makes reference to a Baptist minister who was asked during a television show in San Francisco whether he believed that men who have sex with other men should be stoned to death, as it is written in the Book of Leviticus. He replied: 'That's what it says. ... That's what God says. ... That's what the Bible says.' In this case, the minister gave ultimate allegiance to the Bible, and would like biblical injunctions to be followed by the state, even if they go against human rights principles. To assert that this statement is an obvious indication of fundamentalism is as clear as holy water. However, it is sometimes not so easy to find traces of fundamentalism in the language used by lay people who belong to these extreme religious groups.

When assessing the importance of monotheistic fundamentalist groups in Australia, the Australian census is not of much help. In their categorisation, the Australian Bureau of Statistics groups all Islamic groups under Islam (340,395 people in 2006, that is 1.7% of the Australian population), and all Jewish groups (88,834 people, that is 0.45% of the population) under Judaism. There is no information on any sub-groups that might be fundamentalist. Further, even if Christian groups (close to 12.7 million, that is 64% of the population) are more detailed than their religious counterparts, there is no specific category for fundamentalists. Even if we could list some Christian groups in Australia that are more prone to being fundamentalist than others, it does not mean that all members of the denomination will be fundamentalists. For example, in the 1998 Australian Community Survey (Black *et al.* 2004), to the question 'different religions and philosophies have different versions of the truth and may be equally right in their own way', 67% of Pentecostals, 45% of Baptists, 19% of Presbyterian, 10% of Anglican and 9% of Catholics rejected that non-fundamentalist statement. To find traces of Biblical fundamentalism, respondents were asked to choose one of the following statements:

- 'the Bible is God's Word and all it says is true',
- 'the Bible was written by people inspired by God, but it contains some human errors',
- 'the Bible is a good book because it was written by wise people, but God had nothing to do with it', and
- 'the Bible was written by people who lived so long ago that it is worth very little today'.

Eighty-five % of Pentecostals, 67% of Baptists, 25% of Catholics and 14% of Anglicans chose the first option. Even if Pentecostals (close to 210,000 people or 1.1% of the Australian population) – one of the fastest growing religious groups in Australia – and Baptists (316,746 people in the 2006 census, which is 1.6% of the population) tend to show greater signs of fundamentalism compared to other Christian groups, not all of their members are necessarily so. On the other hand, there are also signs of fundamentalist beliefs among Catholics and Anglicans which on the whole are not fundamentalist groups.

In research in Switzerland, Stolz and Favre (2005) find that within what they indicated to be fundamentalist groups in their survey, only 66.9% of them agreed to the statement that 'The Bible is the actual word of God and it is to be taken literally word for word'. However, this group nevertheless scores the highest proportion of people believing in that statement compared to non-fundamentalist types of evangelical groups. To the statement that 'There is truth only in one religion', these fundamentalist groups again rate at the highest level with 88.7% in agreement.[5]

The Australian and Swiss surveys reveal that although some indicators give us an idea of which type of groups are likely to be fundamentalist, they only represent the majority of members and not all of them.

If we move to Muslim fundamentalism, we discover that imprecise indicators of fundamentalism have led to a new intelligence strategy, that is 'forensic theology'. This investigation of faith could perhaps help to pinpoint groups that are the most dangerous to liberal societies. Although this is also known as a form of 'ideological surveillance', many security services have worked with experts on Islam to learn the ideological characteristics of religious extremist thoughts, but the forensic work has to be subtle. For example, Grey (2004) points out that the Hamas leader, Abdel Aziz al-Rantissi, killed in an Israeli air strike, declared publicly that 'God declared war against America, Bush, and Sharon'. However, as it could easily be interpreted that this Palestinian group is involved in acts of terrorism in the west, a closer investigation by Grey (2004) reveals that groups like Hamas and Hizbollah tend to be opposed to worldwide jihad (as expressed by bin Laden) and are not connected to global terror groups because they only focus on the occupied territories in Israel/Palestine (see Chapter 11).

Waldman (2006) gives an account of how in a court of justice the beliefs of a person can lead them to condemnation for their intentions rather than just their actions. This 'forensic theological' approach to fighting fundamentalist religious terrorism can lead to damaging conclusions when it comes to judging a faith and what criminal actions its members might commit. For example, an Associate Professor at New York University, Haykel, was asked to give an expert opinion at the judgement of a suspected terrorist. He drew a difference between people who ask God to kill enemies or Jews or

Americans, and people who ask other people to do it. Some violent statements can be an invocation to God exclusively rather than an exhortation to people to commit violence in the name of religion. One of the discussions in the trial of a suspected terrorist was about whether the person was a terrorist for listening to the fundamentalist speech of al-Kousi.

As the journalist writes about Haykel,

> Bin Laden, he said, made similar prayers, but then took it a step further by telling Muslims they had a duty to kill. According to Haykel, al-Kousi [an Egyptian preacher] never took that step: 'He was very clear when he was actually saying you should do something versus what he hoped God would do or he hoped would eventually happen with God's intercession'. Real jihadists, he said, are 'absolutely explicit when they intend violence'. There is no obfuscation, there is no double entendre. (Waldman 2006: 87)

Conclusion

This chapter argues that it is difficult and sometimes dangerous to measure fundamentalism in some religious groups. Fundamentalism cannot be generalised and is open to various interpretations. Further, there are so many levels of belief and involvement in fundamentalist groups that it can be dangerous to assume everyone in the group has distinctive fundamentalist beliefs. Having fundamentalist beliefs in whatever religion is only a step towards committing violent action in the name of religion, and there is a wide gap between those who share fundamentalist ideas, and those ready to become a terrorist.

The previous chapters have analysed what happens on the edge of postmodernity when it comes to religion. On one side we see hyper-consumerist religions that embrace changes, and on the other side, hypo-consumerist groups that are selective in the changes that they agree with. The following chapters analyse groups that are within these extremes. The next one deals with Buddhism and its westernisation process within postmodernity. Chapter 10 explores Christianity and the challenges that this major religion faces with current changes. Chapter 11 deals with Islam and how moderate groups are reworking the ideal of modernity/postmodernity.

Notes

1. Watkinson (2004) argues that these groups promote ideas that go against other groups such as those that support the equality of women, children and sexual

minorities, and wonders if fundamentalist groups are in need of protection under the Universal Declaration of Human Rights, or if it should be equality-seeking groups that need protection from them?

2. As Bruce (1992: 44) points out, another characteristic of the change in these fundamentalist groups between the 1920s and 1980s is that the early movement's 'bogeyman' was the remote threat of communism, whereas it is now the closer 'menace' of secular humanism.

3. *The Guardian Weekly*, December 10–16 2004.

4. On the other hand, right-wing Christian Zionists, even if not Jews, are also supporting the contemporary restoration of the state of Israel as a sign of the imminent return of Jesus as the Christian Messiah.

5. Stolz and Favre (2005) also discover that in Swizerland, fundamentalist groups manage to retain their offspring in their religious groups but do not have much success attracting converts from outside. Whereas other more moderate forms of evangelical groups not only retain their own off-spring but also attract off-spring from outside.

9 Buddhism, Its Westernisation and the Easternisation of the West

Introduction

While I have been writing this book, the Olympic torch has travelled around the world to promote the 2008 Olympic games in Beijing. After leaving Paris, talks were emerging to end its journey because of the tension the flame generated wherever it went. Although this sporting event has been part of popular culture for more than a century and was conceived to promote peace among all countries of the world, it has been turned into a political event by some to put pressure on the Chinese government to stop human rights abuses in Tibet.

China entered Tibet in 1949 and took full control of the country in 1959. Since then, Tibet's leader, the Dalai Lama, has lived in exile in the north of India. For Tibetans, he is a 'god-king' who is the temporal leader of Tibet and the spiritual leader of Tibetan Buddhism. For many in the international community, he is seen as one of the great apostles of non-violence alongside Nelson Mandela and Mahatma Gandhi. Chinese officials, on the other hand have portrayed him as 'a wolf in a monk's robe, a monster with a human face but the heart of a beast' (Ramesh 2008).

Since the occupation of Tibet, many Tibetan monks have allegedly been persecuted, tortured and killed by agents of the Chinese government. Some Tibetans have abandoned their occupied land and migrated to other parts of the world to practice and promote their religion in the west. They also have worked for the return of the Dalai Lama and the freedom and/or autonomy of Tibet. Further, the Dalai Lama himself has been touring the globe as a world leader in Buddhism and as the head of a country under occupation. Officially, he does not ask for total independence from China but rather seeks internal autonomy for Tibet under Chinese control.

The protests around the Olympic torch have been used to remind the world community of the lack of human rights in such a small part of the world. Tibet is a country in the Himalayas far removed from western societies. It is hard to access, does not have much material wealth, and is not a strategic region. However, there is a strong concern from westerners about this little piece of a far away land; even though there are many bigger and closer places to the west which are struggling, they do not generate as much sympathy. One reason is perhaps the growth of western Buddhism and the widespread view that the Dalai Lama is a world spiritual leader.

Protests at Olympic torch events around the world have not only been conducted by Tibetans in exile but also by westerners sympathetic to the Tibetan cause. Perhaps the support is so widespread because, as Lenoir (1999: 100) points out, the majority of westerners seem to be receptive to the message of the Buddha. Western sensitivities towards Buddhism, and more specifically towards Tibetan Buddhism, did not happen overnight; and this phenomenon is the primary focus of this chapter.

This chapter first explores Buddhism and its various sub-schools of thought. It later focuses on Buddhism in the western world and more specifically on its westernisation. Indeed, questions arise when westerners are inspired by a 'foreign' religion and 'adapt' it to their own way of life. It then explores the thesis of the 'easternisation' of the west and analyses western spiritual consumer practices within Buddhism.

Siddhartha Gautama

Siddhartha Gautama was born a prince in 563 BC in what is now called Nepal. In his youth, he led a sheltered life in his palace. He was only exposed to beauty and knew almost nothing of the outside world. Before he left the palace for good, he only went outside of its protected walls four times. During his first three trips, he encountered evidence of human sickness, old age and death for the first time. On his fourth trip, he saw a wandering holy man in rags who greatly impressed him. In him, Siddhartha noticed a radiant tranquillity not found in other people. After fathering a son from his cousin at the age of 29, he left the palace to seek the best spiritual teachers of the day. His quest was to learn spiritual techniques that might put an end to human suffering.

He spent six years learning from various teachers about meditation, yoga and self-mortification but was still unsatisfied. He believed that if he were to continue in this way he would not find the cause of human suffering, so he left his teachers to find his own spiritual path.

Eventually, he sat meditating under a tree, determined not to move until he had found the nature of suffering and the ways to overcome it. His state of meditation became so deep that he remembered his past lives, understood the effect of karma on rebirth, and recognised the spiritual faults that obscure the mind from 'reality'. He then became known as the 'awakened one' because he had achieved liberation from all delusion and mental suffering and stopped his cycle of death and rebirth.

After achieving this, he became an itinerant teacher for 45 years and with the monks who followed him, started the Buddhist community known as the Sangha. This Sangha, according to Chakravarti (1986), was a type of parallel society where people could escape the attitude of inequality inherent in the hierarchical structure of Brahmanical society and culture at that time. After 54 years of teaching, he left instructions on the spiritual path (*Dharma*) and monastic rules (*Vinaya*) to guide his followers and died without appointing a successor. His teachings were memorised and passed down in oral form for over three hundred years. It was only in the first century BC that they were written down.

Beliefs and Practices

In Weber's term, the Buddha (meaning the awakened one) was an exemplary prophet: he led through his own example and life. Indeed, the Buddha encouraged his followers to experiment and follow the teachings that work for them. Buddhism is thus more of an experimental religion rather than one that asks for blind faith and obedience, and it is not perceived as a dogmatic religion with a fixed set of beliefs.

Nevertheless, there were Four Noble Truths espoused by the Buddha. These are:
1. All life is permeated by the reality of suffering (*dukkha*). Pain is experienced from birth, through life with its sickness, unsatisfactory nature, dejection and despair, and eventually death.
2. The cause of such suffering is craving, desire and a thirst for pleasure and existence. All these lead to a continuous cycle of death and rebirth (*samsara*).
3. This cause can be eliminated by the cessation of craving and desire, and the cultivation of non-attachment.
4. The path that leads to the cessation of suffering is the Noble Eightfold Path. Its eight aspects involve right views, right attitudes, right speech, right conduct, right livelihood, right effort, right mindfulness and right contemplation.

Buddhists are concerned about reaching 'enlightenment', which means becoming awakened like the Buddha and putting an end to reincarnation and suffering. The goal is to escape from the cycle of repeated birth and death. If a Buddhist cannot reach enlightenment during his or her lifetime, he or she can nevertheless work to improve the quality of his or her next reincarnation which would allow him or her to reach enlightenment in a forthcoming life.

To help a Buddhist on his or her quest to escape from the circle of re-births, meditation and merit are of great help. Meditation promotes self-discipline, self-control and purification, and helps to improve the control of thoughts and desire. Merit comes from acting the right way, be it mental, verbal or physical. A monk might beg for food and this helps him or her to banish pride. A lay person might give to a monk, and through this generosity might gain a better rebirth through good karma.

It is worth mentioning that Siddhartha Gautama is the Buddha who started this new religion, but he is not the only Buddha. Everyone who is believed to have attained Enlightenment or Nirvana, and who delays his or her escape from the cycle of rebirth to help others attain the same goal, is also a Buddha. A person who reaches Nirvana but who does not teach others about the religious path (*dharma*) is seen as a type of saint called an arhat.

The Three Main Schools

Buddhism, like Christianity and Islam, does not have one lineage and is not one homogeneous group. It is, however, customary to combine all Buddhist sub-groups into three main lineages. These are Therevada, Mahayana and Vajrayana.

Therevada (Southern Buddhism) or the School of the Elders

Most Buddhists from this tradition live in southern Asia (e.g. Sri Lanka, Burma, Cambodia, Laos and Thailand). Smaller groups are found in Southern Vietnam, Bangladesh, India, and other countries where people from this tradition have migrated to.

This tradition tries to remain true to the original teaching of the Buddha and is strongly based on the authority of the Sangha. The ideal is to become a monk who achieves the goal of enlightenment. For this reason, there is a strong focus on monasticism where monks work out their own path to salvation. These fully ordained members are almost all male. Because of the highly disciplined lifestyle and gender imbalance, this tradition lacks the universal appeal to touch westerners the same way that the other traditions do.

Mayahana (Eastern Buddhism) or The Great Vehicle

This school emerged in the 3rd century BC and spread to China, Japan, Korea and Vietnam, and of course, elsewhere with migrant groups from this tradition. As a movement, it slowly developed from within monastic communities. However, contrary to Therevada, this path was also deemed an appropriate way to spiritual liberation for the laity as well as for the Sangha. It is because of its opening to the general population that this tradition is called The Great Vehicle. In short, the Mahayana tradition places less emphasis on monasticism than Theravada and reaching enlightenment is open to everyone: lay and ordained, and male and female. In this tradition, the person who delays his or her Buddhahood through compassion to help other people attain it is known as a Bodhisattva.

Vajrayana (Northern Buddhism) or The Diamond Tradition

This tradition developed in the northern countries of Tibet, Mongolia and the Himalayas, parts of China and central Asia. Its name comes from 'Vajra' (meaning lighting bolt or diamond) which symbolises the end of duality. It claims to be a secret tradition taught by the Buddha to a select groups of monks and was taught in a language that only the initiate could understand. People from this tradition use symbols to convey meanings and in comparison to the other two traditions it has developed colourful rituals.

The Vajrayana tradition uses magical and sacramental rites, as well as mantras (sacred chants) and mandalas (sacred design) to focus the mind. Mantras can be written, chanted or visualised and are used in meditation and devotional practices. Mandalas can be drawn or made out of sand. The contemplation or the making of a mandala is supposed to awaken one's spiritual potential and is a symbolic representation of the cosmos. Mandalas can also be viewed as maps of people's spiritual journeys. These sacred formulae or symbols are intended to convey meaning to those who meditate on or recite them.

Growth of Convert Buddhism

From a western perspective, there are two main types of Buddhist, the convert Buddhist (also called in more colloquial fashion from an Anglo-Saxon perspective, 'non ethnic', 'white', 'non-Asian', or 'Anglo-Saxon') and the Ethnic Buddhist (also called the 'Asian' or 'immigrant'). Ethnic Buddhists often link their religious practice with various social and cultural activities to maintain their ethnic identity.

In the Australian census, the number of Buddhists has grown from 199,812 in 1996, to 357,813 in 2002, and to 418,749 in 2006. In terms of percentage of the Australian population, this means a growth from 1.1% in 1996 to 2.1% ten years later. Barker (2007) attributes increases prior to 1996 primarily to migration movements but mainly to Australian-born converts after that. She estimates that only 45,000 of the 158,000 new Buddhists appearing in the 2001 census were migrants and that 40% of the Australian Buddhist population might now be converts. It should be noted that these figures only represent people who identify as Buddhists. There may be many more people who engage in Buddhist practices but who are not recorded in the census. To understand the growth of Buddhism in the west and the increase in the number of convert Buddhists, Baumann (2001) and Spuler (2000a) suggest a few key periods in the development of this process. The following is a summary of their ideas.

Early Contacts. In the 19th century, the publication of books on Buddhism and translations of Buddhist texts began to appear in the west. It was not a period in which Asians exported Buddhism, but more a period when western orientalists imported these texts to their world. Buddhism was treated more like a curious textual or philosophical object rather than a lived religion.

Buddhist converts and initial institutions. Converts began to appear in the 1880s and the first Buddhist organisations outside of Asia were formed in the 1890s. For example, the Theosophical Society (see Chapter 7) promoted eastern spirituality, including Buddhism, through its centres. It was one of the first group to teach Buddhism as a religion for westerners, and many of the early British Buddhists came from this society (Cush 1996). The first British monk, Ananda Metteyya (1872–1923) created the Buddhist Society of Great Britain and Ireland in 1907 (Baumann 2001).

Practising Buddhism in the first half of the 20th century. The aftermath of WWI saw an increase in interest in Buddhism, and Buddhist activities in the west. These developed more strongly in Germany and the UK. However, the number of Asian Buddhists coming to the western world was limited and so this growth was not so widespread.

Spread and Pluralisation. In the 1950s and 60s there was an increase in diversity of Buddhist lineages available to westerners and a greater general interest in Buddhist meditative practices. Buddhist teachers from various traditions travelled from Asia to many western countries to create centres and win converts. It was during this time that the Beat Generation (see below) developed an interest in this religion and helped to popularise it.

> Buddhism was no longer dominated by a single main tradition, as had been the case in Europe with Theravada and in the U.S. with Mahayana Buddhism. Rather, since the 1950s, Buddhist teachers of various traditions emerged from

Asia to win converts and to found centers. A plurality of Buddhist traditions emerged, substantially supplemented by various Buddhist strands formed by immigrant Buddhists. Secondly, the shift from intellectual interest to practical application deepened and spread through increased interest in meditation. Meditation practices served as a significant mediator to transplant Buddhist traditions from Asia to Southern and Western regions. (Baumann 2001: 17–18)

Rapid increase. By the mid 1970s, Tibetan Buddhists were teaching in Europe, North America and Australia, and greatly contributed to the expansion of Tibetan Buddhism. This was a 'very minor current in Asian Buddhism, but of major importance in the West' (Lenoir 1999: 104). With the end of the Vietnam War in 1974–75, refugees from Laos, Cambodia and Vietnam also arrived in western countries to promote their version of Buddhism. It was also a period which saw a growth of interest in Buddhism from Japan such as Zen Buddhism and Soka Gakkai. Not only was there a heavy influx of Asian migrants to the west but there was also increased interest in Buddhist practices and beliefs from westerners. For example, in Britain, from 1979 to 2000, the 'number of [Buddhists] organizations quintupled from seventy-four to 400 groups and centers' (Baumann 2001: 18). These organisations almost doubled from 167 to 308 in Australia during the 1990s.

Lenoir (1999) explains these developments by limiting them to two phases. The first period was between the middle of the 19th century to the middle of the 20th century which was distinguished by an intellectual interest in Buddhism. The second period started in the 1960s, when the focus became more pragmatic and received stronger existential, spiritual and psychological characteristics. Lenoir surveyed Buddhist converts during this time and found that fewer than 10% wanted to achieve the ultimate goal of this religion, which is freedom from rebirth. For the large majority, Buddhist meditation was practiced as a psycho-corporeal technique to make its practitioners healthier mentally and physically. Most practitioners sought 'spiritual health' and 'happiness', and only 30% of those who believed in reincarnation declared that they wanted to free themselves from the circle of rebirth. The catalyst of this change of interest in the 1960s, which has changed the way Buddhism is practiced in western world, was partly caused by the Beat Generation.

Buddhism and the Beat Generation

The significant growth in interest in Buddhism began with the influence of the Beat Generation in the 1950s and 1960s. Previously, western groups had introduced Buddhism to western societies (e.g. the Theosophical Society), but they did not popularise Buddhism to the extent that the Beat Generation did. Baumann (2001) makes reference to this phase as 'Beat Zen'.

The term 'Beat Generation' makes reference to members of a movement which rejected the social and political systems of the west in the 1950s. They expressed their contempt for western contemporary society by rejecting regular work and material possessions. They espoused anarchism, communal living and drugs. The key figures of this movement were Allen Ginsberg, Jack Kerouac, William Burroughs and Alan Watts. They were the predecessors of the counter-cultural movement of the 1960s. As Allen Ginsberg mentioned regarding the interest of this generation in eastern thought:

> What we [the Beats] were proposing was some new sense of spiritual consciousness. We were interested in non-violence, sexual freedom, the exploration of psychedelic drugs and sensitivity. We were aware that the entire government … was corrupt. We were interested in eastern thought and meditation. We had quite an open heart and open mind (Allen Ginsberg [quoted by Oldmeadow (1999: 56)]).

Ginsberg was introduced to Buddhist texts by Kerouac in the early 1950s. In the early 60s, Ginsberg, who was among the best known poets of his time, visited India with a fellow poet, Gary Snyder, to seek spiritual teachers. From the early 70s, Ginsberg was an involved Buddhist practitioner who developed close links with Tibetan masters. This poet had turned eastwards and the intersection of his meditational practice and the writing of his poetry contributed to make this religion more visible in western societies.

Although the Beat Generation popularised Buddhism in the west, the form of Buddhism that they used was not seen as authentic from an 'Asian' perspective. They were viewed by traditionalists as having Americanised Vajyarana or Tibetan Buddhism in three ways:

1. they democratised this Buddhist lineage by disassembling its patriarchal and authoritarian power structures and moving it away from a monastic to a lay orientation;
2. they feminised it by including women at all levels of practice and leadership and;
3. they integrated Buddhism with the exigencies of the everyday life in late 20th-century America. Their vision of Buddhism was engaged with the most pressing sociopolitical issues of the day, which is in sharp contrast with the monastic lifestyle of Tibetan monks who tend to withdraw from everyday life (Oldmeadow 1999).[1]

The Beat and counter-cultural involvement in Eastern spirituality was not without precedent; nor was it either ephemeral or trivial and, indeed, it is still bearing fruit. The adherence of a rapidly growing and highly significant portion of the Western intelligentsia – artists, writers, philosophers, social activists prominently – to Eastern religious forms (most notably from the Tibetan and Japanese branches of Buddhism), and the assimilation of Asian modes of spiritual experience and cultural expression into Western forms, is one of the more remarkable cultural metamorphoses of the late 20th century, one has yet barely recognised let alone understood. More particularly, the impact of the Tibetan Diaspora on the West, especially the USA, demands more serious attention (Oldmeadow 1999: 67).

The Beat Generation was the precursor of the 1960s counter-culture movement. People from this movement were singing peace, love, universal harmony, and were protesting against materialism, racism and the Vietnam War. Since the days of the beatniks, according to Roszak (1969), post-war youth developed an eclectic taste for mystic, occult and magical phenomena, including western Buddhism (see next section), which has been responsible, in part, for the 'easternisation' of the west (see forthcoming section).

The Westernisation of Buddhism

In the US, Cadge (2004) analyses the way Therevada Buddhists in the west deal with gender issues. She compares and contrasts two organisations: one started and attended by first generation Thai immigrants, and another funded and attended by 'white' converts. With Therevada Buddhism in Asia, only men can become monks or teachers. Although the 'ethnic' organisation teaches that men and women are equal when it comes to learning and participating in the religion, the same gender inequalities about leadership have continued in the new continent. However, women in this US 'ethnic' organisation are involved in some teaching roles in ways that would not be permitted in Thailand.

In the 'convert' organisation, on the other hand, followers are critical of the patriarchal way Therevada Buddhism is practised in Asia and want to allow both men and women to take on leadership tasks and roles. However, despite these concerns to get rid of any gender bias at the leadership level, Cadge (2004) still notices gender inequalities in this group. For instance, more women are involved in volunteering than men and many other tasks performed in the centres are gender-typified (e.g. cooking and cleaning).

In another research, Mellor (1991) discovers that the adoption of Buddhism by British people is not a simple transfer of the religion from Asia to the UK, but that practices go through a process of translation. He underlines that Buddhism among UK converts is channelled in new ways that have many of the features of the Protestant Christian discourse. For him, British Buddhist groups are a significantly new cultural development because of this hybridisation.

Still on this argument about the westernisation of Buddhism, Hahlbohm-Helmus (2000) finds out that after 1959, high-ranking Tibetan Buddhists were sponsored to come to the west by patrons in Europe, North and South America, Australia, Japan and Taiwan to offer their religious teachings and rituals. They tended to teach their traditional version of Tibetan Buddhism as practised in their home country. They also received financial and political support for working towards the independence of Tibet from China. From the 1980s, the People's Republic of China adopted a more liberal position to politics and many Tibetans were then allowed to visit their relatives in exile in India. They also started to emigrate. It is during this time that the increase of 'ethnic' Tibetan Buddhists slowed down in the west as some went back to India and/or travelled to central Asia. This did not stop the new formation of western groups, but the importance of keeping Tibetan culture intact from its endangerment under the Chinese occupation diminished in favour of teaching meditation techniques to improve the well-being and daily lives of westerners. Training in Tibetan Buddhism, according to Hahlbohm-Helmus (2000), became less traditional and was adapted to a western model.

As with Lenoir (1999) already mentioned above, Hamilton (2002) discovers that western Buddhism tends to focus more on the development of the self through a type of this-worldly enlightenment rather than on escaping the circle of death and rebirth. There is more of a focus on meditation for positive mental well-being than escaping suffering by avoiding karma. In the case of Tibetan Buddhism, research suggests that the west has taken from it what suits it as if this religion is a 'museum of a fantasised past'. Other research points out that as this religion might have been reinterpreted rather than translated, it raises the issue that it might have 'sold out' to the west.

These significant studies at least confirm that when Buddhism is imported into western societies, it goes through change and adapts itself to the receiving country. As the western world is experiencing a postmodern phase with an emphasis on the self (as seen in Chapter 5), Lenoir is right to point out that it is no longer possible for any tradition to impose itself on an individual, as might have been the case in pre-modernity and modernity. In the case of western versions of Buddhism, it is more the individual who chooses a tradition and adapts it to his or her personal needs. Thus, when comparing western Buddhism to so-called authentic versions from Asia, one would expect to find people who believe and practise a form of Buddhism recreated in their own way.

Focusing on the example of Zen Buddhism, Spuler (2000b) argues that since the birth of Buddhism, this branch of religion has undergone many processes of acculturation, and that from its migration from India to China, Korea and Japan, it has always adapted itself to the receiving country. In fact,

Spuler finds it difficult to establish the 'authentic' version of this religion because of the changes it has undergone over three millennia. The Zen Buddhism that originally spread in the west before being totally westernised was not even the so-called traditional Japanese version. The masters who spread Zen to the west did so because of its decline in Japan, which resulted from it being too centred on priest's rituals rather than on people's quest towards illumination. Spuler (2000b) underlines that, in general, Buddhist practitioners accept that when Buddhism gets in contact with a new culture, it has to change to adapt itself to the new environment. This acceptance has been greater with Zen Buddhism because of its inherent lack of structure than with Tibetan Buddhism, which often attempts to maintain its 'ethnic' identity.

The point is taken from Spuler (2000b) that the westernisation of Buddhism is just another type of acculturation across the long history of this religion. But as Lenoir (2001) admits, even if Buddhism has changed its forms when meeting various Asian sub-cultures in the past, the changes that occurred when this religion entered modernity and post-modernity, especially in the west, have been greater than with any previous encounters. He even refers to a shock rather than a simple change to emphasise the weight of this specific acculturation process.

The Easternisation of the West

It is one thing to say that Buddhism has been westernised in the west; it is another one to say that Buddhism, and other eastern spiritualities, are part of a process of an 'easternisation' of the west. Indeed, as Buddhism and other 'imports' from the east have been so successful in the west, especially with the 'spiritual explosion' of the 1960s, one might wonder if the importation of eastern religions such as Buddhism could not have impacted on western culture as well.

Campbell (1999) makes reference to a process of 'easternisation' which goes beyond the simple import of spices, yogurt, practices such as yoga and acupuncture and whole religious beliefs such as those from Hinduism and Buddhism. He argues that:

> the traditional Western cultural paradigm no longer dominates in so-called 'Western' societies, but that it has been replaced by an 'Eastern' one. This fundamental change may have been assisted by the introduction of obviously Eastern ideas and influences into the West, but equally important have been internal indigenous developments within that system, developments which have precipitated this 'paradigm shift' (Campbell 1999: 41).

As indicators of this shift, Campbell (1999) cites the development of environmentalism (and more specifically that of deep ecology), the emergence of the human potential movement and various psychotherapy practices, the religions of the self, and the increasing belief in reincarnation. He argues that this shift had been contained to a minority within the 1960s counter-culture movement. However, a critical change happened in the 1980s when these creeds became more acceptable among the population at large. Eastern religions, and especially Buddhism, have been westernised in the west, and through this process of hybridisation, the west is paradoxically being easternised.

Further (to make the matter even more complicated), it appears that these westernised versions of eastern religions are being exported back to Asia, in a type of reverse orientalism (Hill 2000). For example, Howell (2006) finds out in Indonesia that many Muslim and non-Muslim middle-class people have developed an interest in new western spiritualities and have been actively involved in spiritual groups which have directly been imported from North America and Europe, rather than from Asia where they were initially formed. As another example, Lenoir (2001) makes reference to his fieldwork in Tibet where he spoke to Tibetan monks. He discovered that the monks were opposed to what they call 'spiritual materialism', which is about the consumerist approach to religions and spiritualities as explained in Chapter 5. They also made reference to the fact that because western life is strongly influencing various lifestyles in Asia, postmodern approaches to picking and choosing spiritualities and religions are also spreading within the Tibetan Diaspora in India.

The comment below might shed some light on these cultural transactions between east and west:

> it is not unusual for a more refined, reformed and allegedly purified version of a tradition to be actually re-exported back to the East and then re-imported again into the West as the 'authentic' tradition as opposed to folk or allegedly debased forms (Hamilton 2002: 247).

In the light of these exchanges between west and east, Hamilton (2002) argues from a broader perspective that processes of easternisation and westernisation might simply be aspects of globalisation.

Western Buddhism and Consumption

Taking into account the westernisation of Buddhism, we might wonder whether convert Buddhists are close to being as hyper-consumerist as the New Agers we have seen in Chapter 5, and whom we will explore at length in Chapter

12. Could it be that westerners who convert to Buddhism are as likely to shop around for another religion as often as New Agers and that conversion to Buddhism is more like choosing a religion from a shop shelf?

To answer this question, Cush (1996) conducted fieldwork with British Buddhist groups in the 1990s and found that some of her respondents from the western Buddhist community wanted greater orthodoxy and scholarship in their study and practice of Buddhism, and that the connection with New Age eclectic spiritualities had to stop. Some respondents from her 1990s research accepted that there are many valid religious paths and that Buddhism is just one of them. They also believed, however, that it is important to stick to one path in order to spiritually move forward. According to these western Buddhists, commitment to one path is not found among New Agers. They believed that New Agers tend to go in too many spiritual directions (see Chapter 12) and dilute Buddhist teachings through their so-called superficial and self-indulgent approach to spirituality. This finding was different from her studies in the mid-1970s when she found that British Buddhists and the New Agers seemed to be closer because of their common inclusion within the 'counterculture' or 'alternative society' of the time.

Phillips and Aarons (2005) also conducted research in Australia to assess whether convert Buddhists were as eclectic in their religious outlook as New Agers. In 1996, it was estimated that 1 in 13 Australian Buddhists were westerners (i.e. both parents were born in Australia or from another English-speaking country), which is a 30% increase from 1991. Phillips and Aarons (2005) sent a survey to a large western Buddhist study centre in a major Australian regional city and reached a response rate of 169 participants. Through their analysis, they are able to argue that convert Buddhists are more inclined to focus on their interest in Buddhism over a sustained period of time rather than follow Buddhism as one of multiple religious paths as practiced in New Age circles. While their survey discovers some evidence of New Age-style Buddhism among convert Buddhists, it is quite low compared to those with a much more traditional approach. They find a greater tendency toward engagement with Buddhism rather than a basic consumerist attitude.

From the same research, but in another article, Phillips and Aarons (2007) explore the possibility that eastern spiritual practices might offer westerners a solution to disenchantment with their westerner identity. They discover that converts to Buddhism in Australia do have a weaker attachment to western markers of identity such as social class, political party, ethnicity, gender, than the rest of the Australian population. They conclude that Australians involved with eastern spirituality are less prone to characterise themselves with western conceptions of self-identity. They also found that this disenchantment with western forms of identity is at its highest among convert Buddhists when they are involved in Buddhist practices but do not identify as

Buddhists. Paradoxically, it is the people who believe in Buddhism without belonging who are the furthest away from western types of identity than Buddhists who believe in, and feel they belong to, their religion.

Although Buddhism has been westernised and is now offered as one major 'religious product' to westerners, people involved in Buddhism do not consume this religion to the same extent as hyper-religious consumers (e.g. New Agers). However, they do not necessarily attempt to find and live the 'authentic' Buddhist way of life as they are more focused on meditation techniques for self-development than in the search to escape the cycle of rebirth.

Conclusion

This chapter has used Buddhism as a case study of a religion at the core of cultural exchanges between the west and the east. This religion has been westernised in the west and, paradoxically, might have also to some extent easternised the west. While the westernisation of Buddhism is only another process of acculturation of this religion, it is a process that has caused many changes. It seems that westerners involved in this religion are more interested in meditation practices focusing on self-development rather than on working towards the ultimate goal of escaping the cycle of rebirth as originally explained by Siddhartha. Interestingly, research also points to the fact that parts of the east are re-importing westernised versions of Buddhism rather than looking in their 'own backyard' for more traditional ones. The extent and implications of this re-importation process are unknown at this stage.

Note

1. On the other hand, a key figure in the movement, Alan Watts, was also the person who tried to bring Zen Buddhism to the western world in its 'authentic' form.

10 Christianity: Churches and Sects in a Post-Christian World

Introduction

At the same time that the third episode of *Lord of the Rings* was winning a series of Oscars as if they were given on an assembly line, a low production movie from Quebec, *The Barbarian Invasion*, received the prize for the best foreign movie. In this Canadian movie a young woman working for Sothebys visiting Quebec is contacted by a Catholic priest. The priest mentions that his church has a collection of old works of art that he is hoping to sell to international art collectors. The young woman is interested by this possible deal and pays a visit to a sort of Catholic store room. In this place reminiscent of an old and forgotten attic, an old priest shows her around the various art pieces covered with dust and cobwebs. Not only does this setting portray Catholicism in the western world as a decaying institution, but when the young woman tells the priest that these antiques are worth nothing, the metaphor about the decline of the relevance of the Church is reenforced.

As we have seen in Chapter 4, fewer people attend churches, and the political and cultural influences of mainstream Christian religions are no longer what they were in yesteryears. This movie is not only retelling what sociologists of religion have been analysing for years in terms of membership dropouts, it also emphasises that the Catholic Church has less power in a consumer world as its works of art are not of much value.

Following the illustration from this movie, this chapter quickly gives an account of the type of religious organisations found in the sociological literature to situate what a church is. It then moves to a new sociological narrative, the post-Christian argument, which claims that Christianity is losing momentum in the western world. However, even if parts of Christianity are attempting to grow through changes operated by Vatican II and the advent of the mega and emerging churches phenomenon, Christianity seems to be more of a success story outside of the western world. This chapter therefore finishes by arguing that although Christianity is in decline in the western world, it is strongly growing in the developing world, a phenomenon which has been called the next Christianity.

Christianity in a Snapshot

Although Christ died in 33 AD, Christianity did not become an official religion until 312 AD when the Christian Constantine became the Roman emperor. His successors went further by proclaiming that Christianity was not only permitted in the Empire, but was to be the only religion allowed. The Church obtained a religious monopoly in the Empire and became closely linked with the government. Later, Christianity went through many periods of consolidation, expansion and schism. Two of these schisms were the creation of the Orthodox Church and the Reformation.

Towards the end of the third century AD, the Roman Empire became too large to manage, and the Emperor Diocletian split it in two: an eastern half (Greece, Asia Minor, Palestine and Egypt) and a western half (Italy, Spain, and Gaul). Gradually, the two parts started to grow independently, and the church followed this division. In the Eastern Empire, the Church became closely identified with the State, whereas in the west, the Church retained its independence. In 1054, both churches excommunicated one another. The Eastern Church is now known as the Orthodox Church and the western one as the (Roman) Catholic Church.

The united western Christendom suffered a further blow in 1517 when Martin Luther nailed his 95 theses on the door of a church in Wittenberg. This led to the Reformation, which challenged the idea that divine authority should be mediated by a religious hierarchy and that the Bible could not be interpreted by individuals. The Christian religion could thus be practised individually, rather than within a vast institutionalised community led by a Pope. This Reformation led to the mushrooming of Protestant groups.

The churches that follow Luther (usually called Lutheran) remain somewhat closer to the Catholic tradition by retaining the office of the Bishop and the use of altars, rituals and picture. Those that follow the teachings of John Calvin (1509–64) (e.g. Presbyterians and Congregationalists) are further distanced from Catholicism because they removed all ornament in their churches. In general, Reformation Churches tend to have a more democratic organisation than the Catholic Church by giving decision-making to a local church rather than a centralised one.

The Church of England, otherwise known as the Anglican or the Episcopalian Church, stands between the Roman Catholic Church and the Churches of the Reformation by containing elements of both. During the reign of Henry VIII, when the Church of England was formed, the main question was not about the church's doctrine or sacramental life (as happened with the Reformation) but was about the authority of the Pope.

Religious Organisations

What is a church in a sociological sense? Ernst Troeltsch (1950) was one of the first to answer this question by trying to sociologically differentiate different types of religious organisations. For him, a church is a large organisation that usually professes to embrace all members of a society. Members of a church are usually by birth or marriage and few demands are made on them. They tend to come from the middle and upper levels of society, and are led by a formal organisation with a strong hierarchy of paid professionals. Churches are usually ideologically conservative and tend to support the status quo.

Although at the time of Troeltsch (1865–1923) a church could claim to embrace all members of a society, this has become a different matter in today's multicultural world. As many new religions have migrated to, and flourished within, the western world, a church can no longer claim to cover a whole nation under its wings and directly influence its state. As Davie (2000: 53) underlines, 'State churches no longer have the power to dominate...; they may, however, have retained the capacity to represent, to speak on behalf of the religious sector of modern societies, an important if reduced element.'

Sects, on the other hand, are smaller and have more power over their members than any other type of religious organisations. Contrary to churches, they tend to be against the status quo and are world rejecting. Whereas churches are in communication with the power of the state, sects are antagonistic and sometimes even refuse to cooperate with it. Their members tend to come from a lower class or from people who are opposed to the state. Members can be expected to withdraw from the outside world and devote their entire time to the beliefs and activities of their group. Sometimes, sects have a 'charismatic' leader rather than a hierarchy of paid officials. Such groups have some similarities with the world rejecting New Religious Movements that will be described in Chapter 12.

As already seen in Chapter 4, Troeltsch also created another ideal type of religious organisation, which he called from a sociological perspective 'mysticism'. This type is close to the world affirming New Religious Movements and New Age networks which will be explored in Chapter 12. They are small loosely knit groups organised around some common spiritual and religious interests but are lacking a well contained belief system. These groups tend to be more tolerant, and leave to each of its members their own authority in religious and spiritual matters. Mystic groups/networks have often divergent opinions and are often short lived.

Later, the American sociologist, H.R. Nieburh added a fourth type to Troeltsch's typology to cover the middle ground between church and sect.

He called this type 'denomination' (e.g. the Salvation Army and the Methodist in their current form). Many people are born into this type of religious organisation and some can also join them. Like churches, they have a professional ministry and are large. These groups are not exclusive and are relatively undemanding of their members. In the 19th and beginning of the 20th century, churches and sects were groups that strongly believed they had the monopoly of truth whereas denominations did not.

These are four ideal types of religious organisations and many religious groups have moved from being one type to another according to their own development and changing surroundings. A religious group is thus not limited to being one of these types across its history and location. For example, the Methodists, the Salvation Army and the Baptists started as sects. While growing in size and longevity, they made peace with the external world and have now become denominations. The Anglican, Lutheran and Orthodox churches could be seen as ex-churches in countries like the US, Canada, Australia and New Zealand because they have been transplanted from countries where they were national churches, and have become just one religious group among many. Thus, from a sociological point of view, they might be understood as denominations rather than churches.

Decline of Christianity in the Western World

Before making a claim about Christianity in the western world in general, I would like first to focus on Australia as a case study. Australia is a former English penal colony where the Anglican religion was first used as a tool for social control despite claims of a separation of church and state. It saw its religious homogeneity change after WWII as post-war migration and conversion to new religious movements transformed the cultural, religious, and ethnic profile of Australia society. As shown in Table 5, in 1947, Anglicans represented 39% of the population. In 2006, they have dropped to 18.7% and are no longer the largest religious group in Australia. Catholics, on the other hand, thanks to migration movements since 1933 from, for example, Italy, Malta and the former Yugoslavia, have become the largest group with 26.7% of the population. They outnumbered the Anglicans for the first time in the 1986 census. What is also worth noting is that Australia is becoming a less Christian country; from 88% of the population in 1947 to 64% in 2006. Without going into too much detail, on the other hand, non-mainstream Christian groups such as the Pentecostals and non-Christian groups are growing in Australia. In the 'other' census category which includes groups such as Bahá'í, Japanese religions, Scientology and Witchcraft, there has been an increase of 33% between 1996 and 2001. In the same timeframe, Buddhism increased by 79%, Hinduism by 42%, and Muslims by 40% (Bouma (2006). It is also important to mention that the 'no religion' category, although it has decreased by 1.5% since 1996, has grown from 6.7% of the population in 1971 to 18.6% in 2006.

Because of changes in the social and religious fabric of a country like Australia, fewer people claim to be Christian. This is due to the intensifying competition among non-Christian religious groups that have migrated to Australia and the growth of people claiming to be of 'no religion'. For this reason, although Christianity is still the dominant group, it is losing momentum.

The Australian example is an ideal case study for the western world. The west has historically been referred to as the Christian civilisation or 'Christendom', but this identification is making less and less sense. More and more people are turning away from organised religion, and more and more non-Christian religious groups are attracting people (e.g. the Bahá'í faith [see Possamai and Possamai-Inesedy 2007a]). Christianity is no longer the dominant religious group in western societies but has become part of the mix 'n' match characteristic of today's religion/spirituality. Although this is the case in Europe and Australia, one should remember that the USA is exceptional in the sense that its people adhere the most strongly to Christian values. However, as Hunt (2002: 99) points out, there has been an increase in the American population involved in a faith outside of Protestantism, Catholicism and Judaism.

This has been referred to as the post-Christian thesis, which also extends to the drop in Christian values among the general population as culture is changing. Cupitt (1998: 219) gives a simple example:

> Amongst Cambridge undergraduates in the mid-1950s well over 90 per cent professed belief in God and 55 per cent claimed to practise religion. The decline of these figures was slow at first, but now is proceeding very rapidly. In 1994 a poll reported that 34 per cent professed belief in God, and only 10 per cent claimed to practice religion.

This is translated in many surveys in western societies, such as the European ones used by Lambert (1995), who discovers a drop out in the number of people who believe in a personal God and in an absolute morality, and an increase of believers in the theory of reincarnation. These results support the argument that these countries are becoming post-Christian.

Don Cupitt (1998) theorised this post-Christianity thesis, and explained its existence in connection with the advent of postmodernity. Indeed, as previously seen in this book, the idea of a better future has collapsed, the age of Authority is over, and truth can no longer be universal (except among certain extreme fundamentalist groups). Cupitt (1998: 219) comments that 30 years

Table 5 The size and proportion of selected Australian religious groups in the 1947, 1971, 1996, 2001 and 2006 Censuses.

Religious Identification*	1947 000s	%	1971 000s	%	1996 000s	%	2001 000s	%	2006 000s	%
CHRISTIAN										
Anglican	2957	39.0	3953	31.0	3903	22.0	3881	20.7	3718	18.7
Baptist	114	1.5	176	1.4	295	1.7	309	1.7	316	1.6
Catholic	1570	20.7	3443	27.0	4799	27.0	5002	26.7	5126	25.8
Lutheran	67	0.9	197	1.5	250	1.4	250	1.3	251	1.3
MPCRU**	1678	22.1	2199	17.2	2011	11.3	1887	10.1	1734	8.7
Orthodox	17	0.2	339	2.7	497	2.8	529	2.8	544	2.7
Pentecostal	—	—	—	—	175	1.0	195	1.0	219	1.1
OCG***	270	3.8	683	5.4	653	4.4	711	3.7	777	3.9
Total Christian	**6,673**	**88.0**	**10,990**	**86.2**	**12,583**	**70.6**	**12,764**	**68.0**	**12685**	**63.9**
BUDDHISTS	—	—	—	—	200	1.1	358	1.9	418	2.1
HINDUS	—	—	—	—	67	0.4	95	0.5	148	0.7
JEWS	32	0.4	62	0.5	80	0.5	84	0.4	88	0.4
MUSLIMS	—	—	22	0.2	201	1.1	282	1.5	340	1.7
OTHER	4	0.1	14	0.1	69	0.4	92	0.5	109	0.5
Total	**37**	**0.5**	**99**	**0.8**	**617**	**3.5**	**911**	**4.8**	**1105**	**5.6**
Inadequate desc	19	0.2	29	0.2	54	0.3	352	1.9	108	0.6
No Religion	26	0.3	856	6.7	2949	16.5	2905	15.5	3706	18.6
Not Stated	825	10.9	781	6.1	1551	8.7	1836	9.8	2223	11.3
Total Population	**7,579**	**100**	**12,756**	**100**	**17,753**	**100**	**18,769**	**100**	**19,855**	**100**

* Only those Christian groups larger that 1% and other groups 0.4% and larger in 2001 have been included.
** MPCRU combines the data for the Methodist, Presbyterian, Congregational, Reformed and Uniting Churches. The Uniting Church was formed in 1977 in a merger of Congregational, Methodist and about half of the Presbyterians. Source: Australian Bureau of Statistics.
*** OCG – Other Christian Groups less than 1%.

Source: Bouma (2006: 53) for all columns but that of 2006. All information has been taken directly and indirectly from the Australian Bureau of Statistics.

ago a large majority of the western world felt the need to pay at least lip-service to Christianity; but things have now changed. In his work, he hopes for a mutation in Christianity or a new religion that may succeed Christianity and replace the void left by postmodern beliefs. The remaining parts of this chapter study these mutations without addressing Cupitt's religious agenda.

Vatican II

The Second Vatican Council was the most important event of the Catholic Church in the 20th century. It started in 1962 with Pope John XXIII (who died in 1963) and was finished in 1965 by Paul VI. All the bishops in the world were invited to this council to discuss how to 'open the windows of the Church' to the rest of the world. As an outcome, it issued 16 documents which dealt with various matters such as the promotion of Christian unity, the recognition that non-Christian religions are true and have holy revelations, and the right of all people for religious freedom. However, the documents on liturgy, on Divine Revelation, on the Church itself and on its role in the modern world were those that brought the most changes within the Catholic Church.

Before that time, masses were performed in Latin. After Vatican II, masses were given in vernacular (e.g. English in England, French in France, and German in Germany) and churches' rituals were redesigned to encourage the active participation of those present. For several centuries, Catholics had been discouraged from reading the scriptures themselves and were asked to rely on their priest and teachers to interpret them. With this major change, people were strongly encouraged to read them for themselves. It also encouraged the laity to become more involved at the organisational level.

Although the Catholic teaching is still the same, what Vatican II did is to re-express it in a language more suitable to the late 20th century. The Council wanted to open its old image of an elitist church withdrawn within itself to one that is open to people from all levels and religions and involved in the everyday realities of the world.

Paradoxically, after Vatican II, mass attendance went down. The number of priests, sisters and brothers is still declining and their average age is increasing. The way the clergy deals with people has also changed. For example, in some Catholic institutions like schools and hospitals, many positions that used to be filled by religious people are now taken by lay people. Some people have attributed the drop in Catholic Mass attendance and religious participation to Vatican II, whereas many others suggest this might have happened because of the postmodern social and cultural changes that have already been explored in this book.

Still today, Catholics have not dealt with these changes in the same way. Some see these changes as a tragedy that bishops have been powerless to control; some have embraced Vatican II because of the willingness of the Church to adapt itself to current social and cultural changes; and others think that Vatican II has not gone far enough. Catholics tend to be classified according to their responses to these changes. These include ideal types such as the Revolutionary, the Traditional, the Progressive, and the Conservative.

The Revolutionary Group within the Catholic Church views the changes that Vatican II brought as not sufficient enough. Liberation Theology is such a group which is mainly found in Latin America and has been led by people like Hugo Assmann, Leonardo Boff, Gustavo Gutiérrez and Juan Luis Segundo. This theology combines Marxism and Christianity and challenges the status quo in their country to promote social change especially for the benefit of the poor. It believes that a radical structural change is essential and criticises the current bourgeoisie and the church if the religious organisation is on the side of the rich and powerful. The Christian message here is one of liberation rather than justification. It works towards changing institutional structures that are the causes of poverty.

Traditional Groups, on the other hand, react against Vatican II and want the Church to go back to its older vision. Some of these groups fit with the Catholic integralist type explored in Chapter 8. They tend to be Catholic ascetic and promote orthodox Catholic teaching. The Opus Dei is a case is point. This group was created in Madrid by Josemaria Escriva in 1928. Contrary to Liberation Theology, it pursues success and liberal materialism, and wants to restore the Church and Papacy from the changes that it took with Vatican II. According to Davie (2000: 144–46), Opus Dei saw the changes in liturgy brought by Vatican II as disruptive and their priests have continued to celebrate mass in Latin with their backs turned to the congregation. Although the group displays the characteristics of a religious order, it is more a group of lay people who are still active in everyday life and have a family. There are even various levels of involvement within that group. 'Numeraries' make a vow of celibacy and live in Opus Dei dwellings. 'Associates' are like numeraries but do not live in Opus Dei houses. The majority of members of this group are called 'supernumeraries'. They can be married and work in a secular job. 'Co-operators' offer various types of support to the group but are not seen as members. Further, this group has a personal prelature, which is a new category in Catholicism. This refers to a worldwide diocese which has a strong level of independence from local bishops.

There are progressive groups among Catholics who believe that more could have been done since Vatican II but not to the revolutionary extreme of Liberation Theology. They want more social reform within the Church such as allowing priests to get married, recognising homosexuality among Catholics, and allowing methods of sexual contraception. For this group, a Third Vatican Council should be put in place to push the work of the Second one further.

The last group is the conservative one, which refers to Catholics who have approved the outcomes of Vatican II but do not believe in any more changes such as allowing priests to get married. The late John Paul II and his successor, Pope Benedict XVI, would fit into this category, as would the large majority of Catholic Cardinals. This group wants bishops to send Catholic messages in the public arena but do not want the clergy to get involved in politics. These 'conservatives' would not view a Third Vatican Council in a good light. In particular, John Paul II openly opposed Liberation Theology and fought against communism for most of his life, starting in his native Poland. He did not accept that Catholicism could be merged with aspects of Marxism.

Christianity Further Reaching for the Popular

The time when a church was at the centre of a community and could attract the local flock is gone. Apart from the US, as seen in Chapter 4, the rest of the western world has seen a strong decline in church attendance. However, in all parts of the world, some churches are working on bringing a flock ready to commute back inside its walls. Some churches are reaching out to the population by tapping into their own local culture and loosening their ties to the official elitist tradition (e.g. to pews, to prayers books and to Jacobean language). To deal with a new and highly mobile society that moves through networked communities, and to adapt to a new spirit of the times dominated by consumerism, some churches are attempting to attract people by narratives rather than rhetorical arguments. This is done to counteract and/or diminish the post-Christian phenomenon now underway in the western world.

For example, the Catholic Church, after attempting to denigrate aspects of popular religion within its faith during modernity, is now re-evaluating its cult of saints and the Virgin and is supporting it more strongly in postmodernity. This is demonstrated by the late Pope John Paul II's interest in pilgrimages. Voyé (1998) writes about this change within Catholicism and underlines the helpful notion of the relegitimation of popular religion since the advent of postmodernity. This process helps the Catholic Church to be seen as giving more meaning to the life of non-elitist Catholics. Of course, this process is happening within the Anglican Church as well. An example is the renewed interest in an old and populist aspect of religion – exorcism. As Pentecostals and Charismatic groups are growing in the western world, so are beliefs about the devil and exorcism, which are strongly promoted in these groups. According to Milner (2000), the Church of England, although looking in a positive light at the growth of interest in spirituality that these new groups are bringing, worry about this re-emergence of interest in exorcism. This is not because exorcism is viewed as a superstition, but because the techniques of this religious ritual employed by these groups can easily lead to dangerous excesses. Exorcism, for the Anglican Church, should be mainly an act of healing and grace. They encourage norms of self-restraint instead of touching the body of the possessed, and in particular not his or her sexual parts. With the growth of popular religion, the Church of England has recently renewed its approach to this phenomenon to meet today's religious demand by offering a spiritual technique of healing that is more controlled and bureaucratised. By doing this, it reaches people to whom popular (rather than theological) aspects of religion give meaning.

Other Christian groups are part of this relegitimation process as well and some of them show great interest in mega-churches as already seen in Chapter 5. Drane (2006b: 122–23) notes that, 'According to Charisma News Service (www.charisma.com), in 1970 there were only ten mega-churches in the USA, rising to 250 by 1990, and not far short of 800 by 2004 – with many more aspiring to such status'.

These mega-churches tend to be loosely connected to a denomination, if at all, and they tend to be a suburban phenomenon. Karnes et al. (2007) discovered that in the US, congregants are often young adult, urban and professional, and often commute long distances to these churches which are more likely to be built in wealthy neighbourhoods than in poor ones. This indicates that in a world of church competition, people are ready to travel long distances to have the church service of their choice rather than walk down to their local church a few streets away from their home.

However, within this movement of churches attempting to become more popular, some insiders, although agreeing on the changes necessary to adapt to postmodern culture, see mega-churches as offering uninventive pre-packaged worship and theology (Drane 2006a). As a reaction to this, emerging churches[1] in western societies have recently started to develop. They also ask questions about the nature of the church and of its engagement in the world, and want to make the Gospel accessible to unchurched people. They try to create the ambiance of an art gallery or café rather than that of an arena or rock concert found in mega-churches (Bader-Saye 2006). In a recent report from Wayne Brighton, a researcher with the General Synod Office of the Anglican Church, the Church was recommended to have a more community-based approach, including café churches (Price 2004). These café churches have people sitting at tables and chairs, drinking and/or eating and chatting. Other examples are churches in pubs, cyber churches, 15-minute long commuter churches designed for the 21st-century overly busy workers on their way to work with little time to spare for a more conventional church services, and skate churches with ramps inside or outside the church hall where skating is mixed with Bible readings. The latter example is explained on the Internet by the organisers as:

> A weekly outreach where we provide a supervised environment for young skaters on the Sunshine Coast [Australia] to enjoy. An outdoor smooth car-park is transformed into a gnarly street park with fun boxes, flat rails, grind boxes, picnic tables, pole jam, fridge bank, manual pads and more. Safety gear is provided as well as expert advice and instruction. The session wraps up with a relevant, low key devotion that applies God's truth to our everyday circumstances.[2]

Some of these churches mix pop music with liturgy. In his analysis of the infamous Nine O'Clock Service in Sheffield, UK, Till (2006: 91) discovered that it is difficult for the church to compete with the 'visual and aural impact that multimedia experiences in nightclubs and on television have upon young people', and that more people go clubbing each weekend than attend church. To deal with the competition, the Nine O'Clock Service was a service given in a local church at 9 PM after the last conventional service, and was strongly influenced by the clubbing culture and its electronic pop music for its liturgies. Its first service was given in 1986 and it developed quickly. At one stage, it had more staff and more attendees than Sheffield Cathedral. Although the service was stopped because it led to one of the biggest sex scandals the Church of England had ever seen (Till 2006: 102), it was influential in the development of alternative types of worship in churches. As Till (2006: 105) concludes:

> [The Nine O'clock Service] saw itself as an alternative solution and it learnt from secular culture how to use music and the arts to reach and inspire people. In club culture it found new forms of communal expression developed by secular DJs, clubbers, musicians, and promoters. It took what was useful from club culture while disapproving of and expressly forbidding the use of drugs and other aspects of excessive hedonism (ironically also forbidding any sexual activity outside of marriage).

Many of the liturgies used in the mega and emerging churches use Christian music – a type of music where evangelicals have experimented with musical style far more than lyrical content. As McIntyre (2007) points out, these lyrics are like rock and pop music with its gigs and celebrities, but without the sex and drugs. The teens who buy this music are found to be part of a consumer culture specifically aimed at a Christian lifestyle.

By using a style of sociation more appropriate to a society dominated by consumer and popular culture than having people preached at from a pulpit, it is hoped to increase church attendance and to have the gospel reach a larger audience. As seen in Chapter 4, although church attendance in the US is far more healthy than in Europe, it nevertheless does not stop this new continent to seek for a growing popularity in these new forms of faith activity as they are competing with other churches for members.

Drane (2006b: 4) defines this complex new phenomenon across continents as such:

> On the one hand, 'emerging church' is being used as a shorthand way of describing a genuine concern among leaders of traditional denominations to engage in a meaningful missional way with the changing culture, and as part of that engagement to ask fundamental questions about the nature of the Church as well as about an appropriate contextualization of Christian faith that will honour the tradition while also making the Gospel accessible to otherwise unchurched people. … There is, however, another image of 'emerging church', consisting of Christians who have become angry and disillusioned with their previous experience of church (predominantly at the conservative evangelical, fundamentalist and sometimes charismatic end of the spectrum), and who have established their own faith communities that – far from being accountable to any larger tradition – are fiercely independent, and often highly critical of those who remain within what they regard as the spiritually bankrupt Establishment. … this second type is more typical of 'emerging churches' in North America, while the first is more typical of the English scene (and to a lesser extent of Australia and New Zealand).

The astute observer to this new phenomenon will realise that, as Bader-Saye (2006) points out, there are two types of adaptation by these churches to the postmodern world. One type is concerned with a cultural and stylistic change only and not with a change in theology or ecclesiasticism. By being 'hip' or 'cool' in their engagement with the changes of today, these churches are simply packaging the gospel for a new generation. This type is called 'Evangelical Pragmatists'. Bader-Saye (2006) also refers to another type, the 'Post-Evangelical Emergents' where both methodology and theology, form and content, have been adapted to today's concerns.

The church did not wait for the advent of postmodern culture to attempt to become more popular. There are well known cases in history (e.g. Vatican II as seen above) that prove the contrary. However, what makes this process different nowadays is that parts of Christianity aim to adapt themselves to not only people's local culture but to their lifestyle as well. Indeed, the point is for the religious group to tailor its 'religious product' to a particular niche (e.g. skate church to a particular sub-culture), a process called lifestyling.

The Next Christianity

Whereas the western world is facing a post-Christian 'religious-scape' that some Christian groups are trying to counteract, this decline is far from happening in the developing world. It is growing at such a high level that Jenkins (2002) sees that Christians are becoming a growing majority in the 'Rest' of the world. It is estimated that by 2025, close to three quarters of all Catholics will be in Africa, Asia and Latin America. By 2050, 50% of the Christian population will be in Africa and Latin America, whereas 17% will be in Asia. This Next Christianity dominated by developing countries is already more conservative than in the north. As Jenkins points out, the Catholic faith rising in Africa and Asia is more traditional and is more at ease with notion of authority and spiritual charisma than in the west. Catholicism within this Next Christianity looks like a pre-Vatican II faith. Jenkins (2002: 64) summarises these differences:

> The cultural gap between Christians of the North and the South will increase rather than diminish in the coming decades, for reasons that recall Luther's time. During the early modern period Northern and Southern Europe were divided between the Protestantism of the word and the Catholicism of the senses – between a religious culture of preaching, hymns, and Bible reading, and one of statues, rituals, and processions. Today we might see as a parallel the impact of electronic technologies which is being felt at very different rates in the Northern and Southern worlds. The new-media revolution is occurring in Europe, North America, and the Pacific Rim while other parts of the globe are focusing on – indeed, still catching up with – the traditional world of book learning. Northern communities will move to ever more decentralized and privatized forms of faith as Southerners maintain older ideals of community and traditional authority.

Jenkins is unsure about the unification between northern and southern Christians. Within the northern countries, there is a push to impose liberal stances in doctrine and morals (e.g. complete transparency in church administration, increase lay participation in decision making, abolition of mandatory clerical celibacy, and ordination of women to the priesthood). However, if this push were to happen to the conservative southern Christianity as well, it could create a new schism. Jenkins envisions a scenario for Catholics in which if a Third Vatican Council were to be put into place to complete the changes started by Pope John XXIII, it might revert the whole of Catholicism to a pre-Vatican II situation if this Council were to be dominated by conservative Christians from the south. In other words, and not only specific to Catholicism, if the north were to work on a new Reformation following the current liberal vision with the Church, it could turn out to rather become a new Counter-Reformation led from the south.

Conclusion

This chapter has quickly covered what is happening in Christianity at the moment from a sociological point of view. We live in a post-Christian period in the west in which fewer and fewer people embrace Christian values and attend churches. To remedy this problem, some Christian groups are acting on making their religion more relevant for today's postmodern life which is exemplified by the creation of mega and café churches. However, the situation in the southern hemisphere appears to be different to the north where Christianity is growing so strongly that this process has been called the Next Christianity. This Next Christianity is more conservative than the more liberal north and favours pre-Vatican II values.

Notes

1. Also called Next Wave, New Paradigm and Liquid Church (De Groot 2006).
2. Internet site; http://www.ywamwaves.com/ministries.ministries3.ews (16/08/ 2007).

11 The Multiple-Modernities of Islam?

Introduction

The story 'V for Vendetta' is a narrative set up in the UK in the near future that explores various philosophical, political and sociological issues. The story takes an idealist (in its philosophical sense) approach to the world, like the sociology of Durkheim and Weber, by arguing that ideas (rather than economics) are what drive the world. It is through ideas that the main character of the story 'V' is fighting against a fascist English government which works hand-in-hand with the Church to control the population.

In the 1980s, it was first written as a graphic novel by Alan Moore and drawn by David Lloyd as an allegory against the neo-liberalism of Thatcher's government. When the movie came out at the beginning of the 21st century, the allegory was still strong, but in reference to the Bush administration.

'V' is a terrorist fighting to raise people's consciousness about the way they are mistreated. His goal is to make people realise that they can overthrow their fascist government if they wish. The task is hard because in this dystopia, all dissident voices have been shut down, and all works of art and philosophy that could make people think against the dominant ideology are forbidden. Because they are against the law, controversial books have been hidden by 'V' and other characters. One of these books is the Koran, which, if found by the police, could cause the owner to be imprisoned or executed by the government. In the movie, the book is represented as a piece of philosophical and religious beauty that has become dangerous under an oppressive regime.

This holy book only appears in the movie and is not found in the graphic novel. The placement of this book in this post 9/11 version is quite indicative that the authors wanted to show how, in a story in which terrorism has a large part, the Koran can be a source of inspiration for peace and beauty and not for violence. The movie was quite clear in separating Islam from terrorism, which is what this chapter is also doing. Because of 9/11, western representations of Islam have dramatically changed and have generalised, especially in the media, a view of the religion in negative and stereotypical ways (see e.g. Cahill et al. 2004). This chapter rather focuses on the diversity that exists within Islam, and the sociocultural conditions of the Islamic world.

Even if the very large majority of Muslims are not involved in violence, the context in which Muslims are living can be problematic as the secularisation process of their countries, pushed by pre-WWII western colonialist forces, have failed to create the wealthy and equitable societies that were promised by their governments. As a consequence, many Muslims see Islam as an alternative to secularisation in bringing their societies back on sound economic, political and social tracks. The challenge for moderate and liberal Muslims today, within and outside western countries might be on working with the dominant western ideology to create a modernity which would fit with their belief system.

Islam in a Nutshell

Islam means 'surrender' and its confession of faith is 'There is no god but God and Muhammad is his Prophet'. This religion started with Mohammed (*ca.* 570–632 AD) who was born in Mecca. During his time, Mecca was already a centre of pilgrimage and was dominated by the pagan group, *Quraysh*. The town held the *Ka'bah,* which was a sacred building used as a sanctuary. Before the beginning of Islam, Mecca was already centripetal to many nomadic Arabs, who came to the city for its annual pilgrimage festivals and fairs.

In 610, Mohammed was said to have become the messenger of God (*rasûl Allâh*). He started to preach his revelations from God to the people of Mecca from 613 to 622 and many merchants from Medina came to see him every year. Slowly the ideas he preached in Mecca were also developing in Medina. In 622, the Prophet was forced to leave Mecca and went to Medina. This year is central to the Islamic faith and is called the Hijrah (i.e. the Emigration of the Prophet and his believers). It marks the beginning of the Arabian era as much as the birth of Christ marks that of Christianity.

Over the years Mohammed's forces in Medina grew to a point that an army was ready. In the 10th year of the Arabian era (or 632 AD for Christians), Mohammed personally led the great pilgrimage (called the *Hajj*) to Mecca and Islam became the new dominant religion of the region.

It is important to note that when Islam was born, it did not refute Christianity and Judaism. Twenty-eight Christian and Judaic prophets are mentioned in the Koran, such as Adam, Moses, Jesus (whose divinity is denied) and John the Baptist. They are all described as legitimate prophets who also brought the word of God, and Mohammed was but the special prophet of the Muslims.

In a nutshell, there are two main books for Islam: the Koran, which contains the words of Allah transmitted by Mohammed between 610 and 612, and the Hadith, which comprises stories by people who knew the prophet. Central to Islam are the Five Pillars (i.e. five ritual acts). These are:

1. The Confession of Faith (*Shahada*). This is a process that proclaims there is no god but God and Mohammed is his prophet.
2. The Prayers (*Salat*). These are said five times a day and should be preceded by an ablution. The recitation of the Prayers involves repeating a few sets of Arabic phrases, a few prostrations towards Mecca, and some other ritual incantations.
3. Fasting (*Sawm*). During daylight hours in the ninth month of the lunar calendar, Muslims do not eat or drink. This period is known as the holy month of Ramadan.
4. Pilgrimage (the *hajj*). All Muslims must go on a pilgrimage to Mecca at least once in their lifetime
5. A Tax or Tithing (*zakah*). Muslims should contribute to a religious tax for the poor, the needy, the new converts or the religious student with no means of support. This tax can also contribute to a Holy War.

Before his death, Mohammed appointed his chief advisor, Abu-Bakr, to succeed him after his death to lead the prayer. This succession gave birth to the area of the 'rightly guided' *Khukafaa* (Caliphs), these being Abu-Bakr (632–34), Omar (634–44), Uthman (644–56), and Ali (656–61). Ali was defeated by Muawiyya (the founder of the Umayya dynasty) and forced to move from Mecca to Damascus. This created the Shiite/Sunni schism within the Muslim religion. For the Shiite (also called Shia, Shiite, Shî'î), only descendants of the Prophet's daughter, Fatimah, and her husband Ali have the right to lead Muslims. For the Sunni, a ruler does not need to be in a direct line of descendents from the prophet but can be chosen for their wisdom and piety.

Shiite Islam has also many sub-movements. For example, a schism within Shiites happened when there was an issue of succession over the seventh Imam.[1] This led to the creation of the Ismaili (Isma'ili), a Shiite sect whose adherents believe that Ismail, the son of the sixth Imam, was the rightful seventh Imam. Moving away from this sect, but staying within Shiite Islam, another break in the religious leadership lineage happened at a later stage. The 12th Imam got kidnapped and was never found. Some Shiites in Iran believe that he is in hiding and that Islam will be the world religion when this Hidden Imam (called the Mahdi) reappears. Today, this form of Shiite Islam predominates in Iran and has large communities in Iraq and Lebanon.

Another large group which cuts across both Sunni and Shiite Islam is called Sufism. It is organised in Brotherhoods and Orders with an allegiance to a spiritual master. Sufism aims to reach spiritual union with God.

There are many different Islamic groups within and outside these three large 'families' of Islamic faith. As Tayob (1999) underlines when it comes to modern Islamic writings, believers agree on certain core beliefs, but they often disagree on worship practices, on how to understand the Koran and on the paths towards religious and social development.

Modernisation and /or Re-Islamisation?

As discussed in Chapter 4, the rise of modernity in western countries during the 17th century gave us democracy, science and the capitalist economy. The western world, which once lagged behind the Muslim world, became more scientifically advanced, wealthier and more powerful. During the 18th and 19th centuries, many Muslim nations were colonised by European na-tions, and many Muslims have felt extremely humiliated by this experience. While European countries pushed the colonisation process in the name of modernity in Muslim countries, many European and local colonised thinkers believed that Islam would slowly become secularised. These colonised thinkers, especially those who had gained a degree or had lived in a western society, predicted that the Islamic world would move towards the modern world and embrace science, democracy and capitalism.

When comparing the secularisation process between the western and Islamic worlds, Tayob (2005) argues that the question of power and the push factor of the elites underscore differences. He does not argue that these factors were not important with regard to the advent of secularisation in the western world. Rather, he suggests that they were only by-products of other key factors such as rationalisation and urbanisation in the west, whereas for the secularisation process in the Islamic world in the context of international relations, power and its imposition by the elites is crucial to understanding secularisation. Tayob (2005: 125–26) states:

> Secularisation in Muslim contexts cannot be dissociated from the political dimension of colonialism and the weakness of the Muslim state in relation to European states. Power seems to have been written into the debate over secularisation when Muslim states tried to assert their authority and indepen-dence against rising European powers.

On the path to modernisation, some Muslim states attempted to force changes within their societies: that included reinterpreting Islamic thought and leading their people towards secularisation. The moment in history that marked the strength of this process was when Mustafa Kemal Atatürk (1881–1938) founded the Turkish republic after the fall of the Ottoman Empire. The honorific title of Atatürk (Father of Turks) was bestowed upon him by Turkey's national parliament in 1934. During his presidency of Turkey between 1923 and 1938, he westernised and secularised his country by abolishing the caliphate system and relegating Islam to the private sphere. The adornment of the fez became prohibited and the traditional Islamic female scarf was banned in public institutions. Atatürk's new government followed the political structures of the west by creating western-style parliaments, bureaucracies and armies.

In this new republic, religion was placed under the control of the state, which resulted in the persecution of some religious leaders (Turam 2004). Indeed, Turkey's new civil code became hostile to Islam rather than separate from it. As a symbol of these sociocultural reforms, Atatürk moved the capital of Turkey from Istanbul to Ankara in 1923.

This moment in history was read by Europeans and newly secularised Muslim countries as an indicator that Islam, like other religions, would slowly move away from people's concerns, at least in the public sphere. This process of secularisation was followed in many de-colonised Muslim countries after WWII. This was done in cooperation with the western world through loans, direct aid, increased trade and military cooperation. Unfortunately, many of those former Muslim countries did not rise to the economic and social level of European countries as expected. Debt and inflation tended to slow down their prosperity and weaken their democracy. In many cases, nepotism and corruption led to many social injustices.

It was in part due to the widespread social inequality in the Muslim world that later in the 20th century, Muslim religious movements increasingly wanted to reverse the dream of secularisation and re-Islamise their countries, which they believed had been lost to secular government. Their claim is that Islamic countries have failed to modernise because Koranic law was not implemented. By working on a return to original Islam, some Muslims believe that their countries will be on the path to economic and social development, as well as political power which could restore the Muslim world to its former supremacy. This came as a surprise to the western world when the large majority of scholars believed that the demise of Islam, like religion in general, was a *fait accompli*. Islam was wrongly believed to be relegated exclusively to the private sphere and irrelevant as a belief system in modernised Islamic countries (Tayob 1999).

Kepel (2002) works on two levels of re-islamisation: one from above (i.e. an emphasis on politics and the state) and one from below (i.e. an emphasis on social movements/networks). Inspired by his work, I will discuss the Islamic revolution in Iran in 1979, which showed to the world that the re-islamisation process could happen from above. I will also discuss the case of the Intifada during the 1980s in the Palestinian occupied lands and the Algerian civil war in the same period, which indicated that re-islamisation can also happen from below. These cases studies are not the most recent ones, but they are crucial as it is around that time that the world community became acutely aware that Islam was attempting to re-emerge in the public sphere, i.e. well before 9/11.

Re-Islamisation from Above: The Case Study of Iran

Until 1979, Iran was governed by Mohammed Reza Shah Pahlavi (the Shah). During his secularist and authoritarian regime, all radical, moderate and liberal Islamic groups were prevented from participation in political decision-making. The Shah's secularist project involved reducing to the minimum any religious group's influence and political power. To this end, the SAVAK, a ruthless secret police, was working with the government. However, despite the efforts of the Shah to control the traditional clergy, the numbers of mosques increased in the 1960s and 1970s.

The Islamic revolution in Iran started in February 1979 when the Ayatollah (an Iranian Shiite religious leader) Khomeini returned to Teheran from his exile of 14 years in Turkey, Iraq and France to overthrow the Shah's regime. Many Islamic students from the elite classes followed the Ayatollah because they were frustrated by the previous government, which prevented their rise to power within the country's social structure. They believed, like Khomeini, that their society had to be ruled by Islamic law. It thus became logical for the leader of their society to be the person most knowledgeable of that law.

Khomeini made himself further known globally through the Salman Rushdie affair. In September 1988, Rushdie's novel *The Satanic Verses* was published in the UK. This led to widespread negative reactions from Muslims, such as those from the Leicester Islamic Foundation who sent a circular to the Muslim community in the UK denouncing the book as blasphemous, only a few weeks after its publication. At a later stage, the burning of the book in Bradford town hall square took place in front of around a thousand people. These acts of protestation reached a higher level when the Ayatollah Khomeini announced from Tehran that:

> I inform all intrepid Muslims in the world that the author of the book, *The Satanic Verses*, which is against Islam, the Prophet and the Koran, and all those who have published it knowingly are condemned to death. I call on courageous Muslims to execute them as soon as possible, wherever they may be, so that in future no one may dare to insult what Muslims hold sacred. (Quoted by Kepel (1994: 139)

He issued a fatwa (i.e. a legal judgement based on the Holy Texts of Islam) condemning Rushdie, a person outside of the Muslim world, to death.

This was something that was without precedent. According to Kepel (1994), this event was of such high importance in the Muslim world because a fatwa should have only concerned Shiites who are lead by Ayatollah's spiritual authority. By making this judgement on behalf of all the Muslims of the world, he was attempting to proclaim himself the religious guide of the whole Muslim world. Through this, and many other activities, Khomeini was trying to export his Iranian revolution abroad. Indeed, he believed that nationalism was a western construct that should be eradicated and he dreamed of the creation of a global Islamic state not restricted by any national borders.

Re-Islamisation from Below: Palestine and Its Intifada

The case of the first Intifada (i.e. the uprise against oppression) in Palestine/Israel during the 1980s is a perfect case study of this process. However, before reaching this time, one needs to go back a century earlier to understand the complex situation that prevailed on both sides.

The modern creation of the state of Israel happened through a long process. Jews have suffered many years of anti-Semitism in Europe and many of them were longing to return to the biblical land of Israel. A catalyst for this desire was the Louis Dreyfus affair in 1894, when a French army officer was accused of treason and sent to jail. He was innocent, but because he was from a Jewish background, he was used as a scapegoat by French authorities. This created indignation among many French intellectuals who protested against Dreyfus's imprisonment because it did not fit with their belief in equality, justice and freedom (see the concluding chapter of this book for more details). One of these intellectuals was Theodore Herzl, a founder of Zionism, which is a movement dedicated to the creation of a Jewish state that would welcome the Jewish diaspora.

At that time the land that is now Israel was called Palestine and was under the rule of the Ottoman Empire. When Palestine became part of a British protectorate (1922–48) as a consequence of the fall of the Ottoman Empire after WWI, there were around 55,000 Jews and 700,000 Arabs on this land. While the Zionist movement was growing in strength in the rest of the world, WWII broke, bringing with it the systematic extermination of six millions Jews by the Nazi regime and its supporters. This genocide on such a large scale made Jews feel that the only solution for their protection from another possible extermination was to create a state where they could have a government and an army looking after them and their interests. After WWII, many of the Jews who survived the Nazi Holocaust migrated to Palestine in the hope of finding and building a place where they could be protected from anti-Semitism.

Faced with this new reality, the newly formed United Nations proposed to partition the land into two states; one Jewish and one Arab. The Arabs rejected this proposal and fighting broke out in Palestine. In 1948, Zionists declared independence for the new State of Israel. Four surrounding Arab states attacked the newly formed state in retaliation but lost the war. At the time of the creation of Israel, the territory had around 650,000 Jews and 1,300,000 Arabs. Since that time, many Palestinians have been living in refugee camps in some bordering countries, while many of them were pushed to Gaza and the West Bank where they have been living as second-class citizens under the strict control of Israel. In 2006 there were 5.4 million Jews (i.e. 76% of the population), less than in the US (6.15 millions in 2002), and 1.4 million Arabs. The full history of the conflict between Jews and Palestinians is too complex for this book to cover in detail, and for this reason, I am mainly focusing on the first Intifada (i.e. the first Palestinian uprising).

By 1987, Palestinians in the occupied lands had been living under the Israeli occupation for 20 years. The international community did not seem to show any signs of sympathy to their cause and Yasser Arafat's Palestine Liberation Organisation (PLO), which had been involved in acts of diplomacy and terrorism outside of Palestine, was still not reaching its goal of freeing Palestine. Until that time, the fight for the liberation of Palestine was led by a secular group and no mention of Islamic mobilisation was found in the vocabulary of the PLO. Inside Palestine, frustration and anger had been growing strongly since the creation of Israel. This finally broke out into a full-scale Intifada or uprising in December 1987. The rebellion led by young Islamist militants and the Hamas Islamic Resistance Movement started by throwing stones at the Israeli army that controlled the occupied territories. The reaction of the army was to shoot at the people and to break their arms. As the Intifada stretched to three years, more Israelis and members of the international community wanted to start negotiations to settle the problem. This led to the Oslo agreements (1993–99) which did not succeed in creating a peace settlement as expected. This failure at the international level led to the second Intifada which became more organised and more violent than the first. It was no longer about simply throwing rocks at the army, but became more about carrying out a series of deadly suicide bombings to push the same concerns of the first Intifada with more violent means.

Before this rebellion, the PLO was working as a secular movement and it took the world by surprise that political activities from within the occupied lands could have been carried out by religious actors. The first Intifada revealed to the world that religious groups could be active in the public sphere for a specific cause.

Re-Islamisation from Below: Algeria and Its Civil War in the Early 1990s

The Palestinian case is not the only one that can illustrate re-islamisation from below. The case of Algeria is also important.

The Algerian *Front Islamique de Libération* (FIS, translated as the Islamic Salvation Front) was founded in 1989 by an elderly sheikh, Abbassi Madani, and a young Islamic preacher, Ali Belhadj. Since the *Front National de Libération* (FNL, translated as the National Liberation Front) took power after the Algerian war of independence against French colonisation, the government became Arabic but remained secularist and favoured secular people who fought within the FNL. After its creation, the FIS quickly capitalised on those who felt economically displaced.

Since the Algerian revolt against France, Algeria was a one-party democracy. In 1989 the government opened itself to multipartism. In December 1991 the FIS won the municipal election and in January the following year the previous government, opposed to the idea of giving a religio-political party more power, tried to regain control. Religion had to be prevented from being involved at the political level by the secularist government. In March 1992 the FIS was banned, and in 1992, the FNL President Boudiaf was assassinated by the FIS. These actions led the country into civil war until the end of the 1990s. It came as a surprise to the international community that political tension of such magnitude could involve religious actors wanting to re-emerge in the public sphere.

Modernisation or Anti-Modernisation in Islam?

Many Arabic, Persian, and Turkish countries became modernised after the fall of the Ottoman Empire and were on a secularist path following the western model. This has been interpreted as a social and political failure by many Islamic groups that have contested the western model. What needs to be underlined here is that these forms of protest were not necessarily directed against the western world (although some were, such as the FIS against France), but mainly against secular Arabic governments that have become oppressive to their own people and which have been perceived as corrupted.

What is at sake for Muslims now, has been perfectly spelled out by Turner (2007: 406–407)

> The principal challenge for Islam in the new global environment is how to sustain an Islamic identity in the context of modernization, the secular state

and multiculturalism. However, the revival of Islam is taking place alongside a revival of Christianity in Asia, especially among Protestant and charismatic groups, and hence, the problem of creating civil societies that can sustain co-operation between competitive religious movements has become a major political issue...The specific situation of Muslim minorities in Western societies after the terrorist attacks on the Twin Towers, and the bombings of civilian targets in Madrid, London and Bali is that Islamic communities are increasingly subject to official scrutiny by secular government agencies.

Within Islam, there are now new developments and movements that work on new Islamic identities in a revived process of modernity. Even if the secularist modernity offered by the western world is seen to have failed, many contemporary Islamic groups do not necessarily reject the project of modernity. For example, there are emerging Islamist feminists who fight for a different reading of the Koran which argues that nowhere is it written in the Koran that women cannot drive a car. In the Turkish context, Göle (2000) writes about some Islamist women in Turkey who want to break away from the moralising Islamic perspective on woman and are inspired by western feminism. These women want to affirm their personality without being dependent on a man and argue that patriarchal oppression exists in all societies and is not exclusively restricted to capitalist systems. They point out that the source of their oppression is not western or Islamic values but Muslim men. In the case of Iran, Afshar (2007) deals within a Shiite context and explores how elite Islamist women are contesting religious interpretation by misogynistic males. These women also argue that there is no contradiction between feminism and Islam and that the problem of oppression arises from men from different classes who justify patriarchy with their own religious interpretation.

There are also Islamic movements that aim to promote modernism, tolerance and democracy without rejecting their religion. These are 'liberal' Islamist groups such as the Darqawiyya movement which is a form of Sufism aiming at restoring European Islam. This movement claims that as centuries ago parts of Spain were Muslim, there is no need to look to North Africa or the Middle East to find inspiration for becoming Muslim. By rediscovering the 'authentic' European form of Islam that had been practised in Granada and Cordoba during their Muslim rule, there would be the possibility of working with a contemporary European Muslim identity.

In Turkey, the Gülen movement does not show signs of wanting the creation of a Turkish Islamist state. It is even opposed to the idea of the state applying the Sharia'a law and argues that these laws should be followed in the private sphere only. The aim for this movement is to create a self-disciplined Islam among themselves and in harmony with secular political institutions. Turam (2004: 261) underlines that this movement is almost inexistent in the Arab-Muslim world and Iran, but that it is expanding in the recently independent secular countries of Central Asia, such as Kazakhstan, and in the west because of its bargaining abilities with secular states.

Recent research from Hassan (2007) can help us understand why this movement is more popular in Turkey and former Arabic communist countries than Arabic countries in North Africa or in the Middle East. In his research, he surveyed 6300 Muslims in Indonesia, Pakistan, Egypt, Malaysia, Iran, Turkey and Kazakhstan. He discovered that a type of religious renaissance is taking place in these Muslim countries. By this, he makes reference to not only a commitment to Islamic theology but also to a pragmatic application of this theology to the everyday life of its believers. However, this renaissance is not happening at the same level in all the countries he studied. Indeed, Hassan (2007: 470) claims:

> There appear to be two types of religious commitments. One type is characterized by ideological orthodoxy; strong emphasis on ritualism, devotionalism, an image of Islam grounded in traditional readings of sacred scriptures and personal religious experience. The other type is characterized by a lack of ideological orthodoxy, lack of emphasis on ritualism and devotionalism and a non-traditional image of Islam. We can call the first type traditional Muslim piety and the second non-traditional Muslim piety....The traditional type of religious commitment characterizes Indonesia, Pakistan, Malaysia, Egypt and Iran. The non-traditional type is largely a characteristic of the Kazak Muslims. The Turkish case falls in between the two types.

Even if there is no concrete evidence for this argument, it might be deduced from Hassan's analysis that the Gülen movement might develop the strongest where non-traditional Muslim piety dominates, such as in Turkey, Central Asia and within certain westernised Islamic groups.

According to Turner (2007), contemporary commentators on Islam have argued that the problem in having Islam fitting into a western culture and society is that Islam does not recognise the separation of church and state. From a western perspective, Islam would have problems in meeting the Westphalian model, which subordinates religion to politics and removes religion from the public sphere. It might be tempting to argue when comparing Turner (2007) with Hassan (2007) that one should be aware of these two types of piety and that perhaps the Islamic groups more characterised by non-traditional piety are more apt to meet the model for liberal multiculturalism characterised in western societies rather than those that fit with the traditional Muslim type. This non-traditional piety type is found in countries where the public sphere is highly secularised and one might wonder if it would characterise moderate and liberal Islamic groups in western countries as well. It might thus be tempting to raise the assumption that the more traditionalist a Muslim group is, the more difficult the bridge with the Westphalian model will be built.

In the UK context, for example, Hellyer (2007) points out that this country has one of the most ethnically diverse Muslim populations in the world, and that even if there are various active Muslim organisations, none of them can claim the full representation of the Muslim community. Although some of these organisations would like to place Islamic law above state law, thus making the 'universal' rules of Islam superior to the local context, it is far from being the case for all of them as 'evidence suggests that the British Muslim community is committed to a British identity' (Hellyer 2007: 249). While remaining loyal to their faith, they also identify with a British identity and want to create a British Islamic culture. This would involve some innovation and creativity from the Muslim community to adapt itself to this new identity, which might fit with the non-traditionalist Muslim piety type as discovered by Hassan (2007). This appears to be a work in progress for more moderate and liberal groups which aim to bridge the Islamic model with that of the Westphalian one. However, as part of this bridge, efforts from the British and other western states to facilitate the practice of Islam within their territories might also be required.

Islamic Multiple-Modernities?

From the various arguments presented above, it is clear that some Islamic actors are working on Islamic projects of modernity which offer variations from western thinking. Such religio-social actions should be understood within the multiple modernities thesis as already explored in Chapter 4. As Göle (2000: 91) has explicitly written on this topic, it is worth reminding the reader of this thesis within an Islamic context:

> the multiple-modernities project puts the emphasis on the inclusionary dynamic of modernity, on borrowing, blending, and cross-fertilization rather than on the logic of exclusionary divergence, binary oppositions (between traditionals and moderns), or the clash of civilizations (between Islam and the West).

Göle argues that within this contemporary phase which explores the boundaries of modernity within an Islamic context, there is a post-Islamic stage in which Islamism is less and less about following political and revolutionary actions, but is rather about engaging in social and cultural everyday life practices (Göle 2000: 94). 'Post-Islamists' would thus be working on new public spaces, on creating their new visibility and new lifestyles and identities. This post-Islamic stage is working so much on redrawing the initial western project of modernity by bringing Islam into the public space that the author even raises an important question: 'The question that needs to be asked is not whether Islam is compatible with modernity but how Islam and modernity interact with each other, transform one another, and reveal each other's limits' (Göle 2000: 94).

Göle (2002) gives a telling example of how Islam and modernity can test their limits. In 1999, Merve Kavakçi, a computer engineer trained in the USA, became an Istanbul deputy from a pro-Islamic party. When she entered the Turkish parliament for the first time, she was wearing a contemporary long-skirted two-piece suit with fashionable glasses (symbols of modernity), and a white headscarf (symbol of traditionalism and Islam). Men and women deputies stood up and protested against this Islamic display in a republican and public space. Twelve women from the Democratic Left Party were apparently among the most opposed and were shouting 'Merve out, ayatollahs to Iran' and 'Turkey is secular, will remain secular' (Göle 2002: 178). The reaction from these women could be explained by the fact that secularist women, many years ago, were able to enter the Turkish public sphere and end the spatial separation of genders through their emancipation from religion which was symbolised by taking off the veil.

This pro-Islamic deputy shook the status quo of her country by displaying her ease with both modern and Islamic culture in the public sphere. She disturbed both the traditional Muslim groups and the secularist modernist ones, and through this, was working towards a new understanding of modernity in the Turkish context.

In another country, Kamali (2007) deals with the Iranian issue while reminding the reader that the idea of modernity as a single and homogeneous philosophical and social project is a eurocentric construction. Throughout the modern Iranian history, different visions of modernity have been put into place by various governments, from before the Shah until radical Islamic groups took power in 1979. Another project of modernity then came back during the presidency of the liberal Islamist Muhammad Khatami who was defeated at the last election in 2005 by the radical Islamist Mahmoud Ahmadinejad.

Conclusion

From this quick exploration of Islam it is tempting to argue that moderate and liberal Muslims who are attempting to make their religion more visible in the public space and who are creating new Muslim identities are not rejecting modernity, but are working on new versions. Rather than focus on the debate about the acceptance or rejection of modernity by Muslims, it has become more intellectually productive to understand the tension between Islam and modernity as leading instead to the creation of various understandings of modernity with an Islamic touch. This understanding fits with Eisenstadt's (2000) thesis of multiple modernities already explored in Chapter 4. New Islamic multiple modernities will be different across Muslim and western countries and acknowledging these social and cultural changes will lead to a better understanding of Islamic issues in today's world.

Chapters 9, 10 and 11 have given an overview of current changes within three long-time established religions. We have seen the difficulty that Christianity faces with consumerism, the westernisation process that Buddhism experiences, and the new modern projects that Islam is proposing. Changes happen with less established religion as the next two chapters explore. Moving away from established religion, some people want to explore a religion/spirituality outside a conventional setting and join a New Religious Movement, a New Age group, and/or a neo-pagan group. Although these religions/spiritualities have a much shorter history than Buddhism, Christianity, and Islam, they are nevertheless challenged by the fluidity of our contemporary society.

Notes

1.　For the Shiites, the Imam is their divinely inspired leader. For a Sunni, an imam is the leader of congregational prayer in a mosque.

12 New Religious Movements and the Death of the New Age

Introduction

The television show *Xena: Warrior Princess* portrays a female hero who can use a sword as strongly and skilfully as any male warrior. In these stories, which are based in a historically re-invented sword and sorcery fantasy setting populated by gods and goddesses, the main character has been received by the public as a feminist icon or even as a goddess figure by some neo-pagan groups (see Chapter 13). McPhillips and Franzman (2000) summarise well the religious underpinning of this TV series:

> [Xena] participates in the soap opera tradition by reflecting current popular trends, e.g. towards denigration of institutionalized religions and uncritical acceptance of newer forms of religion. This is clearly filtered through the writers' and/or directors' feminist viewpoints regarding religion and religious beliefs. Thus, traditional and institutional religions are presented mostly in caricature, as in the case with the presentation of Islam only under its extreme militant and zealous aspect. Newest forms of religion or spirituality are generally presented in highly positive, uncritical, or naïve ways.

Using *Xena* as a case study, one can thus claim that there are traces in popular culture which indicate that newer forms of religions are favoured over more traditional ones. This is reflected in everyday life with people who have an increased interest in New Religious Movements and New Age Spiritualities. However, this chapter argues that this growth is far from being enough to overtake institutional religions.

Since the 1960s and its counter-culture movement, some people have actively started to explore religion outside of its institutionalised walls. This, of course, is not a new phenomenon if one remembers that movements such as the Theosophical and Anthroposophical Societies, and Occultist groups such as the Golden Dawn, have been around since the 19th century. However, what makes this relevant to our time period is the increase in membership and the growth in variety of these movements. If I may generalise, I argue in this chapter that New Religious Movements (NRMs) were a strong phenomenon in the 1960–70s, and even if many of them still exist today, the taste for alternative spiritualities moved towards New Age Spiritualities in the 1980–90s. While NRMs and New Age spiritualities are still extant today, we would now be in a phase in which people are more interested in the type of spiritualities discussed in Chapter 4.

New Religious Movements (NRMs)

The term NRMs tends to describe new forms of religions which have developed during the 1960s in the western world. Even if some of these groups, such as Theosophy and Spiritualism have appeared in the 19th century – and are thus called old NRMs (Chryssides 1999) – they still remain within the confines of this appellation as they have 'fully' emerged in the public sphere around this period. According to Wallis (1984), within these groups, two large sub-types tend to typify the phenomenon: the world rejecting and the world affirming groups.

The world rejecting NRMs have some affinity with the 'sect' type of religious organisation described in Chapter 10, as they appear to create a sense of community removed from mainstream society. Their membership tends to be more demanding than mainstream religions, and tension with the external world can be high. There is an expectation that members of this type of group would leave their family and work to fully dedicate themselves to a religious life. For example, the Unification Church started in Korea in 1954 and was founded by the Reverend Sun Myung Moon. It landed in California in the early 1960s, and the Moonies, as they were known, had a very slow start in the US until the 1970 when Moon himself moved there. People from this NRM believed that that there was a decline in moral values among young people and that traditional Christian churches had been in decline. Moon wanted to continue the work that Christ had started but was not able to finish: to establish the Kingdom of Heaven on earth. The Moonies did not require communal living but they expected devotees to dedicate most of their time to being involved in, and promoting, the movement. Another example of a world rejecting movement is the International Society for Krishna Consciousness (ISKCON) whose adherents in its early days lived in considerable poverty in an 'ashram' and dedicated much of their time to religious and domestic work. However, even if this group, as well as others like the Children of God, started in this world-rejecting fashion and had been in tension with the outside world, it has since opened itself up and has recently become less world-rejecting.

World-affirming NRMs do not ask their members to reject mainstream society. They tend to believe that human beings have a (godly) potential within themselves that can be developed. Members of these groups do not have to leave their family and/or job. They can be involved in these religious groups while remaining active in everyday society. Groups of that type are Transcendental Meditation and the Church of Scientology. As an example of this type of NRM, Transcendental Meditation asks its members to meditate on a mantra for 20 minutes every morning and evening to help them become more efficient in the here and now. It does not propose a programme of meditation like ISKCON which involves total withdrawal from everyday life. There is also a belief within Transcendental Meditation that if a critical mass of people meditate regularly, the level of what they call the cosmic consciousness will rise and benefit the whole of society by providing a solution to crime and other social ills.

Some of these NRMs have created tension in the western world. For example, several legal battles have surrounded the case of the Church of Scientology, the Children of God or the family, and Ananda Marga. At another level, tension also exists in the media. Indeed, journalists can at times appear to know little objective information about NRMs and as a consequence seem quite negative towards them. These negative sentiments can be seen to create a sense of fear towards new forms of religion.

It is because of these tensions that in Anglo-Saxon cultures the word 'cult' has a strong pejorative connotation in everyday life (e.g. Dillion and Richardson 1994; Pfeifer 1992) whereas the terms 'New Religious Movements' (NRMs) and 'Minority Religions' are more objective appellations used by scholars to describe the same phenomenon. 'Cults' tend to refer to religious groups with an authoritarian leadership that suppresses rational thought, organises deceptive recruitment techniques and coercive mind control, and isolates members from conventional society and former relationships. It is a word used to scare, to worry and to sell in the milieu of sensationalist journalism. For Barker (1986: 332), the term became highly derogatory after the mass suicide/murder of 922 followers of Jim Jones in Guyana in 1978. While numerous NRMs had formerly been treated individually, these deaths shaped the public's perception of NRMs and have all tended to be negatively termed 'cults', even if there exists a considerable diversity among them. If most Anti-Cult Movements' pronouncements tend to be about 'destructive cults', they also have the tendency to lump many NRMs together as though they were a single entity; 'the sins of one being visited on all' (Barker 1995: 297). Indeed, although we cannot forget the atrocities at Waco (1993), and with the Order of the Solar Temple (1994), Aum Shinri-kyo (1995), the Heaven's Gate (1997) group, and the Movement for the Restoration of the Ten Commandments of God in Uganda (2000), one has to be clear that these events only touch a small fraction of the whole field of NRMs and that the very large majority of these religious groups cannot be generalised from them. More will be presented on this topic in the concluding chapter of this book.

When making predictions on the future of NRMs, one of the leading scholars in this field, Introvigne (2004), claims that although the number of movements is increasing, there is no evidence that membership across and within these groups is growing. We seem to be dealing with 2% of the population from most countries in the world that are moving from one group to another. Introvigne (2004: 985) draws the conclusion that 'thousands of new religious movements will continue to compete for the allegiance of a comparatively small percentage of the population prepared to join them'.

Although NRMs do not tend to attract more people today, some of their ideas have spread throughout mainstream society and have, in parts, carried the recent popularity of New Age spiritualities.

New Age Spiritualities

While the number of people reading New Age books or attending workshops has increased rapidly since the 1980–90s, it has not led to many identifying themselves as belonging to 'New Age' religions/spiritualities. As Bruce (1996) notes, the popularity of 'New Age' cannot be measured by the number of people identifying with constituent groups but rather by the extent to which people are influenced in everyday life by the phenomenon.

The term 'New Age' lacks a clear denotation in the academic literature and among the likes of the New Age spokespersons listed by York (1995) such as Gayce and MacLane. However, for convention sakes, it could be argued that at its beginning, this term was connected to that of the Age of Aquarius which is based on the astrological assumption that the sun changes its zodiacal sign every 2160 years, according to the astrological law of the precession of equinoxes (Le Cour 1995). This migration into another zodiac is supposed to create important modifications on earth and just such a profound alteration is about to happen in the third millennium. The sun is leaving the zodiac of Pisces and will gradually enter the zodiac of Aquarius, affecting the behaviour and attitudes of every living creature. This is referred as the coming of the Age of Aquarius. If we associate the word 'New Age' with the 'Age of Aquarius', we could define New Agers as spiritual actors who believe in this Aquarian coming and follow a syncretic spirituality, which interprets the world as monistic (the cosmos is perceived as having its elements deeply interrelated. It recognises a single ultimate principle, being, or force, underlying all reality, and rejects the notion of dualism, e.g. mind/body); whose actors are attempting to develop their Human Potential Ethic (actors work on themselves for personal growth); and whose actors are seeking Spiritual Knowledge (the way to develop oneself is through a pursuit of knowledge, be it the knowledge of the universe or of the self, the two being sometimes interrelated). There are other ideal types of New Agers who view the world as monistic, who work at developing their Human Potential Ethic and who seek spiritual knowledge, but do not believe in the Age of Aquarius. For more information, see Possamai (2005a).

We have seen in Chapter 10 that the western world is slowly turning into a post-Christian one. However, one should not assume that people leaving churches move to the New Age. There is a relative lack of penetration of New Age beliefs or practices into the Christian churches as found in recent research by Heelas and Woodhead (2005), who conducted research in Kendal, a town of around 28,000 people in the north of England. The town was used as a testing ground, or 'spiritual laboratory' as one of the respondents put it. As part of the fieldwork, the authors mapped the locality, visited each congregation and group from the holistic milieu at least once, conducted archival research, identified and researched representative case studies, counted people who attended congregational and holistic services, and administered a questionnaire to both groups. The researchers discovered that 2,207 people (i.e. 7.9%) were active in the congregations of Kendal and 600 people (i.e. 1.6%) in its holistic milieu. Overall, they found very little overlap between the congregational domain and holistic spirituality. Only around 4% of congregational members had participated in the previous week in holistic activities, and only 6.4% agreed with the statement that 'alternative or complementary non-church forms of spirituality have things to teach Christianity' (Heelas and Woodhead 2005: 31–32).

According to the authors, the Kendal figures do not seem to deviate from the UK national picture. While it is clear from the book that the congregational domain is declining while the holistic milieu is growing, it is far from being a spiritual revolution; it is more of a 'mini-revolution'. Taking into account their own findings and those of others, they claim that whether it be Kendal or the UK nationally, if the holistic milieu continues to grow at the same rate since it started in the 1970s, and if the congregational milieu still declines at the same rate, the 'full-blown' spiritual revolution in the UK will only take place during the third decade of the third millennium. By 'full-blown' revolution, the authors understand a situation in which the congregational domain and holistic milieu have become much the same size.

Further, the authors also discovered that the relatively small growth of the holistic milieu does not compensate for the larger decline of the congregational domain. Indeed, the fall in numbers of Christian churchgoers is much higher than the growth of the New Age and other NRMs. As Bruce (2002: 81) states, 'even the most generous estimates of the New Age are unlikely to have the new spiritual seekers filling the space left by the decline of just one denomination'. The New Age, as it appears, does not provide a spiritual refuge for all dissatisfied Christians: many of these church leavers can also become nonreligious.

Following on from these findings, Possamai, Bellamy and Castel (2006) found that after analysing the results of a 2001 survey of a random sample of churchgoers in Australia, these people do not have much affinity with the New Age: a result which fits with the current literature. However, when looking more closely at the sample, it is clear that Catholics have the highest affinity with the New Age among all Christian groups, and evangelical groups have the least affinity. The research also found that churchgoers in their teens are more inclined to alternative ideas.

Paradoxically, I discovered in Possamai (2005a) that the use of the term 'New Age' is dead while its beliefs and practices are still alive. In 1996–97, I interviewed 35 people in Melbourne who might 'commonly' be described as New Agers. However, 71% of the participants negatively criticised New Age, and 9%, even if positive towards it, did not consider themselves as New Agers. Some negative comments were:

> It's like a train labelled New Age and everybody's jumping on it. And it started off very good, a very good term. But now there's a lot of people out trying to make big money on it for all the wrong reasons.

> And the other thing I find most irritating about the New Age movement is how gullible people are.

> So I guess I'm a bit of a, you know I'm not your typical New Age, totally immersed in it sort of person [...]. I mean my personal feeling is that I like to keep my feet on the ground a bit [...].

These findings are confirmed by Introvigne (2001) who makes reference to the Next-Age, which is a movement from within the New Age that aims to move away from the commercialised aspect of what is commonly known as 'New Age'. Geoffroy (2001) also notices some concerns with the commercialisation of these spiritualities in Quebec. As many insiders tend to dissociate themselves from the label 'New Age', many of them would rather claim to be involved in the type of alternative spiritualities already discussed in Chapter 4. Instead of stating they are involved in the New Age they would rather claim to be involved in spiritualities in its broader sense.

The Affinity Networking Capital

I have explained two phenomena in the last two sections that have rarely been linked together in the literature. Sociologists have developed tools of analysis such as the Church-Sect typology seen in Chapter 10 that are not fit to understand New Age Spiritualities. For this reason, many sociologists of religion developed new ways of understanding this new phenomenon that appeared in strength in the 1980–90s. However, no conceptual tool has been developed to link these two new religious and spiritual activities as the challenge lies in combining the various typologies of religious groups with contemporary forms of networking. Therefore, this section aims to focus on the way spiritual actors across NRMs and New Age network as discovered in Possamai (2005a).

As the insider Judith explains:

> [...] I'm a solitaire [...] I don't belong to any group, no. I don't belong to any rigorously defined group any more than most people would say, somebody may be a computer programmer and they belong to the group of computer programmers but they don't necessarily know them. But they'll have a lot of friends who are. They'll all pull together. And if somebody's particularly good at some particular part of that job then they'll probably teach the others. If they're particularly strong in some other area the information is passed on. And it is more about information being passed on. It's a network I suppose more than anything else. A bit of a Web.

There would thus be a network, a web, in which people in NRMs, New Age groups and in alternative spiritualities exchange ideas. Even the most religious individualists are not isolated. People in this religious sub-field attend seminars, workshops, conferences, reading groups, and exchange ideas. They visit many kinds of religious associations and very few stay all their lives in only one. They also visit psychic fairs and New Age festivals for a 'bit of shopping' and select the new books and/or new practices on the market, always out to discover something new and to enrich their spiritual experience, until finding 'what feels right to them'.

This leads us to move towards the new network paradigm in the sociology of religion which includes concepts such as the Bund (Hetherington 1994), neo-tribes (Maffesoli 1988), situationalistic networks (Lipovetsky 1987), the Segmented Polycentric Integrated Network (York 1995), and the Web (Corrywright 2003; 2004). Explaining the subtle differences between these terms is beyond the scope of this book, so I will work more specifically with that of the Bund.

This term was created by the German Schmalenbach in the 1920s. Hetherington (1994) summarises it as: 'An elective form of sociation, in which the main characteristics are that it is small scale, spatially proximate and maintained through the affectual solidarity its members have for one another in pursuit of a particular set of shared beliefs' (1994: 2).

The Bund has its solidarity more focused on affective-emotional links. It is elective, and for its members: 'Schmalenbach shows that it is an intentional act of joining together with strangers that is the basis of their common feeling and mutual solidarity' (Hetherington 1994: 13).

The term Bund has, as its central theme, the affective and emotional elements which appear to correlate with the intuitive form of authority located in the inner self. Indeed, when insiders (Possamai 2005a) describe how to follow a spiritual path, they often underline the importance of listening to intuition, to know what feels right for them, i.e. if they experience an affinity with a group or a person, it is worth listening to their 'gut feeling' about whether to stay with this group or person. The mode of locating authority in the inner self facilitates 'spiritual mobility', i.e. the eclecticism (often affectual) in spiritualities. However, stating that these spiritual workers evolve in networks is not enough to make a fully satisfying sociological account. The networks are not random and are part of a specific milieu which the next section explores.

The Cultic Milieu and the Network Paradigm

Before moving further in this section, another note must be made with regard to the politics of the use of the word 'cult' and 'NRMs'. At the beginning of this chapter, I explained the tension created when using the word 'cult', especially in the media. A way to avoid this is to use the word 'NRMs' or 'Minority Religions' instead. However, that said, it does not mean that all sociologists of religion follow this convention. For example, Campbell (1972) and Stark and Bainbridge (1985) use the word 'cult' to refer to 'NRMs' without any pejorative connotation. Since their work is central to this section, I will be true to their vocabulary for the remainder of this chapter.

The cultic milieu is a concept which takes into account the fluid form of aggregation of spiritual workers. This term was coined by Campbell (1972) who refers to it as the cultural underground of society. It includes all deviant belief-systems and their associated practices, e.g. unorthodox science, deviant medicine, the world of the occult and the magical, mysticism, and alien intelligences. A major flaw in this concept is that it focuses on the belief that there is a lack of organisation in this cultic milieu; accordingly it does not take into consideration more organised religious groups (York 1995). The task for this section is thus to take the more organised groups into account, and to combine these groups and the cultic milieu with the recent network paradigm.

As a first step towards this, Stark and Bainbridge (1985) provide a typology which includes three levels of cult activities supposedly covering the whole cult environment. In this typology (see below), cults vary in terms of their level of organisation. However, Stark and Bainbridge's perspective tends to focus more on the production of spiritualities and takes less into consideration the different modes of consumption of these spiritualities, i.e. the plurality of reasons why spiritual actors visit these cults.

These actors do not consume spirituality passively, and they do not necessarily take it for granted. Inspired by de Certeau (1988), the production of spirituality is indeed not received passively, but is contested and again re-appropriated. And if we compare spirituality to a message, there is resistance from the original message and as de Certeau writes about texts in general, '[t]he reader takes neither the position of the author, nor an author's position. He invents in texts something different from what they intended' (1988: 169). Indeed, as described in Chapter 5 on consumerism, hyper religious consumers no longer accept the religious 'set menu' offered by 'traditional religions' – or even by new religious movements – but are more interested in 'religion à la carte'. They free themselves from ascriptive bonds and thus, presumably, weaken social ties to any particular religious group. This type of subjectivism dictates that one should find one's own path, which includes experimenting and exploring spiritual practices and reading a great number of books, etc., until one feels confident enough to decide which spiritual path to follow. This exploration can take many years and it is stressed that time is sometimes necessary before finding the most suitable path.

These spiritual actors are seekers (Balch and Taylor 1978: 54–55; Sutcliffe 2003) and they network. They shop around in cults and in the cultic milieu; and consume the spirituality on offer. Their inner self appears to be the arbiter of their spiritual quest. These actors focus on constructing their own identity, their own personality, and on generating their own knowledge. These consumers are mobile and their tastes fluctuate, and as seen in Chapter 5, they are part of what Bauman (1998) calls post-modern religions; they consume products to gather and to enhance sensation.

Explaining the cultic milieu only in regard to the production of spirituality does not aid in the understanding of the movements of spiritual seekers among ideal types of cults. A way to explain this networking would be thus to focus more specifically on the movements of these social actors between what is produced and what is consumed. Thus, to provide a more comprehensive look at cults – some more organised than others – within the cultic milieu, I wish to build a two-dimensional model based on the production and consumption of spirituality. I will apply three works (Campbell 1978a; Gillen 1987; Stark and Bainbridge 1985) that are highly relevant to the understanding of this milieu.

First Axis: Production of Spirituality

Stark and Bainbridge's (1985) conception of cults is especially relevant to a description of cult structure, i.e. their type of organisation that produces spirituality. The authors propose a typology of three ideal types: the audience cult, the client cult and the cult movement.

1) Audience cults are the most diffuse and least organised type of cult. They often do not gather physically but produce cult doctrines entirely through magazines, books, newspapers, radio, and television. There are virtually no aspects of formal organisation to these activities. They 'deal in myth, weak magic, and esoteric entertainment. Audience cults operate primarily through the mass media but sometimes attract crowds of consumers to lectures, fairs, and the like' (Stark and Bainbridge 1981b: 430). These audience cults are involved mainly in what the Jorgensens (1982: 375) call psychic fairs; a synonym with 'New Age' festivals.

> The obvious function of psychic fairs is to make money and disseminate information, yet they also provide a crucial basis for social network and solidarity. In the course of psychic fairs, members of the community make new friends, exchange ideas and services, reaffirm established relationships, develop business arrangements, present positive images to the public, make converts, and recruit members.

However in this kind of fair, I find not only audience cults but also client cults that are more organised, but which also need to sell their 'spiritual' products.

2) Client cults are considered by Stark and Bainbrige (1985: 26) as audience cults organised among those offering the cult service. No successful effort is made to weld the clients into a social movement or to have their all-embracing mobilisation. The leaders dispense magical services – e.g. those of astrologers, tarot card readers, psychics, healers, water dowsers. The authors compare the relationship between those promulgating cult doctrine and those partaking of it as the relationship between therapist and patient or between consultant and client. 'Indeed, client involvement is so partial that clients often retain an active commitment to another religious movement or institution' (1985:26).

3) Cult movements (Stark and Bainbridge 1985: 29–30) are full-fledged religious organisations. Many of them are very weak organisations, others can function much like conventional sects and attempt to create social change. The degree to which these movements mobilise their members differs considerably within this ideal type. However, unlike the other cult types, they tend to provide a meaning of the universe for their members.

Stark and Bainbridge summarise their typology as follows:

In general, cult movements are higher in tension with the sociocultural environment, because they present more total challenges to conventional beliefs and practices than do client cults (which focus on narrow areas of human concern) and audience cults (which tend merely to offer vague vicarious satisfactions and entertainment) (1981a: 322).

Second Axis: Consumption of Spirituality

Bruce Campbell (1978a) defines ideal types of cults through the way they handle the tension between the sacred within and the profane. He posits two ideal types: the illumination cult and the instrumental cult. Campbell developed this typology to describe different forms of aggregation, whereas I will 'paraphrase' his typology to analyse the different modes of consumption in the cultic milieu. I have already touched on this typology in Chapter 6 when I addressed what Jediists could gain from being inspired by the characterisation of a Jedi knight. However, I am extending here the analysis of this typology.

The author describes what I call the teleology of the being, i.e. that these spiritual actors will try to reach what they believe is the ultimate way of being and this will influence their mode of consumption. If one person believes his or her salvation is in the extramundane, by developing his or her divine spark he or she will consume certain means in relation to this soteriology, e.g. use of yoga for meditation. If another person fixes a goal in the intramundane to reach a state of well-being, of realisation, he or she will consume other media, or the same means but with a different conception, e.g. use of yoga to diminish stress. I have also found in the work of Paul Gillen (1987) another kind of teleology offered by some cults that is mainly entertainment, e.g. use of Tarot cards to socialise and have fun. Because of this teleology of the being, the spiritual actor shops around cults to find what can help him or her. There is no one teleology or mode of consumption shared by them, but many; and these are what this axis explores.

1) The Illumination cult,

> referred to by others as the mystical form of cults, corresponds to Troeltsch's technical mysticism [see Chapter 4]: a timeless, universal religion concerned with the development of the eternal self. This type emphasises detachment from the personality and the search for direct inner personal experience of the divine within (Campbell 1978: 233).

Campbell suggests that this kind of cult gives to its members a belief in a sacred within that influences their teleology for illumination, i.e. a mystic, a wise man, a wise woman, a sage, a saint, etc. Spirituality is here an end in itself, and will be consumed to fulfil this goal. Thus, by 'illumination', I refer to a quest for a direct inner personal experience of the divine within, or for a greater individual potential.

2) The instrumental cult,

> referred to by others as the self-adjustment type, offers the individual tech-
> niques by which to better himself [sic] and his [sic] place in the world. Inner
> experience is sought for its effects, its ability to transform the everyday empiri-
> cal personality so that it can better meet the demands made upon it (Campbell
> 1978: 233).

The teleology of their members is to become a more 'powerful' person in the intra-mundane and focus their attention, not on an inner experience, but on concrete effects, e.g. to develop their intelligence, their charisma, and to feel better in their body. The spirituality consumed, in this sense, is a means to external ends. Thus, by 'instrumental', I refer to some techniques an individual uses to better himself or herself, and to become more effective and efficient in worldly pursuits.

3) The entertainment cult is a concept borrowed from Paul Gillen (1987) which originally dealt with the pleasure of Spiritualism. The author observed spiritualist groups, as seen in Chapter 7, and he realises that 'spirit messages entertain in many ways, but most distinctively by the evocation of a sugges-tive indeterminacy. Like the patterns of the Rorschach test, they provoke interpretation but refuse to support a definite meaning' (Gillen 1987: 226). He also describes the activity of the medium as an attempt to hold the interest of his or her audience, like a television channel will do to raise its ratings. In another research, Luhrmann (1994: 222) argues that people turn to modern magic, 'because they seek for powerful emotional and imagina-tive religious experience, but not for a religion per se'. Heelas (1993: 111) also refers to yuppie (like) people who consume a more Disney-esque – i.e. entertaining – spirituality. Some people will thus involve themselves in a cult simply for a good time.

The Grid

The first axis shows the level of organisation of the cults (Audience, Client and Movement) and describes the production of spiritualities in the cultic milieu. The second axis describes the reason behind the consumption of these spiritualities (illuminational, instrumental and entertainment). The cross-ing of the axes gives nine ideal types of cult which are at the meeting place between the production and consumption of spirituality, and which cover the whole cultic milieu. Spiritual actors of the alternative type mainly net-work among these ideal types and it will be impossible to associate any of them with strictly one ideal type.

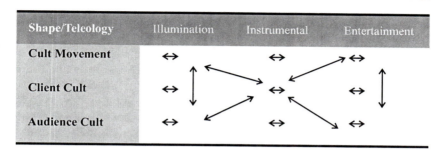

Figure 4 The cultic milieu and its affectual network.

Figure 4 describes what the cultic milieu is. It is an imaginary place of many cults with different organisations and teleologies which offers a networking space for spiritual actors. Some of them attract members, others clients or patients, and others, spectators. In this milieu, the many needs of seekers (e.g. finding spirituality, healing tools, having fun) are fulfilled; however, these needs vary. One person might visit a cult movement, e.g. the Theosophical Society, to develop his/her 'higher' self and another might just enjoy the talks and workshops that this society offers. On the other hand, someone on a 'deep' spiritual path might go to an audience cult to discover new techniques of enlightenment. Accordingly the nine types of cults portrayed within the grid demonstrate not only different reasons why spiritual actors use them, but also the plurality of actors from NRMs, New Age groups and alternative spiritualities evolving within the cultic milieu.

However, even if these actors could be described as being involved in a cultic milieu and its NRMs, they are not restricted to it. The cultic milieu, being underground, is not the only place seekers visit to enrich their spirituality. As explored in Possamai (2005a), some might have been born into a particular religion or have been atheistic, but none of them necessarily follow the steps of their parents. On their spiritual paths, after having rejected their spiritual establishment, many of my informants visited 'New Age' and non-'New Age' groups and often continue to experience tension and conflict within those groups because they want to find their own subjective religion. For example, it is not uncommon for people to go to a born-again Christian movement (not an element of a cultic milieu) first before being involved in these alternative spiritualities; and vice versa. Some spiritual actors sometimes go to church or are interested in Buddhism and visit its temples. They sometimes join a sect and stay in it for a few months. When one of my informants, Tom, said in his interview (Possamai 2005a) that the best way to learn spirituality was to 'get out into life and live it', he was referring to a life beyond the cultic milieu.

We could speculate on the recent change of the degree of activity of certain spiritual actors within this cultic milieu and its networks. And for this purpose, the work of Sutcliffe (2003) will be of help. In his analysis of these alternative spiritualities in the UK, he points out two different time periods. Before the 1970s, spiritual actors tended to be ascetic, puritanical and other-worldly, whereas afterwards, they became emotionally expressive, hedonistic and firmly this-worldly. Those before the 1970s tended to be subcultural pioneers and were serial seekers. Those who started to 'seek' in the 1970s were countercultural baby boomers and acted like multiple seekers. He explains these terms as such:

> A 'serial' seeker has changed religious or spiritual allegiance, typically more than once. Adhesion to each 'spiritual path' may last months, years or decades, and any number of sequential affiliations may be pursued over the course of a lifetime. [...] In contrast, multiple seeking proceeds multi-directionally and synchronically: an array of spiritual resources are exploited more or less simultaneously. Ideas, methods and techniques are decontextualised and reconstituted in new settings and adventurous juxtapositions (Sutcliffe 2003: 204).

Based on Sutcliffe's analysis, we could extrapolate that since the 1970s spiritual actors have increased their level of involvement in the cultic milieu as multiple seekers tend to move across networks faster than serial seekers. We could then conclude that the networking pace within this cultic milieu is more intense than it was before the 1970s.

Conclusion

This chapter has argued that although NRMs still exist today, they are not growing like they were in their heyday in the 1960–70s. During this time, people wanted to explore religion outside of the institutional type and explore various groups, but while some of them were fully integrated to everyday life, others wanted to remain on its margins. This push against authoritarianism was progressed even further by religious actors who did not want to belong to a religious institution or to a NRM, but who wanted to seek spiritualities strictly for themselves and by themselves. New Age spiritualities became stronger in its intensity in the 1980–90s; however, as seen with the cultic milieu and its affectual networks, people move quite easily from NRMs to New Age groups, and back and forth.

Because of the negative connotation that the phrase 'New Age' has received, people involved in alternative spiritualities would rather say that they are simply interested in the type of spiritualities seen in Chapter 4. In sociological terms, they would be of the technical spiritual type as they are not bounded by a belief in one specific religion and/or group. Within this cultic milieu, another type of religious group called neo-paganism which is not a NRM or a New Age group, but which shares many characteristics with them, evolves. The next chapter also explores the networking impact of this group, but in the light of consumer culture and cyber-space. Through this case study, this chapter advances the preceding discussions on consumerism and the Internet further.

13 Witchcraft, the Internet, and Consumerism

Introduction

In light of the structure of this book, one would expect a chapter on witch-craft to start with an account of *Charmed, Buffy the Vampire Slayer, Sabrina,* or *The Craft.* However, what I want to do instead is compare and contrast two recent representations of paganism and neo-paganism in works of popular culture where witchcraft is not central.

I have already presented *Sin City* from Frank Miller in Chapter 3. For this chapter, I want to present another of his works (with Lynn Varley), called *300,* also adapted for the big screen. There is a scene in which King Leonidas, the 480 BC Spartan King must convince the Ephors, priests to the old gods, to raise an army against the imminent invasion of the Persian King, Xerxes. To reach the temple, he has to travel away from the urban center of Sparta and climb a remote mountain. When he arrives at the temple, King Leonidas uses reason to convince the priests of the need to defend his country. The priests only want to trust the words of the Oracle, a young and beautiful woman who can predict the future when in a trance. In this instance, her message goes against the need to protect Sparta from the imminent invasion.

Oracles, although not necessarily young and beautiful, are quite common in ancient pagan societies and were often believed to have strong powers of divination even if sometimes their message was difficult to decipher (e.g. the myth of Oedipus). However, in this story based in ancient Greece, we are shown that the divine inspiration given by the Oracle is in conflict with the reason of King Leonidas. We also discover later in the story that the priests were paid by an envoy of Xerxes to make the Oracle say something to disadvantage the Spartans. This vision, needless to say, presents this type of pagan religious activity as superstitious and open to corruption.

In the movie *The Matrix,* Neo discovers that the world he has been living in is a pure illusion called the Matrix. He believed for most of his life that he was in the 20th century but discovered after meeting Morpheus that he was in fact living in the 24th century dominated by Artificial Intelligences. Although his body has been a prisoner of the 24th century, his mind has been living in a permanent dream within the 20th century. Once he realises that the Matrix is but an illusion, he is able to use the latent powers of one who is able to bend the 'reality' of his dream world. In this story, like King Leonidas, he has to meet with an Oracle to know his future.

This setting, when compared to the first story, is quite different. This Oracle is a postmodern representation of a pagan figure and lives in an apartment in a busy global city. She is not surrounded by a hierarchy of priests but by people with extraordinary inner powers such as telekinesis. When Neo finds the Oracle, he does not see a young and desirable woman, but a middle-aged African-American who looks like a sweet and caring mother figure. Although the movie is full of special effects, she does not go into a trance. She simply tells her prophesy without any props. Whereas the scene from *300* made the reader/viewer believe that nothing from the Oracle could be trusted, the scene from the Matrix shows that no money could corrupt this special talent.

Through these two examples from popular culture, I want to emphasise that the magic found in the hands of certain individuals, when mixed with money and special artifice, are perceived with superstition, whereas if it is from a down-to-earth person who has nothing to gain, this may become more believable for the reader/viewer.

People involved in neo-paganism and witchcraft deal with magical rituals. Some of these claim to be able to see the future by using of a pack of Tarot cards. However, one should note that the claim to see the future is not restricted to this religion. Depending on the setting in works of popular culture, magical abilities can be portrayed positively as has been done in *The Matrix*. And, as Berger and Ezzy (2007) argue, of all the new and revived minority religions of the last few years, Witchcraft has been one of the fastest growing thanks to its wide and positive representations in mainstream culture, such as in shows like *Charmed* and *Buffy*. This growth in popularity might have democratised people's access to this revived old religion but it has also inscribed it into consumer culture in an extended way. We will come back to this consumerist aspect after covering the basis of this religion and its place on the Internet.

It should be noted that neo-pagans evolve in the cultic milieu described in the previous chapter. This chapter adds to the model of the cultic milieu and its affinity networks from the last chapter by showing that groups and individuals on the Internet can also be part of this milieu as well. As the networking activities in the cultic milieu have grown in intensity since the 1970s with the appearance of multiple seekers, this same intensity has been again increased with the advent of cyber-religions.

Neo-paganism is one of many groups that are hard to sociologically typify. Although it has been associated with New Age spiritualities because of certain similarities, it is quite different, as I have argued in a previous work (Possamai 2005a). Further, neo-paganism has been poorly studied as a New Religious Movement as it is more of a conglomeration of covens, networks and individuals than a movement as such. Also, because it is presented as a revival of an old religion that predates Christianity, insiders find it hard to claim that it is new. Nevertheless, whatever their resemblances and differences with New Age spiritualities and New Religious Movements (which is beyond the scope of this chapter), neo-paganism can tell us more about the use of religion on the Internet and in consumer culture. This follows after a sociological exploration of this religion.

Neo-Paganism and Modern Occultism: The Invention of a Tradition

The Romantic period of the 19th century in Europe saw the revival of witchcraft. More specifically, in late 19th-century Germany, the pan-Germanic movement (*Volkstumbewegung*) had some strong connections with German paganism (Noll 1996). In Anglo-Saxon culture, it was claimed that neo-paganism was a nature religion that had continued through the Middle Ages into the present. As claimed by Charles Leland's *Aradia, or the Gospel of the Witches* (published in 1899 and one of the main sources of contemporary witchcraft), Aradia refers to the old religion (i.e. ancient paganism) whose chief deity is Diana. While staying in Italy in 1866, the American writer claimed to have found a manuscript containing the ancient secrets of Italian Witchcraft. Continuing on this line of thinking, Margaret Murnay published her *Witch-Cult in Western Europe* in 1921. In it, she claimed that this ancient religion had survived into the Middle Ages and at least into the early modern period. Ideas from these books continued for a while, and a number of historians and folklorists followed their lead, but they did not create the type of neo-paganism under study.

Neo-paganism must also be located in relation to modern occultism. By modern occultism I refer to the movement started by Eliphas Lévi (1810–75) in France as seen in Chapter 7. Many new initiatory orders were created from this movement, such as the Hermetic Order of the Golden Dawn by Samuel Mathers in the UK. Although today cabbalistic magic, high magic and occultism appear together with neo-paganism, this association with Occultism has caused dissension, however the link has always been there (Hume 1995: 6).

T.M. Luhrmann (1994: 41–44) traces the roots of neo-paganism to the occultist Hermetic Order of the Golden Dawn, an initiatory society founded in 1887. The Hermetic Order fragmented and one of the new groups, formed in 1922 by Dion Fortune, was called the Society of the Inner Light. This society influenced new groups coming out of the Occultist stream, but they were not yet identifiably neo-pagan. Luhrmann (1994) calls the groups influenced by Dion Fortune, the Western Mysteries groups, because they see themselves as the continuation of the mystery traditions of the west, e.g. Eleusis, Mithraism, and Druidism. According to Luhrmann, these groups demand far more intellectual engagement than witchcraft. The practitioners of Western Mysteries are grouped in fraternities or lodges. They tend to be Christian, often work on cabbalistic principles and appear to be a contemporary form of modern occultism.

From the 1940s, further fragmentations of occultism resulted in the emergence of exactly the sort of neo-paganism under investigation. Gerald Gardner, who met Aleister Crowley through two occultist groups, the Golden Dawn and the Ordo Templi Orientis (O.T.O., i.e. the Order of the Temple of the East) published fictitious ethnographies of contemporary witches mainly in the late 1940s and the 1950s. He claimed to have been initiated and had revitalised Witchcraft (i.e. neo-paganism) in the western world. For Gardner, witches had ancient knowledge and powers handed down through generations. This reinvention of tradition was claimed to be a revival of ancient nature religions. Witchcraft was organised in covens run by women called 'high priestesses' who presided over rites of initiation for new members of the coven. Gardner shifted the elitist ceremonial magic of the Golden Dawn to a more populist magic that could be performed by everyday people. He also reduced the Judeo-Christian flavour of the Golden Dawn and added neo-pagan ideas derived from the books of Murray and Leland. Prior to Gardner there was no religion called witchcraft (Hume 1997).

The practices and beliefs set by Gardner are sometimes called Gardnerianism and two main ideal types of coven exist: one which sees itself as direct apostolic succession from Gardner's original coven and one which claims a different origin but whose ideas are inspired from Gardner's work. Alex Sanders, and the Alexandrians, are an example of the latter case. Since Gardner, many specific neo-pagan organisations were (and are being) established, but few have endured more than a year or two.

These beliefs are strongly nature based, with the earth perceived as a living entity. Some neo-pagans even go further by arguing that the earth is conscious (i.e. the Gaia hypothesis). Also, as the divine is found in every aspect of nature, consequently the earth is perceived as sacred. Neo-pagans believe in living harmoniously with the earth and are often involved in ecological movements. Indeed, neo-paganism is sometimes referred to as the 'spiritual arm' or the 'spiritual side' of the ecology movement (Hume 1997).

Some pagan environmentalists have also become politically involved in the 'green' movement.

The Goddess is witchcraft's central concept and is used as a metaphor of nature. 'She is in the world, of the world, the very being of the world' (Luhrmann 1994: 49), and within this belief system, every woman can be a goddess, and every man can be a god.

At this stage, it is possible to elaborate the difference between Wiccans, neo-pagans and witches. Most witches are neo-pagans, but not all neo-pagans are witches. It could be argued that a witch is a neo-pagan who practices one or more varieties of magic on top of honouring Nature, whereas a neo-pagan who is not a witch, sees Nature as sacred but does not attempt to practice magic(k) to the same extent. Wiccans are witches, but not all witches are Wiccan. A Wiccan would be someone mainly following Gardnerianism or Alexandrianism (i.e. the system elaborated by Alex Sanders). Unfortunately, there is no certainty of the definitions of those terms because of the wide variety of interpretations among neo-pagans. As Hume (1997: 66–67) underlines from a pagan newsletter, 'Ask four witches to tell you what the Craft is about, and you'll get four different opinions'.

The Variety of Neo-Pagan Experiences

In neo-pagan discourses, there is a strong emphasis on rituals, initiation, Goddess and worship of the Goddess. The following case studies from Possamai (2005a) reflect the diversity of my informants' experience within, and interpretation of, neo-paganism (their use of vocabulary may be different from that of other neo-pagans).

Jennifer is involved in a neo-pagan group for women only, and she often goes to meetings where she engages in rituals with other members.

> The first group that I was in was a group of all women and we would meet weekly and have a circle and do a ritual in the circle. And that ritual would normally be for healing or something like that.

However, some rituals are for herself and performed by herself,

> I've got certain basic rituals that I use and certain basic acknowledgments that I always make. And I try to be really mindful when I make them. Not matter of fact or habitual, but are mindful. And I meditate in my room.

Steve (who already spoke in Chapter 7) is against any rigid structure in groups and is now involved in a networking form of neo-paganism: 'I've done rituals for years. You know for far too long. [...] the last 10 years, yeah I've been basically in occult groups.'

Tensions occurred in those groups and some people wanted to gain more power within the group. For Steve, too much politics was taking time away from the rituals of magic. So, he decided to leave: 'And quite frankly, I did less magic in [my group] than I actually did on my own [...]. So I've always found you get more magic from working by yourself than you do with groups.'

When I asked him if there was some difference between rituals performed in occultist and neo-pagan groups, he answered that

> the pagan movement is [...] quite different. It's totally unregulated. Like the magical pagan scenes are the same, although they'll pretend that they're not. Basically, in the long run and in substance [the techniques from occultist groups and neo-pagan groups are the same], in detail no. A lot of pagans find magic too complicated to learn. So they do it simply. They try and simplify it.

Judith was searching for an initiator in neo-paganism for many years. She never found her 'teacher' and became one herself.

> Wicca to me is a practising Pagan [that is engaging in Paganism using rituals]. It's this difference between a Catholic and a Catholic priest. So if you are a Pagan you are a Catholic. If you are a Wiccan you are a Catholic priest or a sister. That is the way I define it. That's not necessarily how other people use the words. But Wicca does imply that you are a practicing witch.

She also initiated Betty who refuses to be affiliated to any groups. She sees herself as doing rituals close to meditation.

> It is very easy to say that I'm in a coven and I worship. We get together every Tuesday night and we do this ritual and we're worshipping her [the Goddess]. I am a solitary practitioner who tends not to rely on ritual, so I guess I almost see my life as a celebration. I worship her every time [...]. And I guess I would say that I celebrate my relationship with her all the time.

These four case studies do not reflect the wide variety of accounts within the neo-pagan movement. There is not one authority or scripture for all neo-pagans. Indeed they borrow eclectically from many religious and philosophical traditions, and from popular culture as seen in Chapter 2. As a result, neo-paganism is diverse and not centralised. However, some core trends and beliefs are followed by neo-pagans, such as the belief in reincarnation, their ritual, the celebration of seasonal or pastoral changes, and the desire to develop a neo-pagan community.

As touched upon in the extracts above, some neo-pagans are interested in this spirituality without wanting to join a group. Now that neo-pagan books and many Internet sites are widely available, it becomes easy for someone to follow a ritual of self-initiation rather than being under the guidance of a recognised leader. According to Berger *et al.* (2003) there will be more of these neo-pagan individual practitioners in the United States than those who practice in groups. Cowan (2005) points out the difference between those who are trained by a coven or by any other ritual group, and those who are self-initiated and autodidactic. Because these solitaires are sometimes regarded as 'second-class Pagans' by more traditionalist neo-pagans who work off-line, they would benefit most from the Internet; as they would avoid any off-line stigmatisation. We will come back to this notion of the Internet after exploring the more traditional practice of off-line neo-paganism.

Neo-Pagan Rituals and Covens

Not all neo-pagan groups agree on each ritual. Practices vary from an elaborate ceremony to a simple ritual or a simple meditation accomplished by one neo-pagan. Generally, the common practice is to consecrate a sacred space symbolised by a 'circle', and then worship the Goddesses and/or Gods within it. Magic can also be performed within the same circle, which can be drawn in city apartments, in suburban backyards and in country places.

Certain tools are used for these rituals, such as an athame, i.e. a ceremonial knife for casting a circle. Another element of the ritual is the altar which denotes the Aristotelian Elements: Earth, Air, Fire and Water. A pentagram or pentacle is also often used to symbolise Earth, whereas a thurible (or censer) represents Air, a candle or small pot of fire Fire, and a chalice of water symbolises the element Water. Often the witch will own his or her Book of Shadows, which is the witch's handwritten book of spells and magical information.

These tools (and others not mentioned) are part of a complete symbolic system which provides the neo-pagan with a 'map' for entry into other psychic realms and to reach another state of consciousness.

Within the sacred circle, two main activities occur: 1) the solar celebration; and 2) the practice of magic which coincides with the phases of the moon.

1) Wiccans and some other neo-pagans celebrate eight major festivals or sabbats each year; these are religious ceremony deriving from ancient European festivals celebrating seasonal or pastoral changes. They are also called solar celebrations, and are symbolised as the 'Wheel of the Year'.

Traditional dates taken from the northern hemisphere can be considered inadequate for the southern hemisphere. Some neo-pagan groups will keep the original dates, and others have adapted them for the Australian and New-Zealander context (Hume 1999). Table 6 presents a list of these celebrations.

Table 6 Solar Celebrations – Sabbats.

Nth Hemisphere	Sth Hemisphere	Exoteric Name	Esoteric Name
October 31	April 30	November Eve	Samhain
December 21	June 21	Winter Solstice	Yule
February 2	August 1	February Eve	Imbolc (Oimelc) or Brigid
March 21	September 21	Vernal Equinox	Ostara
April 30	October 31	May Eve	Beltaine
June 21	December 21	Summer Solstice	Litha or Midsummer
August 1	February 2	August Eve	Lughnasadh or Lammas
September 21	March 21	Autumnal Equinox	Mabon or Harvest Home

The two most important sabbats are Samhain (the neo-pagan New Year's eve: a night in which the barriers between the worlds of life and death are uncertain and in which the ancestors are supposed to walk among the living) and Beltaine (a fertility festival, i.e. the birth of summer).

2) There are also lunar celebrations which are called esbats, and these are held 13 times per year during the full moon. Magic is often practised during this time for psychic healing sessions, for focusing and directing energy to achieve some results, and for developing the spirituality of its practitioners.

At the end of the Sabbat and Esbat, people usually share food and drinks, exchange story-tellings, bless the goddess and/or god, and open the circle, allowing the space not to be consecrated any longer.

These covens' practices are usually based on the teachings of the pagan revivalist, Gardner and Sanders, with one of the main rituals being the casting of the circle as illustrated by Jayakar (quoted in Jayran in Harvey and Hardman 1996: 209):

> She faces East, saying 'I call the power of Air, and intelligence', lighting the yellow candle. She then faces front and South, saying 'I call the power of Fire, and of the will', lighting the red candle. She then faces West, saying 'I call the power of Water, and of emotions', lighting the blue candle. She then turns behind her to the North, saying 'I call the power of Earth, and of the body', lighting the green candle. She raises her wand to point upwards saying 'The circle is cast. I am between the worlds, beyond the bounds of time, where night and day, birth and death, joy and sorrow, meet as one'.

Covens are organised to celebrate the different pagan celebrations, to perform magic and to exchange knowledge of the Craft. It is usually a group of witches who practice worship together. All covens are totally autonomous and are lead by a High Priest and High Priestess. Covens are traditionally convened at full moon and there is no financial burden on members, who collectively contribute towards the purchase of magical equipment and food, and bring their own tools. Coven organisation is based upon the initiatory forms of modern occultism, and there are three levels of initiations.

The first initiation invites the neophyte to enter the inner-circle of the coven. He or she learns the basis of witchcraft such as casting the circle, setting up the altar, and other basic principles.

For the second initiation, the novice has achieved a higher knowledge of the Craft and is expected to be able to teach a first-degree novice. Before reaching the third level, Wiccans need to choose a neo-pagan of the opposite sex with whom they will form a partnership, which can be symbolic or actual.

For the third degree, it is expected that knowledge of the Craft, i.e. understanding perfectly the different symbols and tools which provide the third degree neo-pagan with a 'map' for entry into other psychic realms, and being able to reach another state of consciousness has been mastered. This level also involves the Great Rite or sacred marriage. This can be enacted by a couple (formed during the second level) as an act of (physical or symbolic) ritual sex. The couple takes on the role of the Goddess and God and performs a sexual union (physical or symbolic) with the deity.

As a New South Wales witch revealed to Lynne Hume (1997: 135):

> My Great Rite was, for me, a most holy and sacred experience. It all has to do with will, intent, and the correct use of energy. It has to do with the flow and use of energy. Physicality is only a very small part. Sex, as sacred sex, creates a lot of energy but is very misunderstood. What occurs in the Great Rite is the persons engaging in sex become the God and the Goddess – if it is done properly. You have to think that inside the person is the God/Goddess. You don't see it as being unfaithful to your own partner or as having merely physical sex. There is a great misuse of the Great Rite, depending on the integrity of the coven.

In those covens, there are often a Craft High Priest and High Priestess who have reached the third degree and who lead the coven.

Cyber-Covens

Since these rituals from the traditional Wicca movement are available on the Internet, it is easy for someone to initiate himself or herself to this religion without finding a mentor. The knowledge of this religion does not appear to be controlled on the Internet by a religious hierarchy. We find here similarities with what happened to esotericism as discussed in Chapter 7.

As Cowan (2005) and Krüger (2005) underline, people who in the past might have been reluctant or afraid to find a coven to gain initiation into neo-paganism can now find various Internet sites with rites for self-initiations and chat rooms to discuss the craft. In these forums and chat rooms, people do not have to show their face and can use a pseudonym. They can even pretend they are from another gender and age. Some might even have more than one cyber-name. The same applies to the chat rooms on Jediism and Matrixism as these hyper-real religions have been able to develop through the fact that people can play with their identities and not suffer from the stigma attached to following a 'nerdy' or 'wacky' religion. Further, people participating in the Cyber-Covens without any fear of off-line discrimination or harassment do not even have to be in the same geographical place.

As Krüger (2005: 5) quotes the insider, Isamara:

> Cyber Wicca is less of a tradition, than in the traditional sense of the craft. The Internet is the ultra-modern age of Wicca, and more and more people are turning to it in their quest to practice The Old Religion. It is the ideal medium for the solitary or eclectic practitioner, to learn from and communicate with others in the craft. It is also ideal for those people unable to meet with and practice with others, and indeed for those who for various reasons, need to remain anonymous. There are now many groups on the Internet that take part in live play and group rituals. This is accomplished through synchronized live imagery and the typed word. When you think about it, magic holds no boundaries; a person practising in England using the same tools, method, and intent, synchronized with a person in America, should and now do, work together in common goal.

Teen Witches tend to learn this religion though books and the Internet, and seem to be quite active in this cyber-space. According to Berger and Ezzy (2007), these young people not only access this religion in cyber-space without fear of harassment but they are also building a sense of belonging with other young witches from all over the world. It appears that a sense of religious community can also be created among people who practise their religion in front of a computer.

This cyber-space adds another dimension to the cultic milieu and its affinity networks seen in the previous chapter. As there are nine ideal types of off-line cultic activities as represented in Figure 7 (see Chapter 12), there would be another layer with another set of nine on-line types of activities where people go back and forth between these on and off-line types.

In these on-line activities, it appears that there is no institution that controls religious knowledge. Indeed, within the rules of communication for respective forums, everyone is allowed to express his or her thoughts and ideas on the craft. One would thus think that there is no hierarchy in cyber-covens, however the reality is different. Krüger (2005) explored a popular on-line forum and discovered that people have ranks, which were reflected by symbols of plastic, silver or golden cauldrons. These individuals were thus integrated into this cyber-coven in a way similar to an off-line coven which has a graduation system through its levels of initiations. As Krüger (2005: 7) states, 'there is no single authority controlling the ritual discourse, but each discussion forum has a complex hierarchy of authority and discursive agency'.

Cowan (2005) recently did an excellent analysis regarding the place of neo-paganism on the Internet and found that although there are many sites and chat rooms, of the many groups that start up, only a few seem to succeed. The life of these cyber-covens can thus be ephemeral. Those who are interested in this on-line religion do not necessarily remain active for a long time. Some might create a new identity and surf sites for some time, but then no longer bother with on-line and/or off-line neo-paganism. Others might be very active in the neo-pagan off-line world and only dabble a little in the on-line world. There are indeed more serious on-line neo-pagans who will dedicate much of their time to their religion, but it does not mean that they will do this for ever. Some might be exclusively on-line neo-pagans and will never associate their pagan on-line identity with their everyday life off-line one. On the other hand, someone starting neo-paganism on-line might slowly become confident with his or her new religious identity and come out in the off-line world with the same identity developed on the Internet. This confidence could be created by a 'sense of belonging' to a cyber-community which can be strong according to Berger and Ezzy (2007).

These cyber-covens are not only 'surfed' for their chat rooms and forums, but also for their on-line rituals. After extensive on-line research, Cowan (2005: 127) lists three interrelated sets of data:

> Texts of off-line rituals that have been uploaded for online reference (i.e., as part of an Internet Book of Shadows), texts of proposed online rituals (that may or may not ever have been performed), and, most important to this discussion, the chat logs (transcripts) of online rituals that have taken place and have been uploaded for archival or illustrative purposes.

In terms of content, the on-line rituals are not much different from the off-line ones. These rituals are mainly found in chat rooms where only a few are invited at a certain time to perform rituals. These are performed live and not many of them are posted on the Internet for posterity. As an illustration, I am again quoting from Cowan (2005: 133–34) who transcribed parts of an on-line ritual:

> .Elspeth> Did anyone bring food they want blessed? :)

> . Terri> no..but I brought a doll.

> .Elspeth> ::watching ghost play with fire::

.Elspeth> Want a blessing, Terri?

.Phyllis> me too!

.Terri> please, Elspeth.

.Terri> ::holds up the doll::

.Randall> ::Watches Elspeth watching Ghost::

.Elspeth>

.Dianne> brought my self

.Elspeth>

.Jill> I have some new crystals=)

.Tina> ::holds up Mama doll::

.Elspeth> ::focusing::

.Elspeth>

.HALLIEJEAN> I'll observe candle

.Phyllis> :holds up Mama doll::

.Jill> can I hold up the crystals?

.Elspeth> Sure. :)

.Elspeth>

.Jill> ::thanks::

.Elspeth> By those who watch... those who guide ... those who guard

.Tina> ::and by my crystals::

.Elspeth> By all the deity known and unknown...

.Elspeth> Send your blessings to these items

.Elspeth> Make them tools of wisdom for us

.Elspeth> That they may aid us on the Path You have sent us on

.Elspeth> ::sketching a symbol of blessing and sending forth::

.Terri> ::smiles::

.Elspeth> :)

.Terri> I felt that. :)

. Tina> :)

.Elspeth> You should have ... Ghost was helping :) ...

.Ann> It hit... felt it in the back of my skull. Thank you. :) ...

.Tina > I felt a warmth in my arms.

The Internet can not only be a place where people network for their religion and in which people practice some rituals on-line, it is also a space where neo-pagan commodities are on offer as the next section covers.

Witchcraft and Consumer Culture

Because of the greater availability of information about neo-paganism on the Internet and in mainstream bookshops, it can easily be argued that this religion has been further democratised. However, as Berger and Ezzy (2007: 32) point out, this has also encouraged the commercialisation of this religion through buying books and religious paraphernalia in shops or on-line.

For example, Ezzy (2003) discovers that spell books published since the late 1980s–early 1990s are aimed at individuals rather than groups, and their ritual is less demanding than what is practised in covens. They are presented in a more simplified and accessible way for the non-initiated who wants to discover more about this religion. Before that time, spell books tended to be aimed at coven-based practitioners and were prepared by small publishing houses. As a consequence of this simplification and individualisation of the spell books, access to this religion has been democratised. This led this religion to be inscribed in consumer culture, as people need to buy items to join rather than be initiated by someone as part of a small group. Practising witchcraft in a coven, Ezzy (2001) argues, does not necessarily involve payment for learning or for participating in this religion.

Finding differences of practice between earlier and recent forms of neo-paganism is not the end of Ezzy's research as he wonders about the various levels of involvement of contemporary witches in consumer culture. For this project, he analysed various Internet sites of relatively famous Australian witches. He finds for example that the site of Deborah Gray would fit with what he calls 'Commodified Witchcraft' because the site promotes hedonistic consumption rather than information and/or tools for self-growth. As he (Ezzy 2001: 37) quotes from her site:

> Goddess of Love Potion. Attract Your Soulmate! … Shrouded in mystery for thousands of years, its magickal powers of seduction are now finally revealed by Australia's 'White Witch', Deborah Gray, who offers it to all those wishing to attract their soulmate, rediscover their true love, and bring passion and desire into their lives.

This site does not give any advice on how neo-paganism can be used to address any contemporary problems from the point-of-view of the religion but offers consumption as a way to deal with these problems. As a contrast, the non-commercial site of the singer Wendy Rule focuses more on developing a self-understanding of her religion rather than on the promotion of commodities. It also engages in ethical and political commentary which is missing from 'commodified witchraft' web sites. This leads Ezzy (2001: 41) to conclude

> Although there is a wide spectrum in between, I characterised commodified Witchcraft as Witchcraft in which the majority of exchanges are commodity exchanges. In contrast, Wicca is characterised by the exchange of both knowledge and goods as gifts, external to the market. These gifts are embedded in familial-like social relationships of mutual and moral obligations. In contrast, commodified Witchcraft involves the exchange of commodities embedded in social relationships that are dissolved by the exchange, with no ongoing obligations.

Ezzy's (2001) research is quite clear in pointing out that even if religion is immersed in consumer culture, there can be religious sub-divisions with regard to the level of its involvement.

Conclusion

This chapter recapitulates many of the findings that this book has identified. By using the case study of Witchcraft, not only did I present a growing religion in the west, but also described the many subtleties that this religion creates when brought onto the Internet and into consumer culture. It is also a religion that is growing thanks to the positive support it finds through works of popular culture, although it has to be noted that not all representations are positive. The next chapter is of another nature. Whereas we have until this stage dealt with a sociology of religion that reflects the lived experiences of generations X and Y, the next deals with a sociology of sociologists of religion. It asks what it means for sociologists of religion to do their job.

Conclusion: What Do Sociologists of Religion in Academia Do Apart from Teaching and Marking? Their Work as Intellectuals

Introduction

In the movie *The Exorcism of Emily Rose*, the Catholic priest who conducted a failed exorcism on Emily is brought to a tribunal. He is accused of not having given her proper care which led to her death. Strong debates happen during the court case between medical doctors who claim that the victim needed a medical treatment to survive and Emily's family and friends who witnessed what they believed was a *bona fide* possession. The debate reaches an impasse because no dialogue exists between these two forms of discourses. One is strongly secular and does not take into account religious/superstitious beliefs. The other is religious and puts faith above science. However, the defence lawyer manages to move the debate further by inviting an anthropologist of religion as an expert witness. This anthropologist has witnessed many cases of exorcism in her fieldwork and is able to give an account that stands between these two opposite discourses. She does not claim that the devil exists and that religious actions should be performed to stop him (or her). She explains that some people believe strongly in him (or her) and that religious rituals are put into place for those who have this religious conviction to free the possessed from such an evil spirit. These rituals can also be interpreted as a form of therapy that allows the person who thinks he or she is possessed to be cured from what could be seen as a form of mental illness. This expert witness provides a key account in the debate by underlining that rituals are a valid form of therapy and that the use of medical drugs is not always necessary to provide treatment.

In this story, we have a person who has studied religious groups quite extensively and is recognised as an expert who can give a rational and objective account in a court of law. If I might equate for this chapter anthropologists with sociologists, I would like to emphasise through this example that not all sociologists of religion are limited to teaching and researching religion within the walls of academia. Some are involved outside of these walls and have been called as expert witnesses in cases such as those from the Church of Scientology and the Children of God to give an account that is not biased in terms of religious and anti-religious beliefs. Other sociologists of religion have been called by the police and various intelligence departments to give account of some religious groups and religious phenomena to prevent the misuse of state executive powers upon certain forms of belief.

Some, on top of being academics, are consultants for various state departments and organisations and/or board members of associations dealing with religious issues. Others are involved in inter-faith programs and promote the celebration of religious diversity through their activities. Some are coming from within a specific religious group, and inform their group about the large sociocultural changes in society that affect their members. For example, some Christian sociologists who are also priests analyse the decline of church attendance and might try to inform their group about ways to adapt to wider sociocultural changes.

Some other sociologists of religion are atheists who underline that the celebration of religious diversity also includes atheism, and that the best protection for religious diversity is a secular state that does not favour any religion above another. Many sociologists of religion are involved in the media and are often asked by radio, television and print journalists to comment on religion in our society.

These sociologists are intellectuals, and as such are instrumental in promoting ideas in our society. However, before going further into this issue, one must first answer a few questions such as, what are intellectuals? And more specifically, what are intellectuals who study religion? What is their role in this diversified, multi-ethnic, multi-creed, and postmodern world?

This chapter deals first with what intellectuals are from a sociological perspective. This perspective has been quite secularist in its approach, and this chapter aims at bridging the gap between the sociological literature and the field of religious studies. The second part focuses on the role of these intellectuals from within this field of research and action, that is, as sociologists of religion. I argue that whatever the work that they do, be it discreet or public, it has a great importance in the process of our civilization. By this, I make reference to the work of Norbert Elias (1995) on the process of civilization, which suggests that there is no such thing as a perfect society, but only one which can be better than what it was in the past. Paradoxically, I will argue, following the work of Habermas and Eisenstadt, that we should strive towards a new project of modernity which includes a more humane and less calculative approach and that religion, among other factors, can bring this process of civilization.

What Are the Intellectuals?

Finding the perfect definition of an intellectual is problematic. It is already a challenge for intellectuals to reach a consensus about concepts such as postmodern, late modern, high modern, post-fordism, post-industrialism. This challenge gets even worst when intellectuals are attempting a consensus about a definition of themselves, especially when their intellectual background can be so diversified. Some of them follow universal principles such as Marxism and functionalism, others are post-modern, post-colonialist, feminist, etc. The problem with such a defining task is that any attempt to define intellectuals is an attempt at self-definition and involves a personal story and agenda. Fortunately, we can find some broad definitions in the literature that might be of help. At a later stage, I will apply them to a case study on New Religious Movements before exploring the role of intellectuals in today's society.

Intellectuals, depending on the definition, have been present in our society for a very long time. One only needs to read Max Weber's (1995) opus on *The Sociology of Religion* to remember that all of the great religious doctrines of Asia are the creation of intellectuals, and that, for example, Manicheanism and Gnosticism, the salvation religions of the Near East, are specifically religions of intellectuals. By comparison, the place of intellectuals, especially lay intellectuals, has not had such a profound importance within the development of mainstream Christianity in the West. We could, of course, discuss the history of intellectuals for a long time in this book, however, I would like to move now to the 19th century and to the birth of the modern intellectual – the type of intellectual that we are familiar with today.

This birth came with the Dreyfus affair in 1898 which we have already mentioned in Chapter 11. Dreyfus was a captain of the French army who was wrongly accused of revealing secret French documents to the Prussians. The French army, at this time, was the stronghold of monarchists and Catholics and was anti-Semitic. Even if Dreyfus saw himself as French, his heritage was Jewish. Because of his background he was used as a scapegoat and sentenced to degradation and deportation for life. He was sent to Devils Island, off the coast of French Guiana, into solitary confinement. Novelists such as Zola, who wrote the famous 'J'accuse', journalists, poets, artists and university professors expressed their discontent with this case and came to see themselves as intellectuals in their fight against prejudice and injustice. It is claimed that the word 'intellectual' was first used with the Dreyfus case when the politician Clemenceau employed it to describe this group. They were called the *Dreyfusard*, and their purpose was demonstrated with the syllogism: 'They complain, therefore they exist'. From this heated event, intellectuals realised their strength and their ability to develop common interests that set them apart from other groups in society. In other words, they saw themselves as a class in themselves who could question traditional values in the name of reason and progress, and thus carry the ideal of the Enlightenment.

Later, social theorists such as Karl Mannheim (1991) and Antonio Gramsci (1971) criticised this approach towards intellectual class consciousness. Mannheim stated that intellectuals transcend class to a certain degree because of their need for a broader point-of-view and their interest in seeing the whole of the social and political structure. The Italian Marxist Gramsci, in his prison notebooks, believed that intellectuals are not a class in themselves, but that they are bound to their class of origin. Intellectuals cannot form a single group, but are divided into sub-groups that emerge from and serve specific classes. The bourgeoisie produces its intellectuals, as does the proletariat. Intellectuals, for Gramsci, thus work for the interest of their own class and are called within this perspective 'organic intellectuals'. He also viewed the role of working class intellectuals as having a key role within the Marxist revolutionary movement.

These intellectuals, be they a class in themselves or not, were supporting the universal ideas of reason and progress that had to be spread all over the world. However, today intellectuals in this postmodern society can no longer offer critiques or a vision that can encompass all or many strata of a specific society. To understand this, Zygmunt Bauman's (1992a; 1992b) work is very helpful. He differentiates between two types of intellectuals that he calls legislators and interpreters. For Bauman, intellectuals tended to be legislators during modernity. And when they made authoritative statements, they were heard. These intellectuals had better access to knowledge than non-intellectuals and because of this, had the right and the social duty to create, support or oppose beliefs and opinions held in various sections of a specific society.

Now in post-modernity, as knowledge has become fragmented, intellectuals can no longer make decisions for others. They can only be mediators in communication between different autonomous groups. The intellectual of today can only interpret his or her knowledge of one specific group, of one specific culture, and/or of one specific field of knowledge and speak about it as an expert. Their role now is to speak on behalf of a particular group, culture, or discipline in a lay language that can be understood by the public and/or by other intellectuals who are experts in other fields of knowledge. Even if Bauman argues that intellectuals must maintain their role as both legislators and interpreters, the trend of today is that they are mainly interpreters. If the legislator was a universal intellectual, the interpreter is specific to one field or group.

In the field of study of religion, an intellectual would be an interpreter of a specific religious group and/or religion and will make this knowledge available to the public, other religions, other intellectuals from within the field of religious studies, and other intellectuals from outside of this field. The intellectual, in this sense, can be a religious or a layperson, but needs to interpret his or her knowledge to other people and groups outside the specific religious group. Two perfect epitomes of this intellectual would be those who are involved in interfaith programs and those who research in the field of religion and share their findings at conferences and media programs.

Being an interpreter does not mean that the intellectual should just reveal his or her knowledge only. There is more to it in this postmodern age. Indeed, for Chomsky (1997), the responsibility of the intellectual is to tell the truth. It is a moral imperative for them to find out and transmit the truth about issues that matter to the right audience. And I believe that if sociologists of religion are interpreters, they need to take this up and be true about religion, be true about its fascinating side, and be true about its fearful side as well.

There are also other responsibilities for the intellectual. For the late Palestinian, Said (1994), intellectuals must denounce corruption, defend the weak, defy imperfect or oppressive authority. Their purpose is to advance human freedom and knowledge. For him, the true intellectual is always an outsider: one who lives at the margins of society in a kind of self-imposed exile. Truth can only be reached by the intellectual if he or she stands apart from a specific society and judges it from the outside. From this, it would be quite interesting to debate whether one can be an intellectual of his or her own religion. The answer is unfortunately beyond the scope of this book.

Intellectuals in the Field of New Religious Movements (NRMs): A Case Study

In the field of study of NRMs, there is a tension between researchers and social activists, which could be crudely generalised as the tension between cult apologists and anti-cultists, also called cult bashers. A cult apologist would be a person who considers the 'conversion' techniques used by these groups to be no different than those employed by more respectable groups. This person will refer to these religious groups as NRMs and/or religious minorities and will tend to be in dialogue with insiders. An anti-cultist would be a person who tends to express the danger of 'cult indoctrination' via so-called 'brainwashing techniques' and lobby for social, political, and legal injunctions against cults. This person would tend to be in contact with the family of a 'cult member' and with apostates. Within this counter-cult group, four categories can be distinguished (Chryssides 1999: 345): 1) secular counter-cult organisations; 2) Christian evangelical counter-cult groups; 3) NRM-specific groups – e.g. Counter Scientology Europe; and 4) organisations that offer the services of deprogrammers – that is, services to abduct members by the use of force and to restore them to 'normality'. These organisations frequently co-operate with each other and network in complex ways.

This field of research is vast and polemic, however we could understand and refine this debate with what we have discovered about the intellectual of the religious. All involved in this field, be they journalists, social workers and social activists, psychologists, sociologists, or NRM's scholarly insiders,[1] are intellectuals but not of the same type. Anti-cultists tend to lump all new religious movements in the same category. They view them as either danger-ous or potentially dangerous. For apologists, there is only a small minority of such groups that are destructive and these have been extensively covered in the media. One would find it hard to forget the mass killing at Waco (1993), in the Order of the Solar Temple (1994), in the Aum Shinri-kyo (1995), in the Heaven's Gate (1997) group, and in the movement for the Restoration of the Ten Commandments of God in Uganda (2000). However, cult apologists tend to make a distinction between specific groups and do not portray all of them as dangerous.

I am tempted to equate anti-cultists with legislators who seek to apply universalistic principles and who aim to influence the public at large. Their definition of cult tends to refer to religious groups with an authoritarian lead-ership which suppress rational thought, organise deceptive recruitment tech-niques, use coercive mind control and isolate members from conventional society and former relationships; and this definition tends to be wrongly applied to all of these minority groups. On the other hand, we could argue that cult apologists would be more interpreters as their work aims at expos-ing what specific NRMs are preaching to the public and to other intellectuals.

We should not forget, even if intellectuals are less heard than in the past, that legislators had great influence over the drafting of the French anti-cult legislation in 2001 which undermined fundamental principles of religious freedom and diversity, not to mention basic principles of human rights. On May 30, 2001, French anti-cult legislation passed through the parliament. Its initial draft called for specific criteria for the dissolution of a 'cult' such as repeated complaints from families against the 'cult'. The legislation also called for prohibition of 'cults' near 'vulnerable' areas (e.g. schools and hospitals), no renaming or reorganisation of dissolved 'cults'; and recognition of the new crime of 'mental manipulation' (i.e. brainwashing). This draft was aimed at providing the state with the means to dissolve any 'cult' that it chose. Following objections by the mainline churches, the initial idea for an

administrative dissolution of 'cults' has been abandoned, and the government may not act so freely or arbitrarily as first expected (Possamai and Lee
2004). This French case in which the anti-cultists has a strong voice as intellectuals over cult apologists is not the only one. In the Post-Aum[2] era in
Japan, the voices of scholars who could offer informed opinions were also
strongly muted in the public sphere by anti-cultists (Reader 2001). Many
other cases could be highlighted in this chapter, however I would like to
move now to the role of the intellectual.

What is the Role of Intellectuals in the Field of Religious Studies?

Habermas' work is vast and complex. For this reason, this section only con-
centrates on one of his key concepts: that of the colonisation of the lifeworld
(Lebenswelt). The systematic colonisation of the lifeworld refers to the re-
placement of the mechanisms of social coordination by those of political and
financial accumulation.

I first deal with his concept of the lifeworld, which can be understood as
everyday life, and will come back to his concept of colonisation. The author
sees in this lifeworld a field where culture, personality, meaning and symbols
meet and where civil society would more or less be active. This lifeworld
would form the basis for communication, that is, communicative action. By
this, Habermas makes reference to individuals' linguistic interaction such as
debates in newspapers and television, conferences, café discussions, etc.
Communicative interactions allow individuals to reach a level of knowledge
of the 'other', that is, an intersubjective recognition. This would enable the
establishment of cooperation between individuals, which is not based on the
maximisation of profit as found in our current consumer society, but that is,
on the contrary, aimed at developing debate about questions dealing with
the quality of life and opening dialogue with others. Thanks to this, human
beings humanise themselves through their interaction with other individuals.
Through this, the plurality of values or the plurality of the visions from our
world is linked to an ethic based on an understanding between movements
and groups, which makes possible the constant renewal of social consensus.

In contrast to communicative action, instrumental reason operates through
a system; the system being the field where we find the instrumental action
of multinational corporations and the political power. When this instrumental
reason spreads through the lifeworld, Habermas makes reference to an effect of colonisation which is growing rapidly in this period of late capitalism
thus reducing all expression of communicative action. By this, he argues that

methods used for making profit are used extensively for the sake of efficiency, even within civil society. This leads to the fetishisation of growth *per se*, and its maximisation process treats other values such as human nature and traditions instrumentally (see similar argument from Castoriadis [1992] in Chapter 5). The effect of corruption from economic factors on the democratic political process, the obscure mixture between news information and entertainment, the transformation of students into consumers and teachers into producers, and the passive civil engagement of westerners, are a few examples of the way the colonisation of the lifeworld happens. The lifeworld tends to be reduced while the system spreads its tentacles. This colonisation of instrumental reason, aimed at the accumulation of profit, increasingly diminishes the strength of communicative action in the lifeworld. The result of this process is a permanent tension between the lifeworld and the system, which threatens the very basis of the Enlightenment project.

In regards to religion, Habermas saw in it an agent of communicative action that was not necessarily taking part in the emancipation project carried by enlightened philosophers. He also thought in the 1980s that religions were agents of legitimation for state intervention in civil society. Now, he admits himself that religions can also be agents of contestation and can offer new ways of being that are not calculative (Habermas 2002: 79). For example, Wallace (2003) uses Habermas' theory to understand Islamic fundamentalism. He demonstrates that the colonisation of the lifeworld can only be in antagonism with religious sensibilities. This antagonism can even exacerbate the conflict with the colonisation forces and provoke a deep religious reaction. From this, Wallace claims that the fundamentalist branches of Islam are in a structural tension with the system.

So, in western societies, what would the role of an intellectual of the religious be in this grand theory? Coming back to our definition of this intellectual as an interpreter, he or she will actively participate in communicative action by various means. He or she could be involved in inter-faith dialogue and thus promote the understanding of various religious groups. He or she can be involved in the research of these groups and transmit the findings in conferences, journals, and books. These actions do not necessarily have to reach the larger community in order to work. All written and oral activities can take part in this communicative action. This action, for Habermas, is fundamental for today's reworked project of modernity. And indeed in a more recent article of his (Habermas 2006), he writes about the challenges that religious citizens have in letting the rest of their society know what their belief systems are about and how they work in a multi-cultural society. Secular citizens also need to develop their understanding of people's faith and to express their right for atheism without undermining religious people in a multi-creed society. Sociologists of religions, as intellectuals of the interpretative type, can work at being a bridge between religious groups, and between religious and secular groups.

We cannot deny that the initial project of modernity has failed, as previously outlined in Chapter 5. However, we should not throw out the baby with the bath water. Great ideals were created, and if the lifeworld had not been so colonised, social outcomes might have been different. One way to create a balance and to make the dream of '(human) reason' come true is by promoting communicative action in a new project of modernity.

Perhaps a way forward for working on the process of civilization is to allow religious people, among a multitude of other social actors, to be part of the Enlightenment project. We can still strive towards the development of reason and progress, but a reason which is not instrumental only and a progress which is not purely material and quantitative. Religion and spirituality, among other factors, could help us turn this reason towards a more human aspect and allow for progress towards a more equitable and qualitative output; a value-oriented output that promotes human rights, human solidarity, justice, and spirituality and that opposes religious extremism and empty secularism. Of course, by allowing such a fusion between faith and reason in a new civilization project that would fit with our multi-cultural and multi-faith world, we should bear in mind that some religious groups and sub-groups are better equipped than others. We should also be careful that in a world in which we can see that anything goes, some religious groups make exclusivist truth claims, use violent means, and are intolerant toward others, and these are not be conducive to this new project of modernity. We should also note that if western societies are moving towards being post-secular, it does not mean they should become anti-secular.

Conclusion

What I am writing about is not the ideal project; it is just a project upon which intellectuals of the religious, such as sociologists of religion like myself, are working hard on. It fits with the creation of a new modern project as part of the multiple modernity thesis. The large majority of these sociologists is involved in inter-faith programs and in the study of religions and is thus already taking part in communicative action. On top of this, with their social and research activities, we are directly or indirectly involved in building a dialogue between religious groups and between religious groups and the secular. By being an intellectual of the interpretative type, sociologists of religion can transmit their knowledge to others. As intellectuals they can take part in the type of communicative action that is conducive to making this fusion between faith and reason possible, and they have to constantly make sure that this ideal does not become perverted or short sighted.

Notes

1. Beckford (2003: 153) makes a reference to some 'organic intellectuals' from ISKCON and the Soka Gakkai who have established their own institutions of higher education where research is being developed and contacts are made with academic researchers.
2. That is the period after 1995 when Aum Shinrikyo led a sarin attack on the Tokyo underground which caused the hospitalisation of thousands of people.

References

AAP (2002). 'Is Jedi now a religion?' *The Age,* August 27.

Afshar, H. (2007). 'Muslim Women and Feminisms: Illustrations from the Iranian Experience'. *Social Compass,* 54 (3), 419–34.

Agence France-Press (2002). 'Jedi census ploy a success'. *The Australian IT,* August 28.

Anonymous (2002). 'Bad Movie Hurts Jedi Down Under'. http://wired-vig.wired.com/news/print/0,1294,54851,00.html,

——— (2003). 'Census return of the Jedi'. (13/02/2003), http://news.bbc.co.uk/1/hi/uk/2757067.stm,

Bader-Saye, S. (2006). 'Improvising Church: An Introduction to the Emerging Church Conversation'. *International Journal for the Study of the Christian Church* 6(1), 12–23.

Bailey, F. (1974). *Changing Esoteric Values.* New York: Lucis Publishing Company.

Balch, R., and Taylor, D. (1978). 'Seekers and Saucers: The Role of the Cultic Milieu in Joining a UFO Cult'. In T. Richardson (ed.), *Conversion Carrers: In and Out of New Religions,* 43–64. Sage Contemporary Social Sciences Issues. New York: Sage.

Barbalet, J. (2008). *Weber, Passion and Profits: 'The Protestant Ethic and the Spirit of Capitalism' in Context.* Cambridge: Cambridge University Press.

Barker, E. (1986). 'Religious Movements: Cult and Anticult Since Jonestown'. *Annual Review of Sociology* 12: 329–46.

——— (1995). 'The Scientific Study of Religion? You Must Be Joking?' *Journal for the Scientific Study of Religion,* 34 (3): 287–310.

Barker, M. (2007). 'Investments in Religious Capital: An Explorative Case Study of Australian Buddhists'. *Journal of Global Buddhism,* (8), http://www.globalbuddhism.org,

Bastide, R. (1996). *Les problèmes de la vie mystique.* Paris: Quadrige/ Presses Universitaires de France.

Baudrillard, J. (1970). *La Société de consommation.* Paris: Gallimard.

——— (1979). *De la séduction.* Paris: Editions Galilée.

——— (1983). *Simulacra and Simulation.* New York: Semiotext(e).

——— (1988). *Jean Baudrillard: Selected Writings.* Cambridge: Polity Press.

——— (1995). The Perfect Crime. (20/06/2001), http://www.simulation.dk/articles/perfect_crime.htm.

Bauman, Z. (1992a) 'Love in Adversity: on the State and the Intellectuals, and the State of the Intellectuals'. *Thesis* 11 (31): 81–104.

——— (1992b) *Intimations of Postmodernity.* London: Routledge.

——— (1994). 'Modernity and the Holocaust'. In *The Polity Reader in Social Theory.* Cambridge: Polity.

——— (1998). 'Postmodern Religion'. In P. Heelas (ed.), *Religion, Modernity and Postmodernity,* 55–78. Oxford: Blackwell.

Baumann, M. (2001). 'Global Buddhism: Developmental Periods, Regional Histories, and a New Analytical Prespective'. *Journal of Global Buddhism*, (2): 1–43, http://jgb.la.psu.edu,

Beaudoin, T. (1998). *Virtual Faith: The Irreverent Quest of Generation X*. London: Jossey-Bass.

Beckford, J. (2001). 'The Construction and Analysis of Religion'. *Social Compass*, 48 (3): 439–41.

——— (2003). *Social Theory and Religion*. Cambridge: Cambridge University Press.

Beit-Hallahmi, B. (2003). 'Scientology: Religion or Racket?' *Marburg Journal of Religion*, 8 (1), http://archiv.ub.uni-marburg.de/mjr/beit.html, 11/01/2007

Bellah, R. (1967). 'Civil Religion in America'. *Daedalus* (96): 1-21.

Bendle, M. (2003). 'Global Jihad and the Battle for the Soul of Islam'. *Australian Religion Studies Review*, 16 (2): 141–52.

——— (2005). 'Max Weber's The Protestant Ethic and the "Spirit" of Capitalism (1905): A Centennial Essay.' *Australian Religion Studies Review* 18 (2): 253–50.

Berger, H., and Ezzy, D. (2007). *Teenage Witches. Magical Youth and the Search for the Self*. New Brunswick, New Jersey, and London: Rutgers University Press.

Berger, H., Leach, E., and Shaffer, L. (2003). *Voices from the Pagan Census: A National Survey of Witches and Neo-Pagans in the United States*. Columbia: University of South Carolina Press.

Beyer, P. (1991). 'Privatization and the Public Influence of Religion in Global Society'. In M. Featherstone (ed.), *Global Culture. Nationalism, Globalization and Modernity*, 373–95. London: Sage Publications.

Black, A., Hughes, P., Bellamy, J., and Kaldor, P. (2004). 'Identity and Religion in Contemporary Australia.' *Australian Religion Studies Review* 17 (1): 53–68.

Bouma, G. (2006). *Australian Soul. Religion and Spirituality in the Twenty-first Century*. Melbourne: Cambridge University Press.

Brown, C. G. (1992). 'A Revisionist Approach to Religious Change'. In S. Bruce (ed.), *Religion and Modernization: Sociologists and Historians Debate the Secularization Thesis*, 31–58. Oxford: Clarendon Press.

Bruce, S. (1992). 'Revelations: The Future of the New Christian Right'. In L. Kaplan (ed.), *Fundamentalism in Comparative Perspective*, 38–73. Amherst: University of Massachusetts Press.

——— (1996). *Religion in the Modern World: From Cathedrals to Cults*. Oxford: Oxford University Press.

——— (2002). *God is Dead: Secularization in the West*. Oxford: Blackwell.

——— (2006). 'Secularization and the Impotence of Individualized Religion'. *The Hedgehog Review*, 8 (1-2): 35–45.

Cadge, W. (2004). 'Gendered Religious Organizations: The Case of Therevada Buddhism in America'. *Gender and Society* 18 (6): 777–93.

Cahill, D., Bouma, G., Dellal, H., and Leahy, M. (2004). *Religion, Cultural Diversity and Safeguarding Australia*. Canberra: Department of Immigration and Multicultural and Indigenous Affairs, Australian Multicultural Foundation.

Campbell, B. (1978). 'A Typology of Cults'. *Sociological Analysis* 39 (3): 228–40.

Campbell, C. (1972). 'The Cult, the Cultic Milieu and Secularization'. *Sociological Yearbook of Religion in Britain*, 5: 119–36.

——— (1978). 'The Secret Religion of the Educated Classes'. *Sociological Analysis* 39 (2): 146–56.

———— (1999). 'The Easternisation of the West'. In B.Wilson and J.Cresswell (eds.), *New Religious Movements. Challenge and response*, 35–48. London and New York: Routledge.

Campbell, H. (2005). 'Making Space for Religion in Internet Studies'. *The Information Society* 21: 309–15.

Carette, J., and King, R. (2005). *Selling Spirituality. The Silent Takeover of Religion.* London and New York: Routledge.

Casanova, J. (1994). *Public Religions in the Modern World.* Chicago and London: University of Chicago Press.

(2006). Rethinking Secularization: A Global Comparative Perspective. *The Hedgehog Review* 8 (1-2): 7–22.

Castoriadis, C. (1992). 'The Retreat from Autonomy: Post-Modernism as Generalised Conformism'. *Thesis Eleven* (31): 14–25.

Chakravarti, U. (1986). 'The Social Philosophy of Buddhism and the Problem of Inequality'. *Social Compass*, 33 (2-3): 199–221.

Chaney, D. (1996). *Lifestyles.* London: Routledge.

Charlesworth, M. (1997). *Religious Inventions: Four Essays.* Melbourne: Cambridge University Press.

Chomsky, N. (1997). *Prespectives on Power: Reflections on Human Nature and the Social Order.* New York: Black Rose Books.

Chryssides, G. (1999). *Exploring New Religions.* London: Cassel.

Cohen, E., Nachman, B.-Y., and Janet, A. (1987). 'Recentering the World: The Quest for "Elective" Centers in a Secularized Universe'. *Sociological Review* 35 (2): 320–46.

Coleman, J. (1992). 'Catholic Integralism as a Fundamentalism'. In L. Kaplan (ed.), *Fundamentalism in Comparative Perspective*, 74–95. Amherst: University of Massachusetts Press.

Corrywright, D. (2003). *Theorectical and Empirical Investigations into New Age Spiritualities.* Bern: Peter Lang.

———— (2004). 'Network Spirituality: The Schumacher-Resurgence-Kumar Nexus'. *Journal of Contemporary Religion* 19 (3): 289–310.

Cosman, C. (2001). 'Introduction'. In E. Durkheim (ed.), *The Elementary Forms of Religious Life*, vii-xli. Oxford: Oxford University Press.

Coupland, D. (1992). *Generation X: Tales for an Accelerated Culture.* London: Abacus.

Cowan, D. (2005). *CyberHenge. Modern Pagans on the Internet.* New York, London: Routledge.

Cranmer, S. (1995). 'The Golden Dawn FAQ'. (26/11/1995), http://www. bartol.udel.edu/~cranmer/cranmer_gdfaq.html

Cubitt, S. (2001). *Simulation and Social Theory.* London: Sage.

Cunningham, C., and Egan, K. (1996). *Christian Spirituality: Themes from the Tradition.* New Jersey: Paulist Press.

Cupitt, D. (1998). 'Post-Christianity'. In P. Heelas (ed.), *Religion, Modernity and Postmodernity*, 218–32. Oxford: Blackwell.

Cush, D. (1996). 'British Buddhism and the New Ag. *Journal of Contemporary Religion* 11 (2): 195–208.

Davie, G. (2000). *Religion in Modern Europe. A Memory Mutates.* Oxford: Oxford University Press.

———— (2002). *Europe: The Exceptional Case. Parameters of Faith in the Modern World*. London: Darton, Longman and Todd.

———— (2006). 'Is Europe an Exceptional Case?' *The Hedgehog Review* 8 (1-2): 23–34.

Dawson, L. (2006). 'Privatisation, Globalisation, and Religious Innovation: Giddens' Theory of Modernity and the Refutation of Secularisation Theory.' In J. Beckford and J. Wallis (eds.), *Theorising Religion. Classical and Contemporary Debates*, 105–119. Aldershot: Ashgate.

de Certeau, M. (1988). *The Practice of Everyday Life*. Berkeley and Los Angeles: University of California Press.

De Groot, K. (2006). 'The Church in Liquid Modernity: A Sociological and Theological Exploration of a Liquid Church.' *International Journal for the Study of the Chrisitan Church* 6 (1): 91–103.

Debord, G. (1995). *The Society of the Spectacle*. New York: Zone Books.

Debray, R. (2005). *Les communions humaines. Pour en finir avec la religion*. Paris: Fayard.

Dillion, J., and Richardson , J. (1994). 'The "Cult" Concept: A Politics of Representation Analysis.' *Syzygy: Journal of Alternative Religion and Culture* 3 (3–4): 185–97.

Drane, J. (2000). *The McDonaldization of the Church: Spirituality, Creativity, and the Future of the Church*. London: Darton, Longman and Todd.

———— (2006a). 'The Emerging Church. A Special Issue.' *International Journal for the Study of the Chrisitan Church* 6 (1).

———— (2006b). 'From Creeds to Burgers: Religious Control, Spiritual Search, and the Future of the World.' In J. Beckford and J. Wallis (eds.), *Theorising Religion. Classical and Contemporary Debates*, 120–31. Aldershot: Ashgate.

Durand, G. (1996). *Science de l'homme et tradition. «Le nouvel esprit anthropologique»*. Paris: Albin Michel.

Durkheim, E. (2001). *The Elementary Forms of Religious Life*. Oxford: Oxford University Press.

Edwards, T. (2000). *Contradictions of Consumption: Concepts, Practices and Politics in Consumer Society*. Buckingham: Open University Press.

Eisenstadt, S. N. (2000). Multiple Modernities. *Daedalus* 129 (1): 1–29.

Eliade, M. (1959). *Cosmos and History. The Myth of the Eternal Return*. New Jersey: Harper and Row.

Elias, N. (1995). 'Technization and Civilization.' *Theory, Culture and Society* 12: 7–42.

Ellwood, T. (2004). 'Invoking Buffy.' In F. Horne (ed.), *Pop Goes the Witch: The Disinformation Guide to 21st Century Witchcraft*, 184–87. New York: The Disinformation Company.

Engels, F. (1959). *Basic Writing on Politics and Philosophy*. Garden City, NY: Anchor Pub. Co.

Ezzy, D. (2001). 'The Commodification of Witchcraft.' *Australian Religion Studies Review* 14 (1): 31–44.

———— (2003). 'New Age Witchcraft? Popular Spell Books and the Re-enchantment of Everyday Life. *Culture and Religion* 4 (1): 47–65.

Faivre, A. (1987). 'Esotericism.' In M. Eliade (ed.), *The Encyclopedia of Religion*, 156–63. New York: Macmillan.
——— (1992). *L'ésoterisme*. Paris: Presses Univeritaries de France.
——— (1994). *Access to Western Esotericism*. New York: State University of New York Press.
Featherstone, M. (1991). *Consumer Culture and Postmodernism*. London: Sage Publications.
Feingold, H. (1983). 'How Unique Is the Holocaust?' In A. Grobman and D. Landes (eds.), *Genocide: Critical Issues of the Holocaust*. Los Angeles: The Simon Wiesanthal Center.
Fiske, J. (1989). *Reading the Popular*. London: Routledge.
Flory, R. (2000). 'Conclusion: Toward a Theory of Generation X Religion.' In R. Flory and D. Miller (eds.), *Gen X Religion*, 231–49. New York: Routledge.
Foucault, M. (1970). *The Order of Things. An Archaeology of the Human Sciences*. New York: Pantheon Books.
Friedman (1992). 'Jewish Zealots: Conservative versus Innovative.' In L. Kaplan (ed.), *Fundamentalism in Comparative Perspective*, 159–76. Amherst: University of Massachusetts Press.
Garret, W. R. (1975). 'Maligned Mysticism: The Maledicted Career of Troeltsch's Third Type.' *Sociological Analysis* 36 (3): 205–23.
Gaze, B., and Jones, M. (1990). *Law, Liberty, and Australian Democracy*. Sydney: The Law Book Co.
Gillen, P. (1987). 'The Pleasures of Spiritualism.' *Australian and New Zealand Journal of Sociology* 23 (2): 217–32.
Göle, N. (2000). 'Snapshots of Islamic modernities.' *Daedalus* 129 (1): 91–117.
——— (2002). 'Islam in Public: New Visibilities and New Imaginaries.' *Public Culture* 14 (1): 173–90.
Gramsci, A. (1971). *Selections from the Prison Notebooks*. London: Lawrence and Wishart.
Greifenhagen, F. V. (2004). 'Islamic Fundalmentalism(s): More than a Pejorative Epithet?' In J. Jaffe and A. Watkinson (eds.), *Contesting Fundalmentalisms*, 63–75. Halifx, Nova Scotia: Fernwood Publishing.
Grey, S. (2004). 'Follow the Mullah.' *The Atlantic Monthly*, 44–47.
Guitton, J., Bogdanov, G., and Bogdanov, I. (1991). *Dieu et la science*. France: Editions Grasset & Fasquelle.
Habermas, J. (2002). *Religion and Rationality. Essays on Reason, God and Modernity*. Cambridge, Massachusetts: MIT Press.
——— (2006). 'Religion in the Public Sphere.' *European Journal of Philosophy* 14 (1): 1–25.
Hadden, J. K. (1987). 'Toward Desacralizing Secularization Theory.' *Social Forces* 65 (608).
Hahlbohm-Helmus, E. (2000). 'Buddhism as Philosophy and Pyschology. Performance Aspects of Tibetan Buddhism "in the West" between 1959 and 1990.' *Recherches Sociologiques* (3): 49–66.
Hamilton, M. (2002).'The Easternisation Thesis: Critical Reflections.' *Religion* 32: 243–58.

Harvey, G. (2000). 'Fantasy in the Study of Religions: Paganism as Observed and Enhanced by Terry Pratchett.' *DISKUS*, 6 www.uni-marbug.de/religionswissenschaft/journal/diskus,

Harvey, G., and Hardman, C. (1996). *Paganism Today: Wiccans, Druids, the Goddess and Ancient Earth Traditions for the Twenty-First Century*. London: Thorsons.

Hassan, R. (2007). 'On Being Religious: Patterns of Religious Commitment in Muslim Societies.' *The Muslim World* 97: 437–78.

Hastings, C., and Laurence, C. (2005). 'Reaching Out to the Converted: Disney Pursues Christian Market.' *Sydney Morning Herald* March 10.

Hay, D. (1990). *Religious Experience Today. Studying the Facts*. London: Mowbray.

Head (2004). 'ASIO, Secrecy and Lack of Accountability.' *Murdoch University Electronic Journal of Law* 11 (4), Http://search.astlii.edu.au/au/journals/MurUEJL/2004/31.html,

Heelas, P. (1993). 'The New Age in Cultural Context: The Premodern, the Modern and the Postmodern.' *Religion* 23: 103–116.

———— (1996) *The New Age Movement*. Oxford: Blackwell.

Heelas, P., and Woodhead, L. (2005). *The Spiritual Revolution: why religion is giving way to spirituality*. Oxford: Blackwell Publishing.

Hellyer, H. A. (2007). 'British Muslims: Past, Present and Future.' *The Muslim World* 97: 225–58.

Hetherington, K. (1994). 'The Contemporary Significance of Schmalenbach's Concept of the Bund.' *The Sociological Review:* 1-25.

Hill, M. (2000). '"Asian Values" as Reverse Orientalism in Singapore.' *Asia Pacific Viewpoint* 41 (2): 177–90.

Holdstock, R. (1978). *Encyclopedia of Science Fiction*. London: Octopus Book.

Houk, J. (1996). 'Anthropological Theory and the Breakdown of Eclectic Folk Religions.' *Journal for the Scientific Study of Religion* 35 (4): 442–47.

Howell, J. (2006). 'The New Spiritualities, East and West: Colonial Legacies and the Global Spiritual Marketplace in Southeast Asia.' *The Australian Religion Studies Review* 19 (1): 19–33.

Hughes, P., Black, A., Bellamy, J., and Kaldor, P. (2004). 'Identity and Religion in Contemporary Australia.' *Australian Religion Studies Review* 17 (1): 53–58.

Hume, L. (1995). 'Guest Editor's Introduction: Modern Pagans in Australia.' *Social Alternatives* 14 (4): 5–8.

———— (1997). *Witchcraft and Paganism in Australia*. Melbourne: University of Melbourne Press.

———— (1999). 'Exporting Nature Religions: Problems in Praxis Down Under.' *Nova Religio* 2 (2): 287–98.

———— (2002). *Ancestral Power. The Dreaming, Consciousness, and Aboriginal Australians*. Melbourne: Melbourne University Press.

———— (2006) 'Liminal Beings and the Undead: Vampires in the 21st Century.' In L. Hume and K. McPhillips (eds.), *Popular Spiritualities. The Politics of Contemporary Enchantment*, 3–16. Aldershot: Ashgate.

Hume, L., and McPhillips, K. (2006). *Popular Spiritualities. The Politics of Contemporary Enchantment*. Aldershot: Ashgate.

Hunt, S. (2002). *Religion in Western Society*. Hampshire and New York: Palgrave.

Huntley, R. (2006). *The World According to Y: Inside the New Adult Generation.* Sydney: Allen & Unwin.

Introvigne, M. (2004). 'The Future of New Religions. *Futures* 36: 979–90.

Ireland, R. (1988). *The Challenge of Secularisation.* Victoria, Australia: Collins Dove.

Jenkins, H. (2003). 'Quentin Taratino's Star Wars? Ditigal Cinema, Media Convergence and Participatory Culture.' In D. Thornburn and H. Jenkins (eds.), *Rethinking Media Change: The Aesthics of Transition.* Cambridge: MIT Press.

Jenkins, P. (2002).'The Next Christianity'. *The Atlantic Monthly*, 53–68.

Johnson, P., and Payne, S. (2004). 'Evangelical Countercult Apologists versus Astrology: An Unresolved Conundrum.' *Australian Religion Studies Review* 17 (2): 73–97.

Jorgensen, D. (1982). 'The Esoteric Community. An Ethnographic Investigation of the Cultic Milieu.' *Urban Life* 10 (4): 383–407.

Kamali, M. (2007). 'Multiple Modernities and Islamism in Iran.' *Social Compass* 54 (3): 373–87.

Kaplan, L. E. (1992). *Fundamentalism in Comparative Perspective.* Amherst: University of Massachusetts Press.

Karaflogka, A. (2002). 'Religious Discourse and Cyberspace.' *Religion* 32: 279–91.

Karnes, K., McIntosh, W., Morris, I. L., and Pearson-Merkowitz, S. (2007). 'Mighty Fortress: Explaining the Spatial Distribution of American Megachurches.' *Journal for the Scientific Study of Religion* 46 (2): 261–68.

Kepel, G. (1994). *The Revenge of God. The Resurgence of Islam, Christianity and Judaism in the Modern World.* Pennsylvania: Pennsylvania State University Press.

———— (2002). *Jihad: The Trail of Political Islam.* Cambridge, Massachusetts: Harvard University Press.

Kilby, C. (1974). 'Mythic and Christian Elements in Tolkien.' In J. W. Montgomerey (ed.), *Myth, Allegory and Gospel: An Interpretation of J.R.R Tolkien/ C.S Lewis/ G.K Chesterton/ Charles Williams*, 119–43. Minneapolis: Bethany Fellowship.

Kinnvall, C. (2004). 'Globalization and Religious Nationalism: Self, Identity, and the Search for Ontological Security.' *Political Psychology* 25 (5): 741–67.

Koenig, P. (2001). 'The Internet as Illustrating the McDonaldisation of Occult Culture.' (30/04/2001), http://www.censur.org/2002/london2001/koenig.htm,

Krüger, O. (2005). 'Discovering the Invisible Internet: Methodological Aspects of Searching Religion on the Internet.' *Online - Heidelberg Journal of religions on the Internet*, 1 (1).

Lacroix, L.-P. S. (2007). 'Le Necronomicon, un grimoire populaire moderne.' In M. Geoffroy, J. G. Vaillancourt and M. Gardaz (eds.), *La mondialisation du phenomène religieux*, 181–202. Montreal: Medias Paul.

Lambert, Y. (1995). 'Vers une ère post-chrétienne?' *Futuribles* (200): 85–111.

———— (2004). 'A Turning Point in Religious Evolution in Europe.' *Journal of Contemporary Religion* 19 (1): 29–45.

Lane, D. (1970). *Politics and Society in the USSR.* London: Weidenfeld & Nicolson.

Langer, B. (1996). 'The Consuming Self.' In A. Kellehar (ed.), *Social Self, Global Culture: An Introduction to Sociological Ideas*, 57–68. Melbourne: Oxford University Press.

LaVey, A. (1972). *The Satanic Bible.* New York: Avon.

Lawrence, B. (1998). 'From Fundamentalism to Fundamentalisms: A Religious Ideology in Multiple Forms.' In P. Heelas (ed.), *Religion, Modernity and Postmodernity*, 88–101. Oxford: Blackwell.

Le Cour, P. (1995). *L'ère du Verseau. Le Secret du Zodiaque et le Proche Avenir de L'humanité.* Paris: Editions Dervy.

Lee, R. (2003). 'The Re-enchantment of the Self: Western Spirituality, Asian Materialism.' *Journal of Contemporary Religion* 18 (3): 351–67.

Lenoir, F. (1999). 'The Adaptation of Buddhism to the West.' *Diogenes* 47 (3): 100–109.

——— (2001). 'Le Buddhisme en France: une tradition dans la modernité. *Recherches Sociologiques* (3): 99–106.

Lewis, J. (2001). 'Who Serves Satan? A Demographic and Ideological Profile.' *Marburg Journal of Religion* 6 (2), http://www.uni-marbug.de/religionswissenschaft/journal/mjr/lewis2.html,

Lipovetsky, G. (1987). *L'empire de l'éphemère. La mode et son destin dans les sociétes modernes.* Paris: Gallimard.

——— (1993). *L'ere du vide. Essais sur l'individualisme contemporian.* Paris: Gallimard.

Lowney, K. (1995). 'Teenage Satanism as Oppostional Youth Culture.' *Journal of Contemporary Ethnography* 23: 454–84.

Luckmann, T. (1967). *The Invisible Religion: The Problems of Religion in Modern Society.* New York: Macmillan.

Luhrmann, T. (1994). *Persuasions of the Witch's Craft. Rtiual Magic in Contemporary England.* London: Picador.

Lyon, D. (2000). *Jesus in Disneyland: Religion in Postmodern Times.* Cambridge: Polity Press.

Maffesoli, M. (1988). *Le tempus des tribus.Le declin de i'individualisme dans les societes de masse.* Paris: MeridiensKlincksieck.

——— (1996). *La contemplation du monde. Figures de style communautaire.* France: Editions Grasset and Faquelles.

Malhotra, A. K. (2001). *An Introduction to Yoga Philosophy: An Annotated Translation of the Yoga Sutras.* Aldershot: Ashgate.

Mannheim, K. (1991). *Ideology and Utopia.* London: Routledge and Kegan Paul.

Marler, P., and Hadaway, C. (2002). '"Being Religious" or "Being Spiritual" in America: A Zero-Sum Proposition?' *Journal for the Scientific Study of Religion* 4 (2): 289–300.

Martin, D. (1995). 'Sociology, Religion and Secularization: An Orientation.' *Religion*, 25: 295–303.

——— (2005). *On Secularization: Towards a Revised General Theory.* Aldershot: Ashgate.

McIntyre, E. H. (2007). 'Brand of Choice: Why Hillsong Music is Winning Sales and Souls.' *Australian Religion Studies Review* 20 (2): 175–94.

McKie, R. (2005). 'Creationist cinema. No science, please, we're fanatics.' *Guardian Weekly*, 1–7.

McPhillips, K., and Franzman, M. (2000). 'Xena: Warrior Princess: Re-Imagining the Religious Cosmos.' *Whoosh!* (44), http://www.whoosh.org/issue44/mcphillips1.html,

Mellor, P. (1991). 'Protestant Buddhism? The Cultural Translation of Buddhism in England.' *Religion* 21: 73–92.

Melucci, A. (1996). *The Playing Self: Person and Meaning in the Planetary Society.* Cambridge: Cambridge University Press.

Milbank, J. (1995). *Theology and Social Theory. Beyond Secular Reason.* Oxford: Blackwell.

Miller, D., and Miller, A. (2000). 'Introduction: Understanding Generation X. Values, Politics, and Religious Commitments.' In R. Flory and D. Miller (eds.), *Gen X Religion*, 1–12. New York: Routledge

Milner, N. (2000). 'Giving the Devil His Due Process: Exorcism in the Church of England.' *Journal of Contemporary Religion* 15 (2): 247–72.

Montenegro, M. (2000). 'Harry Potter, Sorcey and Fantasy.' *CANA: Christian Answers for the New Age.*

Murphy, J. W. (1996). 'There is Nothing Virtual about Virtual Reality.' *ETC.: A Review of General Semantics* 53 (4): 458–64.

Neal, C. (2001). *What's a Christian to do with Harry Potter?* Colorado Springs: WaterBrook Press.

Nelson, G. K. (1987). *Cults, New Religons and Religious Creativity.* London: Routledge and Kegan Paul

New South Wales Anti-Discrimination Board (1984). *Discrimination and Religious Conviction.* Sydney: New South Wales Anti-Discrimination Board.

Noll, R. (1996). *The Jung Cult. Origins of a Charismatic Movement.* London: Fontana Press.

Norris, P., and Inglehart, R. (2004). *Sacred and Secular: Religion and Politics Worldwide.* Cambridge: Cambridge University Press.

Oldmeadow, H. (1999). 'To a Buddhist Beat. Allen Ginsberg on Politics, Poetics and Spirituality.' *Beyond the Divide* 2 (1): 56–67.

Pace, E. (2007). 'Extreme Messianism. The Habad Movement and the *impasse* of the charisma.' *Horizontes Antropologicos* (27): 37–48.

Park, J., and Baker, J. (2007). 'What Would Jesus Buy: American Consumption of Religious and Spiritual Material Goods.' *Journal for the Scientific Study of Religion* 46 (4): 501–17.

Pfeifer, J. (1992). 'The Psychological Framing of Cults: Schematic Representations and Cult Evaluations.' *Journal of Applied Social Psychology* 22 (7): 531–44.

Phillips, T., and Aarons, H. (2005). Choosing Buddhism in Australia: towards a traditional style of reflexive spiritual engagement. *The British Journal of Sociology* 56 (2): 215–32.

———— (2007). 'Looking "East": An Exploratory Analysis of Western Disenchantment.' *International Sociology* 22 (2): 325–42.

Possamai-Inesedy, A. (2002). 'Beck's Risk Society and Giddens' Search for Ontological Security: A Comparative Analysis between the Anthroposophical Society and the Assemblies of God.' *The Australian Religion Studies Review* 15 (1): 44–56.

Possamai, A. (2000). 'A New Look at the Cultic Milieu.' In S.Oakley (ed.), *Sociological Sites/ Sights TASA 2000 Conference Proceedings*. Adelaide: Australian Sociological Association.

———— (2005a). *In Search of New Age Spirituality.* Aldershot: Ashgate.

———— (2005b). *Religion and Popular Culture: A Hyper-real Testament.* Bruxelles, Bern, Berlin, Frankfurt am Main, New York, Oxford, Wein: P.I.E- Peter Lang.

———— (2008a). 'Australia "Shy" De-secularisation Process.' In A. Imotoual and B. Spaler (eds.), *Religion, Spirituality and Social Science*, 23–35. Cambridge: Polity Press.

———— (2008b). 'Popular Religion.' In P. Clarke and P. Beyer (eds.), *The World's Religions: Continuities and Transformations*, 479–92. London: Routledge.

Possamai, A., Bellamy, J., and Castel, K. (2006). 'The Diffusion of New Age Beliefs and Practices Among Australian Church Attenders.' *Fieldwork in Religion* 2 (1): 9–26.

Possamai, A., and Lee, M. (2004). 'New Religious Movements and the Fear of Crime.' *The Journal of Contemporary Religion* 19 (3): 337–52.

Possamai, A., and Possamai-Inesedy, A. (2007a). 'The Baha'i faith and Caodaism: Migration, Change and De-secularization(s).' *Journal of Sociology* 43 (3): 301–18.

———— (2007b). 'Risk Society, Sustainable Development and Religion.' In R.Blancarte and V.Saroglou (eds.), *Religion, Culture and Sustainable Development in the Encyclopedia of Life Support Systems*. Oxford: EOLSS Publishers (Developed under the auspices of UNESCO).

Pratt, D. (2007). 'Religious Fundamentalism: A Paradigm for Terrorism?' *The Australian Religion Studies Review* 20 (2): 195–215.

Presser, S., and Chaves, M. (2007). 'Is Religious Service Attendance Declining?' *Journal for the Scientific Study of Religion* 46 (3): 417–23.

Price, S. (2004). '"Take a pew at God's cafe, sit back and savour a semon."' *The Sun Heral*, 1 August, p.23.

Ramesh, R. (2008). '"Inside the court of the Tibetan god-king."' *The Guardian Weekly* 28 March, p.11.

Reader, I. (2001). 'Consensus Shattered: Japenese Paradigm Shift and Moral Panic in the Post-Aum Era.' *Nova Religion* 4 (2): 225–34.

Richardson, J. (2007). 'The Sociology of Religious Freedom: A Structural and Socio-Legal Analysis.' *Sociology of Religion* 67 (3): 271–94.

Richardson , J. T. (1985). 'Studies of Conversion: Secularization or Re-enchantment?' In P. E. Hammond (ed.), *The Sacred in a Secular Age. Toward Revision in the Scienitific Study of Religion*, 104. Berkeley and Los Angeles: University of California Press.

Riffard, P. A. (1990). *L'ésotérisme*. Paris: Editions Robert Laffont.

Ritzer, G. (1999). *Enchanting a Disenchanted World: Revolutionising the Means of Consumption*. California: Pine Forge Press.

———— (2000). *The Macdonaldisation of Society*. California: Pine Forge Press.

Robinson, W. G. (1997). 'Heaven's Gate: The End?' *Journal of Computer-Mediated Communication* 3 (3), http://ascusc.org/jcmc/vol3/issue3/robinson.html, 25/08/ 2004

Rojek, C., and Turner, B. (1993). *Forget Baudrillard?* London: Routledge.

Roof, W. C. (1999). *Spiritual Marketplace: Baby Boomers and the Remaking of American Religion*. Princeton: Princeton University Press.

Rose, G. (2003). 'That Phantom Menace: A Response to the Supply Side Paradigm of the Rise and Fall of Religious Organisations.' *Australian Religion Studies Review* 16 (1): 90–115.

Rose, P. (2006). 'The Quest for Identity: Spiritual Feminist Ritual as Enactment of Medieval Romance.' In L. Hume and K. McPhillips (eds.), *Popular Spiritualities. The Politics of Contemporary Enchantment*. Aldershot: Ashgate.

Rosenau, P. (1992). *Post-Modernism and the Social Sciences. Insight, Inroads and Intrusions*. Princeton, New Jersey: Princeton University Press.

Ross, M. W. (2005). 'Typing, Doing, and Being: Sexuality and the Internet.' *Journal of Sex Research* 42 (4): 342–53.

Roszak, T. (1969). *The Making of a Counter Culture. Reflections on the Technocratic Society and its Youthful Opposition.* New York: Amchor Books.

Russell, B. (1935). *Religion and Science.* Oxford: Oxford University Press.

Said, E. (1994). *Representations of the Intellectual* New York: Pantheon Books.

Schick, C., Jaffe, J., and Watkinson, A. (2004). *Contesting Fundamentalisms.* Halifax, Nova Scotia: Fernwood Publishing.

Schiller, H. (1996). *Information Inequality: The Deepening Social Crisis in America.* New York: Routledge.

Schlegel, J. L. (1995). *Religions à la carte.* Paris: Hachette.

Simmel, G. (1858–1918) Chapter 4: The Metropolis and Mental Life. In K.H. Wolff (ed. and trans.), *The Sociology of Georg Simmel,* 409–24. Glencoe, Illinois: Free Press.

Smith, M. (1999). 'Strands in the Web: Community-Builiding Strategies in Online Fanzines.' *Journal of Popular Culture* 33 (2): 87–99.

Spuler, M. (2000a). 'Characteristics of Buddhism in Australia.' *Journal of Contemporary Religion* 15 (1): 29–44.

——— (2000b). 'Qu'est-ce que le zen? La reformulation du zen à l'attention de l'Occident.' *Recherches Sociologiques* (3): 33–47.

Stark, R., and Bainbridge, W. S. (1981a). 'Friendship, Religion and the Occult: A Network Study.' *Review of Religious Research* 22 (4): 313–27.

——— (1981b). 'Reply to Jorgensen.' *American Journal of Sociology* 87 (2): 430–33.

——— (1985). *The Future of Religion. Secularization, Revivial and Cult Formation.* Berkeley: University of California Press.

——— (1987). *A Theory of Religion.* California: University of California Press.

Stolz, J., and Favre, O. (2005). 'The Evangelical Milieu: Defining Criteria and Reproduction across the Generations.' *Social Compass* 52 (2): 169–83.

Sutcliffe, S. (2003). *Children of the New Age: A History of Spiritual Practices.* London: Routledge.

Tacey, D. (2000). *Re-Enchantment. The New Australian Spirituality.* Sydney: Harper Collins.

Tamney, J. (2002). *The Resilience of Conservative Religion. The Case of Popular Conservative Protestant Congregations.* Cambridge: Cambridge University Press.

Tayob, A. (2005). 'Secularisation in Islam.' In C. Timmerman and B. Segaret (eds.), *How to Conquer the Barriers to Intercultural Dialogue,* 117–32. Bruxelles, Bern, Berlin, Frankfurt am Main, New York, Oxford, Wein: P.I.E.-Peter Lang.

Tayob, A. I. (1999). 'Defining Islam in the Throes of Modernity.' *Studies in Contemporary Islam* 1 (2): 1–15.

The Australian Human Rights and Equal Opportunity Commission (1998). *Article 18 – Freedom of religion and belief.* Canberra: Commonwealth of Australia.

Till, R. (2006). 'The Nine O'Clock Service: Mixing Club Culture and Postmodern Christianity.' *Culture and Religion* 7 (1): 93–110.

Trevelyan, G. (1984). *A Vision of the Aquarian Age. The Emerging Spiritual World View.* Walpole, New Hampshire: Stillpoint Publishing.

Troeltsch, E. (1950). *The Social Teaching of the Christian Churches.* London: George Allen & Unwin.

Trueheart, C. (1996). 'Welcome to the Next Church.' *The Atlantic Monthly*, 37–58.

Tugend (2001). 'Arab Step up War on Pokemon.' *The Jerusalem Post*, http://www.cesnur.org/2001/pokemon_april01.htm, April 29

Turam, B. (2004). 'The politics of engagement between Islam and the secular state: ambivalences of "civil" society.' *British Journal of Sociology* 55 (2): 259–81.

Turner, B. (2007). 'Islam, Religious Revival and the Sovereign State.' *The Muslim World* 97: 405–18.

Volker, D. (1997). 'De l'usage possible du concept Troeltschien de la religion dans les sciences sociales.' *Revue de l'Histoire des Religions* 214: 2.

Voyé, L. (1998). 'Effacement ou relegitimation de la religion populaire.' *Questions Liturgiques* 79 (1-2): 95–109.

Waldman, A. (2006). 'Prophetic Justice.' *The Atlantic Monthly*, 82–93.

Wallace, A. (2003). 'Reason, Society and Religion. Reflections on 11 September from a Habermasian Perspective.' *Philosophy and Social Criticism* 29 (5): 491–515.

Wallis, J. (2006). 'Spiritualism and the (Re)-Enchantment of Modernity.' In J. Beckford and J. Wallis (eds.), *Theorising Religion. Classical and Contemporary Debates*, 32–43. Aldershot: Ashgate.

Wallis, R. (1984). *The Elementary Forms of the New Religious Life*. London: Routledge & Kegan Paul.

Warner, S. (1993). 'Work in Progress Toward a New Paradigm for the Sociological Study of Religion in the United States.' *American Journal of Sociology* 98 (5): 1044–93.

Watkinson, A. M. (2004). 'Equality Rights and Re-Privatized Public Services: Religious Fundamentalism Meets the Charter.' In C. Schick, J. Jaffe and A. Watkinson (ed.), *Contesting Fundamentalisms*, 137–51. Halifax, Nova Scotia: Fernwood Publishing.

Weber, M. (1970). *Max Weber: Essays in Sociology*, edited by H. H. Gerth and C. W. Mills. London: Routledge.

———— (1995). *The Sociology of Religion*. Boston: Beacon Press.

Werbner, P. (1995). 'Powerful Knowledge in a Global Sufi Cult: Reflections on the Poetics of Travelling Theories.' In W. James (ed.), *The Pursuit of Certainty: Religious and Cultural Formulations*. London: Routledge.

Williams, H. (2003). 'Two Can Play that Game: Hollywood and the Games Industry are Getting Closer Than Ever.' *The Guardian Weekly*, 16–22.

Wilson, B. (1985). 'Secularization: The Inherited Model.' In P. E. Hammond (ed.), *The Sacred in a Secular Age. Toward Revison in the Scientific Study of Religion.'* Berkeley and Los Angeles: University of California Press.

———— (1995). *Religious Toleration and Religious Diversity*. Santa Barbara, California: Institute for the Study of American Religion.

Winslade, J. (2000). 'Techno-Kabbalah: The Perfomative Language of Magick and the Production of Occult Knowledge.' *The Drama Review* 44 (2): 84–100.

Wuthnow, R. (2001). 'Spirituality and Spiritual Practice.' In R. Fenn (ed.), *The Blackwell Companion to Sociology of Religion*, 306–20. Oxford: Blackwell.

Wyn, J., and Woodman, D. (2006). 'Generation, Youth and Social Change in Australia.' *Journal of Youth Studies* 9 (5): 495–514.

York, M. (1995). *The Emerging Network. A Sociology of the New Age and Neo-Pagan Movements*. Maryland, US: Rowmann and Littlefield Publishers.

———— (2001). 'New Age Commodification and Appopriation of Spirituality.' *Journal of Contemporary Religion* 16 (3): 361–72.

Zaidman, N. (2003). 'Commericalization of Religious Objects: A Comparison Between Traditional and New Age Religions.' *Social Compass* 50 (3): 345–60.

Index

Breinigsville, PA USA
21 October 2009
226266BV00003B/2/P

9 781845 533045